Praise for David Bannon's books on grief:

"Brings wisdom and solace to everyone acquainted with grief." —Philip Yancey, author of *Where the Light Fell* and *What's So Amazing About Grace?*

"Remarkable." —*Christianity Today*

"A valuable resource." —*The Christian Century*

"A gorgeous book to help the grieving."
—Jana Riess, author of *Flunking Sainthood*

"Richly beautiful . . . thrums with a real and quiet hope."
—Sarah Clarkson, *From the Vicarage*

"Outstanding." —W. Lee Warren, MD, neurosurgeon, author of *I've Seen the End of You*

"Penetrates and elucidates . . . a marvelous gift."
—Luci Shaw, Writer in Residence, Regent College

"Does not rely on emotional outbursts; rather on sighs, quiet and restrained."
—*The Erlangen News*

"Wonderfully well-researched and yet also moving and deeply personal."
—Timothy Jones, past Visiting Scholar, Princeton Theological Seminary, and author of *Fully Beloved: Meeting God in Our Heartaches and Our Hopes*

"A fascinating text with the power to heal." —Steven S. Bammel, PhD

"Thoughtfully spiritual and honest about the great brokenness of our lives."
—*Hearts and Minds Books*

"Very unique." —*Greenwich Sentinel*

"A book to help the grieving." —*Religion News Service*

"A sacred invitation to embrace grief as part of our own stories . . . a contemplative journey." —*Spectrum Magazine*

A HOPE OBSERVED

Finding Solace Through Shared Stories of Grief

DAVID BANNON

PARACLETE PRESS
BREWSTER, MASSACHUSETTS

2026 First Printing

A Hope Observed: Finding Solace Through Shared Stories of Grief

ISBN 979-8-89348-040-5

Library of Congress Cataloging-in-Publication Data

Names: Bannon, David author
Title: A hope observed : finding solace through shared stories of grief / David Bannon.
Description: Brewster, Massachusetts : Paraclete Press, [2026] | Includes bibliographical references. | Summary: “Bannon shares about his own journey of grief and offers reflections on the grief experienced by biblical or historical figures all paired with Scripture, art, and readings”-- Provided by publisher.
Identifiers: LCCN 2025024918 | ISBN 9798893480405 hardcover
Subjects: LCSH: Bannon, David | Grief--Case studies | Grief--Religious aspects--Christianity | Hope--Case studies | Hope--Religious aspects--Christianity | LCGFT: Case studies
Classification: LCC BF575.G7 B36 2026 | DDC 248.8/6--dc23/eng/20250805
LC record available at https://lccn.loc.gov/2025024918

10 9 8 7 6 5 4 3 2 1

Published by Paraclete Press
Brewster, Massachusetts
www.paracletepress.com

Printed in India

for Jessica

THERE IS NOTHING WE CAN SAY

THAT GOD DOES NOT UNDERSTAND.

THERE IS NOTHING WE CAN SAY

THAT GOD DOES NOT WANT TO HEAR.

Contents

Love

GRIEF BILL OF RIGHTS

My grief matters.
My grief is an act of memory and love.
My grief, like my love, has no time limit.
My grief is the natural and appropriate reaction to loss.
My grief is healthy.
My grief is normal.
My grief is not a process to work through,
a disorder to heal,
a condition to treat,
or an illness to cure.
My grief has only one stage—*grief*.
My grief is my own.
I grieve at my own pace.
I grieve in my own way.
I may speak my grief or remain silent.
I am not crazy.
I am not alone.
How my loved one died is not as important
as *who* that person is to me.
My loved one matters.
Grief is love.

Using This Book

Our grief is our own, as unique as a fingerprint, as fragile as a snowflake. Yet others have crawled through this same valley, stumbling blindly under the shadow of death. In these pages we will meet fellow mourners: presidents and poets; scientists and theologians; writers and filmmakers; artists and musicians; homebodies and wanderers. We may see that they, too, learned death plays no favorites. They too wrestled with questions known to all who grieve: *Why did this happen? Where are my loved ones now? How can I go on?*

The meditations in this book offer a chance to understand loss and find meaning in our lives ahead. Every reading begins with Scripture, for there is no book in all human history as steeped in lessons on how to *grieve, cope, hope*, and *love*. These four themes head each section. Individual entries feature works of art that express these complex emotions in surprising ways. We will also explore startling advances in grief therapy that confirm our suspicions: *Our dead are with God even as we feel them near; we are not crazy; our sorrow is normal, healthy, and expected; grief is love.* A quotation for further reflection ends each reading.

Some topics may interest you immediately; others might seem too painful for now. To help with your personal approach, each meditation stands alone. Open to any page and you will find all the information needed to appreciate that reflection. This leads to some repetition, particularly with dates (I mention 2015 often enough), the credentials of noted experts, aspects of grief that bear revisiting, and a certain poet and bereaved father, Friedrich Rückert. But the convenience seems worth any minor redundancy.

Millions of sufferers across the centuries have found the same solace we seek. This book is filled with some of their stories. And mine. My daughter Jess died in 2015. Her life is as much a part of these pages as the many others we will share together. Until that distant day when we hold our loved ones in our arms again, I pray that our days may be filled with peace and gentle, forgiving memory.

Thank you for sharing with me this communion of grief.

—David Bannon

Grieve

Have mercy on me, Lord, for I am faint; heal me, Lord, for my bones are in agony. My soul is in deep anguish. How long, Lord, how long?

PSALM 6:2–3

Oh, Adonai Elohim, I don't even know how to speak!

JEREMIAH 1:6A (CJB)

A SEPARATE BARGAIN

"She remains, she is here, more beautiful each year."

> *I will lead the blind by ways they have not known, along unfamiliar paths I will guide them; I will turn the darkness into light before them and make the rough places smooth. These are the things I will do; I will not forsake them.*
>
> ISAIAH 42:16

"I'd rather go blind," Etta James sings, than watch the one she loves leave. The first time I heard this song I felt the pull of her powerful emotions. *Yep, that's how it feels during a break-up*, I thought, *though we might not* actually *trade our eyesight!*

After my daughter died, I realized the lyric isn't just bluesy hyperbole. Many bereaved parents have pleaded with God to take them instead. A struggling child puts the lie to any Faustian fantasies of bartering our souls to gain our desires. How many parents, driven to despair, have offered their lives to God or the devil if only their child could survive? Alas, the bargain is not struck. "Dark is the world to me, for all its cities and stars," writes Abraham Heschel. "If not for my faith that God in His silence still listens to a cry, who could stand such agony?"

Who among us has not felt cheated and abandoned by deity as our loved one suffers? Our hearts may at times harbor thoughts of self-recrimination, guilt, a sense of betrayal, abandonment, or misplaced trust. Such feelings are normal.

Johann Wolfgang von Goethe felt wholly changed after the death of his cherished sister, Cornelia. He spoke of her as a sturdy, reliable root that had now been chopped away, leaving him—the branches she once nourished—to wither and die. He had no choice but to surrender to nature, he writes, "which allows us to feel terrible pain for a brief time, but lets us mourn for much longer." A month later, Goethe composed this poem about Cornelia:

> The gods, endless, give all
> to those they love, entire:
> all our joys, endless; all
> our pains, endless, entire.

Goethe is hinting that the gods' largesse may be too extravagant. In giving all, entirely and without reserve, perhaps they give too much. The poet is heartbroken and feeling a tad snide. This is not unexpected. Anger, vindictiveness, and hostility are acknowledged aspects of grief. Many bereaved parents express bitterness, disillusionment, and a sense of betrayal by the divine. They may blame God and perhaps even mock deity's apparent lack of concern.

Etta keens that blindness is preferable to parting. And she's right. I cannot exchange my sight to have my daughter back, but in a very real way, my expressions and perceptions have changed. If eyes are windows to the soul, then in grief our eyes reveal souls that have taken harm. Look in the eyes of other mourners. You may see yourself.

In 2018, *TIME Magazine* photographer Adam Ferguson was assigned seven bereaved parents whose children had died in a school shooting twenty years earlier. "Photographing each parent was complex and hard," Ferguson writes. "No photograph I made seemed able to capture the grief of losing a child." He needn't worry. The people featured on his cover of *TIME* come from many walks of life, yet their eyes tell a shared story that transcends words.

This realization is surprisingly helpful. Looking at photographs of fellow sufferers, I am moved by an ineffable yet wholly palpable quality of grief: a sense of communion. We are not alone. Emily Dickinson may have understood this when she wrote of her grief that she is "still fascinated to presume that some are like my own."

> I measure every Grief I meet
> With narrow, probing, eyes—
> I wonder if It weighs like Mine—
> Or has an Easier size.

> I note that Some—gone patient long—
> At length, renew their smile—
> An imitation of a Light
> That has so little Oil—

Other Romantic poets also reflected on hidden sorrow that lingers under the surface of our eyes. "Leave me to my mourning!" exclaimed bereaved father Friedrich Rückert. "My eyes are accustomed to it now. Each ray of eastern light will darken my soul, adding grief to grief." These words resonate with me. Nature may be soothing, offering hints of joy, yet it is also dangerous and destructive. It is not safe; it is not docile. Perhaps in our grief we see this clearly at last. We may feel that our eyes, and our smiles, as Dickinson wrote, are imitations of a light now bereft of life-giving oil.

Etta continues her song: Somehow she knew it was over; her soul told her to cry. Much of the lyric is about a lost love, but that line speaks to me even now.

Somehow I knew.

When my daughter was a child, we played a game called *I love you more . . .* Usually I started simply: "I love you more than chocolate!" She would chime in, "I love you more than Power Rangers!" (High praise indeed.) And off we would go, one *more than* after another, until sooner or later Jess returned to one of our favorites:

"I love you more than a poke in the eye!"

Jess died around eight o'clock on a Friday evening, January 16, 2015. I was working at the time and felt an odd pressure on my right eye, solid and unmistakable. The next morning, Saturday, I woke with my lid completely covered in mucus. I thought I had an unexpected case of pink eye. That afternoon my sight returned to normal.

Jess's mother was unable to reach me on Friday or Saturday. Finally, on Sunday, January 18, while cooking dinner, I learned that Jess had overdosed on heroin, a victim of the same addiction that led Etta James to write "I'd Rather Go Blind." I was struck dumb, unable to process a reality I knew was true. Later that same year, I came across one of the most famous laments in German literature, again by Friedrich Rückert. It perfectly expresses my bewilderment in those first few days.

> The maid brings news of their
> sister's death to our throng
> of boys; they cry out as one:
> "She is not dead, it is not true."
>
> They stare at her pale lips, her
> cheeks white, dark hair; and
> whisper among themselves:
> "She is not dead, it is not true."
>
> Father weeps, his heart a
> wound; their mother keens;
> still they resist the truth:
> "She is not dead, it is not true."
>
> They were there in the hour
> when she was laid to rest,
> lowered to the cold ground:
> "She is not dead, it is not true."
>
> She remains, she is here,
> more beautiful each year,
> more precious each hour:
> *She is not dead, it is not true.*

"She is not dead," I moan to myself. "Oh dear Lord, it's true, I'd rather be blind." Rückert knew this pain. His boys cry out, they whisper, they resist and ultimately face their sister's death, all the while repeating: *She is not dead, it is not true.* The final stanza's refrain of assurance is almost a sacrament. The religious parallel was no accident.

This song is a "kyrielle by Rückert," observes Michael Neumann, professor emeritus of German literature at Catholic University of Eichstaett-Ingolstadt, referring to a French verse form characterized by refrains in the fourth line of each quatrain. Kyrielle is from the Old French *kiriele*, a derivative of the word *Kýrie*: part of many Christian liturgies, in which "Lord, have mercy" is repeated in the fourth line.

After a loss, we often rely on certain words that offer solace in times of overwhelming sorrow. These take on meaning through repetition and may include a line from a hymn, a passage of Scripture or poetry, a fondly remembered phrase spoken by our dead loved one, or private supplications. They form our liturgies of grief.

David McNeish, a minister with the Church of Scotland, says that this type of personal liturgy can be productive and helpful. He suggests that a constraining one-size-fits-all theology, or a strictly observed model of grief, imposes more harm than relief, denying the "complex and often bewildering phenomenon" of sorrow. Instead, McNeish recommends practical care that focuses on personal context, open listening, and alternative liturgy.

My private liturgy takes a different form. Unlike Rückert's boys, I knew Jess was dead, I knew it was true. Had I the poet's gift, my kyrielle might end each stanza with a different sacramental refrain:

> She remains, she is here,
> more beautiful each year,
> more precious each hour:
> *I love you more . . .*

I would trade places with my daughter in a heartbeat. *If one of us had to die*, I think, *surely it should have been me*. But faced with the reality of this overwhelming grief, I pause over a separate bargain. If one of us must face a world without the other, I would spare Jess this harm.

I'm reminded of a surprising phone call from Jess a few years before she died. A friend's father had just passed. "He was only fifty-five," she said through tearful gasps. "What if it was you? I couldn't stand it. You're my favorite." Now I know, now I see: Grief, too, is an act of love. *Yes, Jess, if one of us must suffer, let it be me. I'd rather go blind than see you in such pain.*

WOULD I BRING HER BACK TO LIFE IF I COULD DO IT?

I would not. IF A WORD WOULD DO IT,

I WOULD BEG FOR STRENGTH TO WITHHOLD THAT WORD.

AND I WOULD HAVE THE STRENGTH; I AM SURE OF IT.

IN HER LOSS I AM ALMOST BANKRUPT,

AND MY LIFE IS A BITTERNESS, *but I am content.*

—MARK TWAIN, ON THE DEATH OF HIS DAUGHTER

Vincent van Gogh,
At Eternity's Gate, 1890,
Kröller-Müller Museum

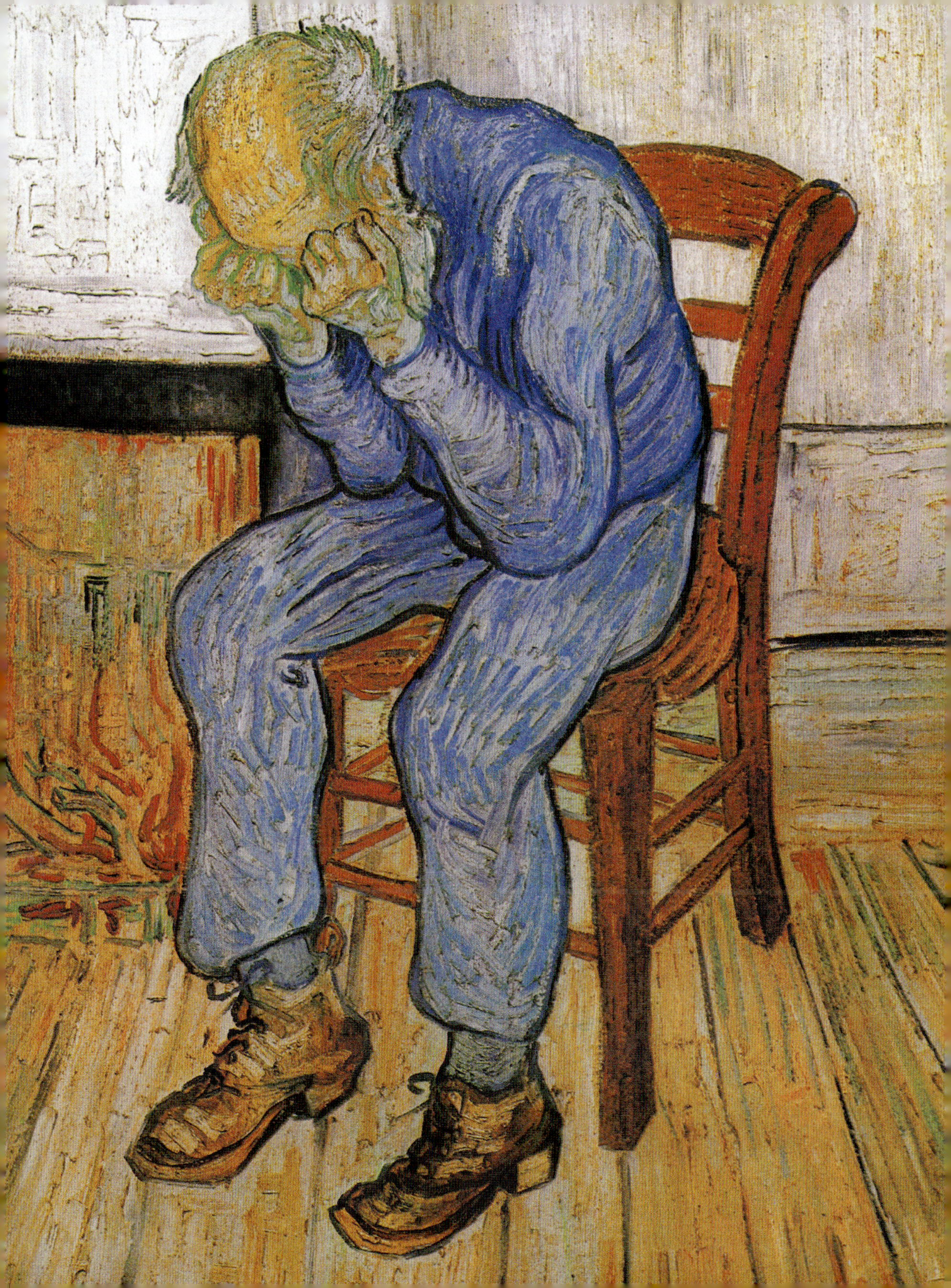

A *REALLY REAL* GOD

"He came that we may be forever with Him—and with them."

Cast all your anxiety on him because he cares for you.

1 PETER 5:7

I heard the scream first. Then the soft chuff of an idling engine, quickly switched off, and silence. I rounded the corner. *Oh, garbage truck,* I thought. *And what, a trike?* I stepped closer.

The metal was mangled, a toddler's tricycle under heavy wheels, and something red and white: the body of a small child, crushed beyond recognition.

I looked up.

A young woman was standing on the sidewalk. Her hands were in her hair, eyes wide with horror, mouth open in soundless agony. Beside her was a heavy-set man in a tan uniform. His shoulders were slumped, palms outstretched. His breath was low, wheezing, shuddering.

I didn't know what to do. So I trudged up the hill to my house.

My mother was on the phone. "Hang on," she said, facing me. "A two-year-old was just killed one street over. A garbage truck backed over him." Then she returned to her call.

I stared for a moment. I didn't eat an afternoon snack. Instead, I went to my room and lay down. Looking at the ceiling, I revisited the tableau in my mind.

The mother's terrible scream and stunned silence. A helpless driver. His truck. The white, as much white as red, so much red.

It was December, 1970. I was seven years old.

I never told anyone what I had seen. My mother was only thirty-two at the time, a child in many ways, as stunned and unable to process what had happened as I had been. Over the years I've worked in the death care field, seen friends and family die, lectured to thousands of students, and today offer support to fellow mourners.

But until now I've kept this story to myself. There is a reason. It's a question of God.

Witnessing such horror was traumatic, but not in the way one might think. My seven-year-old mind did not ponder the mysteries of theodicy—such a paltry word, like biting into a lemon—and I had no doubts about the existence of the divine. In my preteen years, I remained convinced that there is an invisible world that interacts with ours. *There must be*, I thought, *but I'm not so sure they're very nice on the other side.*

That old chestnut of a god that exists but doesn't care didn't suit me either. Even I could see that despite its rationalistic trappings, deism is nonsense. *If God is really real*, I mused as a boy, *then he thinks and feels.* Sure, such thoughts and emotions would be beyond our understanding, but they are palpable, they are alive. *But maybe he doesn't care about what* we *care about.* How could he? A toddler's body had been crushed under wheels that held no belligerence in themselves. Tires were uncaring; a *living* god was not.

Still, I wasn't certain that he was a *reliable* god.

This is when I came to the Holy Bible. I had never been to Sunday School. My reading did not have the benefit of easy answers, or any answers at all, for that matter. The King James Version was no picnic to a preteen. I did a lot of skimming, but once I got the hang of the language, I found the stories irresistible.

I was struck by how fun it was. I had subscribed to *Ellery Queen's Mystery Magazine* when I was twelve, and the Bible wasn't all that different to the irreligious eye: an anthology of tangentially related "books." When read without the burden of reverent instruction, they can be thrilling and more than a little hard to take.

Much of what I read confirmed my suspicions.

When Abraham tried to sacrifice his son, for example, I shook my head and scrawled in the margin: "No way that's God. Freak job. God sent that angel to stop him. I bet Isaac hated his dad."

I had much the same thought when I read about Joshua and Jericho, then that creepy business with Samuel swearing that God told him they should kill all the Amalekite children. Bloody and terrible—and pretty exciting to a young boy, I admit—but if this was God, I didn't see much difference between him and the other gods the Bible tells us to despise.

No one had informed me that people don't bother reading the prophets. So I dove in. I loved them. "They're so weird!" I wrote. And the Book of Revelation? "He's mean. Maybe crazy."

Young people are often frustrated that adults don't seem to listen to them. God, apparently, doesn't mind. Abraham, Moses, David and the prophets were a talkative bunch, but God let them ramble and demand and wheedle. I liked that.

The Gospels were gentle, tender, and heartbreaking to the last. "No happy ending," I scribbled. Yes, the Resurrection was a great day, perhaps *the* great day, but I kept thinking about how Mary watched her son die.

And about a young mother one street over in December of 1970, her mouth open in a scream cut short because no sound could possibly be big enough.

Death is no stranger to us. We need only look around. My daughter died on January 16, 2015. I too know silent keening, sorrow too vast for utterance until roars of anguish rip from my throat. I too know the helplessness of causing unintended harm.

Today I write on grief and facilitate bereavement support groups. "Grief is love," I say, and indeed it is. Grief is also horror, paralysis, and shock. There is no good news at the death of a child, no assurance to silence the screams. "This separation grieves me beyond measure," Martin Luther said after his thirteen-year-old daughter died in his arms in 1542. "It is marvelous to know she is well and truly at peace and yet to be so heartbroken!" If an invisible world is a reality, then a creator is probable, as the deists suggest, and perhaps even plausible. God may well be *really real*, just as I had supposed in my childhood years. I believe so.

For me, God is personal and reliable, concerned with us, mindful of us, though it may be difficult to comprehend the extent and expression of such divine compassion. I have an idea that we know much, much less than we think. Maybe that's how it should be.

The existence of a really real God answers the only question that matters to me now. "Most precious of all joys are those that come from love," writes Benedict Groeschel of the Christ Child. "More than all else we do not want to be separated forever from those we love. He came that we may be forever with Him—and with them."

This is my sole consolation. Our loved ones continue on. We will see them again. They are with us now, as God is with us, walking beside us in the face of

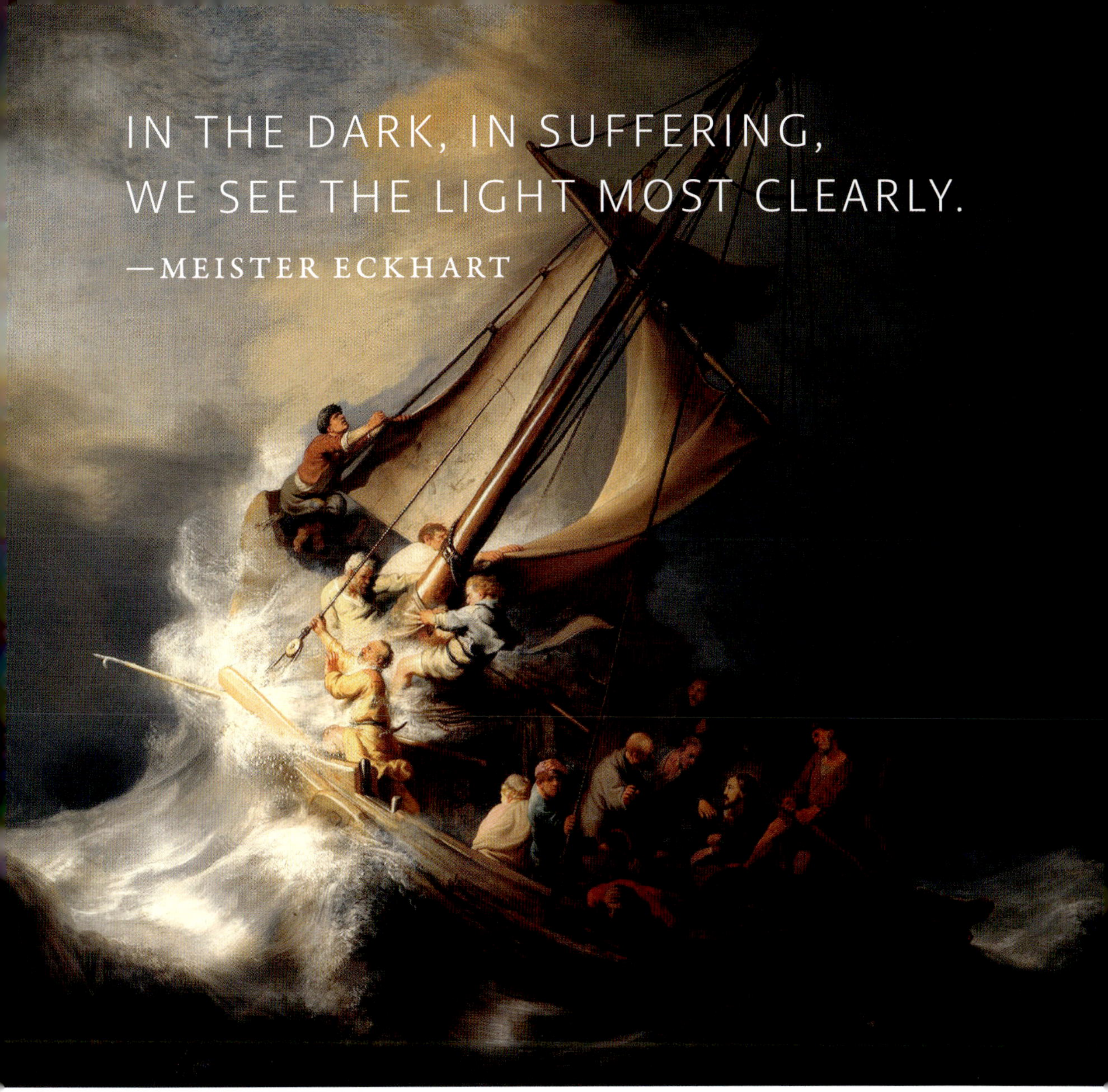

another day. Sometimes it takes courage to believe, but I do. Over many years of joys and sorrows, I have learned nothing to contradict my summation of the Bible, jotted in pencil when I was a child:

"Life stinks. God cares."

Rembrandt van Rijn,
Storm on the Sea of Galilee, 1633,
Location unknown

GRIEF IN ETERNITY

"The question *When is death?* becomes *When is grief?*"

> *I am the Living One; I was dead, and now look, I am alive for ever and ever!*
>
> REVELATION 1:18A

"We haven't talked in three weeks," I once messaged my daughter. "You know how long that is in DAD YEARS???" Jess promptly replied: "Hahahaha! Geez. Well, your little lady loves her dad! I'll give you a call." Which she did.

It seems natural to miss our children when they aren't with us. What kind of father would I have been if I hadn't missed Jess? What kind of father would I be now if I stopped missing her because she is dead? I miss my daughter because I love her. And love has no time limit.

Many Americans are uncomfortable with this kind of talk. Some insist that therapy is called for if we continue to share fond memories of our dead beyond a finite and expected timeline. But not everyone sees it this way. In Egypt, for example, the accepted period of mourning is five years or more. One study in Cairo revealed that a major loss, particularly the death of a child, is expected to cause suffering and grief for decades. An Egyptian mother was thought to be acting quite normally when she experienced days of overwhelming sorrow seven years after her child's passing.

"Grief is expressed so differently from culture to culture," writes respected death researcher Paul Rosenblatt, "that it is absurd to use notions of pathology derived from one culture to evaluate people from another." It is equally unjust to do the same from one person to another, Rosenblatt adds, particularly in the area of a perceived "living spiritual connection" with our dead. "Some people are grieving the permanent end of the relationship," he observes, "while others are grieving the end of one form of the relationship and of those aspects of the relationship that involve concrete actions."

We may accept the advice of others and foolishly expect a quick recovery from loss. A week or so is fine, the thinking goes, a few months if you must, but more seems excessive. "'Time heals,' we are frequently told," writes Charles Corr with Southern Illinois University. "However, this is really not accurate. There are no fixed end points for mourning." Nearly seventy percent of bereaved parents report that it took three to four years to put their child's death into perspective and continue living in any meaningful way. They add that they are forever changed by the loss.

I too am changed. I mourn deeply and love Jess ceaselessly, yet I am also more prone to whimsy and flights of fancy than I was before she died. I was delighted to discover that this is expected. Clinicians have found that many bereaved parents take on some of their child's endearing character traits as a type of personal memorial. I have certainly embraced parts of myself that Jess loved, or that remind me of her.

And so I ask myself, just as Jess might have done, *Is she still with us? Is my daughter free of our time-enslaved existence, wandering at will and interacting with our world? If so, where would she go?* Egypt, for one. She loved it so. And why not? Ancient Egyptians, like modern Christians, saw time as both linear and cyclical.

Okay, okay, bear with me.

We are familiar with the first idea: In our physical world, time is linear; it has a beginning and an end. Many parents, myself included, mark the calendars of our lives before and after the death of our child.

The second aspect is a bit harder to grasp but is solidly in the realm of Christian theology. Eternity is outside of time itself. Describing it as cyclical is perhaps the closest we can come to understanding the unfathomable. After all, what do time and space mean to the God who created both?

C. S. Lewis related that as he anxiously waited for the results from a biopsy, he prayed for a good result. He joked that logic assured him such prayers were likely to be a bit too late, but he wasn't certain. If God is outside of time as we know it, Lewis posited, then surely it would be no difficulty for him to step back to the day the cancer may have begun and heal it—in which case, the test results would be benign. (Which, in fact, they were.) Lewis wasn't far from the ancients in his thinking.

Egyptians saw eternity as both the changeless pattern of all existence and life's continual renewal. They believed that because our dead are eternal, they exist outside of our physical world. They retain their personalities and continue their bonds with us. This ongoing relationship provides a hope for our loved one's presence in this life, they thought, and for a reunion in the next. Perhaps in our modern obsession with therapy, in which "getting over it" is seen as a desirable goal, we have lost an important source of solace.

Prior to the twentieth century, observes Dana Luciano with Rutgers University, mourners made space in their lives for natural and sacred grief. "Grief's time moved, like Sundays, at a different pace from ordinary time," Luciano writes. "It was slower, more capacious, almost spatialized, enabling contradictory feelings (pain and pleasure) to be indulged at once and without traumatic contradiction." This slowing of time facilitated thoughtful introspection and a continuation of the natural affections that perpetuate our essential humanness. "In this light, the altered flow of time experienced by the mourner could (and, I argue, was) understood as a version of sacred time," concludes Luciano, "the regenerative mode that transcended ordinary time in a ritual revisiting of origins." She has a point. For many who grieve, time is far from ordinary.

I learned of my daughter's passing two days after her death. I still refer to that evening as "the day I learned my daughter died" to indicate when my grief began, the onset of my personal timeline of sorrow. One scholar suggests that this chronology is different for each individual. Douglas Davies, an expert in the history, theology, and sociology of death with the University of Durham, coined the phrase *Grief Mean Time* to indicate when actual mourning begins. "Experience counts," he writes. "The question 'when is death?' thus becomes 'when is grief?'" This question offers insight and relief for many of the bereaved.

For example, author Cara Paiuk's father died of cancer shortly after her fourth birthday. As an adult, she relates that her few memories of him are flimsy, flickering, and distorted with time. "What I lost was intangible—an idea, a dream, a whisper of a parent," she writes. "I am mourning a past that never was and a father I will never know." Paiuk relates that her sense of loss seems hazy and undefined.

Journalist Philip Yancey lost his father a month after his first birthday. However, it was not until the author was eighteen that he learned of disturbing events that contributed to the death. "The most important fact of my father's death I learned by chance, from a scrapbook," he says. Yancey's father, a twenty-three-year-old husband and parent of two, died of polio after being removed from his "iron lung" in a doomed attempt at faith healing.

The death had cast a pall over Yancey's life long before he learned that his father's treatment had been cut short against medical advice. This shocking news, though, was something else entirely. "Once exposed," the author confesses, "the mystery of my father's death acquires a new, compulsive power." Although nearly two decades had passed, Yancey's reaction was typical of the first year after a sudden, unexpected loss. Survivors often seem to obsess over the death, replaying it in their minds, filling in details that they do not know and may never learn. In a very real way, an important aspect of Yancey's grief began the moment he read a few newspaper clippings in a family album.

Another beginning of grief may be associated with identity loss, such as occurs with Alzheimer's disease or the slow advancement of dementia, when valued interaction with loved ones declines along with social recognition of the afflicted as a *person*. One study of 129 subjects, conducted by a team of psychologists at the University of Barcelona, found that those who lose loved ones to the slow degradation of these diseases experience a unique form of anticipatory grief: the expected distress, anxiety, and sadness associated with loss; as well as a slow reorganization of the family dynamic; and a growing sense of detachment. With Alzheimer's and dementia, the researchers write, "anticipatory grief is considered an active psychological process of thoughts and emotions that is very different from the mere anticipation of death." Survivors report that they mourned these losses in prelude to the grief that began with the end of biological life.

Davies concludes his essay on *Grief Mean Time* by suggesting that the onset of sorrow is also a start of something else: "Death can mean the beginning of a sensed presence of the dead, or of an eternal God with whom a sensed affinity seems to guarantee one's own immortality."

Ancient Egyptians also saw death as a beginning, using the word "shadow" to symbolize the eternal soul. Our loved ones, like shadows, often seem present but just out of reach. After the soul and life force are reunited, they believed, our dead will become transfigured spirits, known as *akh*: shadows.

"Within these burials and mummies there is a lot of emotion, there is a lot of feeling," observes Basem Gehad, field archaeologist with the Egyptian Ministry of Antiquities. "Beloved people, beloved families. You can hear their voices, you can see their faces." The mayor of Nekheb (modern Elkab) was one such man. Nearly 3,500 years ago, his family inscribed Paheri's tomb with a paradox known to many who grieve. He seemed at once a *part* of this world while existing *apart* from it:

> At night a light is lit for you until the sun shines again.
> "Welcome!" you are greeted in the house of the living.
> You arise by day, beautiful and cleansed of the dark.
> You travel eternity in joy, filled with the praise of God.
> Your soul does not leave you; it is your own forever.

Paheri's inscription describes mixed emotions that many of us know—light and dark, presence and absence, hope and sorrow. Ancient Egyptians believed that earthly ties continue in eternity. They placed palm leaves in circles as a sign of our endless union. A tomb painting for the artisan Pachedu, in Deir el-Medina, uses a sacred palm tree to symbolize his connection to the invisible and physical worlds. Some 3,300 years ago mourners often laid palm fronds before funeral processions to ease their loved one's passing. Egyptians still plant palm leaves on graves in remembrance of their dead.

My daughter's grave is covered with ferns. Wherever I see the hardy plant I am reminded of our bond in life and death. This solace does not alleviate my grief. The pain of her absence remains. Yet at times, if only for a moment, I feel the shadow over my days is transformed into pure spirit. Such thoughts give me a surprising sense of quiet joy.

My fancy again flits to Egypt. I imagine Jess in eternity, perhaps wading through the Nile or standing before the 3,000-year-old statues of Ramesses II at Abu Simbel—while simultaneously feeling her near as I type. This is the first time I've sensed her presence since this morning, and that is a very, very long time in Dad years.

Vincent van Gogh,
Starry Night Over the Rhône, 1888,
Musée d'Orsay

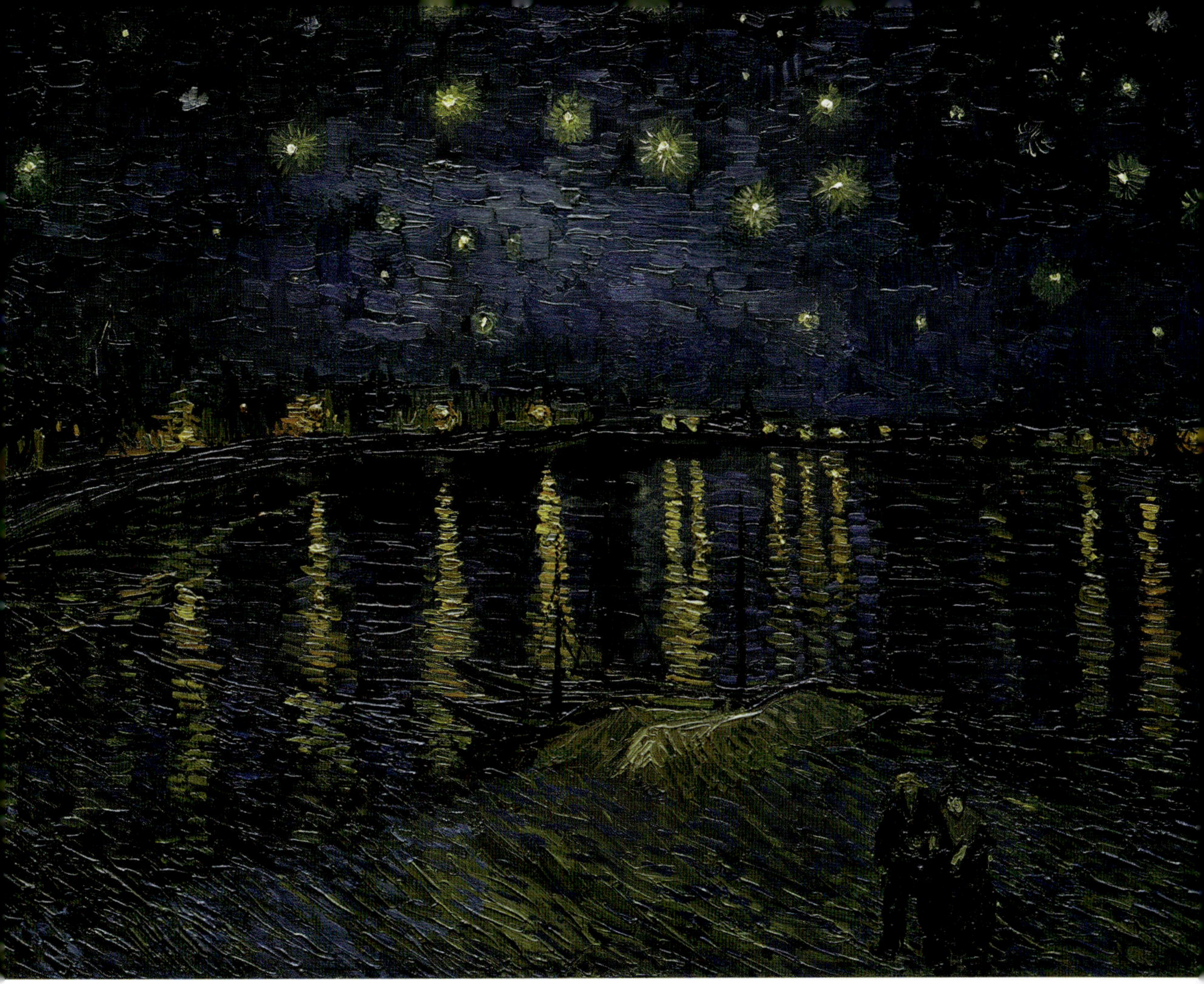

PEOPLE TALK AS IF GRIEF WERE JUST A FEELING—AS IF IT WEREN'T THE CONTINUALLY RENEWED SHOCK OF SETTING OUT AGAIN AND AGAIN ON FAMILIAR ROADS AND BEING BROUGHT UP SHORT BY THE GRIM FRONTIER POST THAT NOW BLOCKS THEM. I, TO BE SURE, BELIEVE THERE IS SOMETHING BEYOND IT: BUT THE MOMENT ONE TRIES TO USE THAT AS A CONSOLATION (THAT IS NOT ITS FUNCTION) THE BELIEF CRUMBLES. IT IS QUITE USELESS KNOCKING AT THE DOOR OF HEAVEN FOR EARTHLY COMFORT: IT'S NOT THE SORT OF COMFORT THEY SUPPLY THERE.

—C. S. LEWIS

MARY SHELLEY WALKS ALONE

"My grief was active, striving, expectant."

> *Can I bring him back again? I will go to him, but he will not return to me.*
>
> 2 SAMUEL 12:23B (CJB)

Each page of *Frankenstein* reflects the tears of its creator. Mary Shelley's fantasy of creating life from death is steeped in regret, anger, helplessness, and abandonment. Yet her artistic expression, for all its horror, is an act of healthy grief.

The book's protagonist, Victor Frankenstein, is a vile creator who refuses his creature a parent's love. The monster's sense of betrayal is heartbreaking. He compares himself to the devil, adding, "Yet even that enemy of God and man had friends and associates in his desolation; I am alone."

These words are nearly prophetic for Mary. Years later, after much grief, she writes, "What I suffer! What I have suffered! Tears are in my eyes when I think of days, weeks, months, even years spent alone—eternally alone." Mary is an orphan, a bereaved parent, and a widow, yet she faces life with rare courage and surprising resolve.

Her mother, Mary Wollstonecraft, dies within ten days of Mary's birth, casting a pall over the child's relationship with her father, philosopher William Godwin. He suffers from narcolepsy, occasionally falling into a deep sleep at table, appearing almost dead, only to awaken later. This troubling illness plays out in front of young Mary, who notes with horror the slender line between life and the appearance of death.

This may be one reason that from an early age Mary spends hours at her mother's grave. It is there, at sixteen, that she frequently meets with the dashing Percy Shelley, aged twenty and married. "Go to the tomb and read," she writes in her journal. "Go with Shelley to the churchyard." And it is there that she first professes her love to Shelley on June 26, 1814. Within a month, they run away together to France. Her stepsister, Jane (later called Claire), joins them.

The couple is well-suited. Shelley is impressed by her beauty, independence, and an intelligence that surpasses his own; Mary enjoys his brilliance, passion, and the equality of their exchanges. "I conversed with him," she writes, "obtained new lights from him, & my mind is satisfied." But their headstrong departure is too much for Godwin. He never forgives Mary.

The couple returns to London for the birth of their first child. Clara is delivered prematurely on February 22, 1815, in Hillingdon. Busy with a newborn, Mary jots only brief daily notes in her journal: "Nurse the baby, read." She wakes in the night of March 5 to breastfeed, but the infant is sleeping so quietly Mary does not rouse her. The next morning, March 6, twelve days after Clara's birth, Mary writes, "Find my baby dead."

She has recurring, vivid dreams of Clara returning to her. "Dream that my little baby came to life again; that it had only been cold, and that we rubbed it before the fire, and it lived," she says, adding, "Awake and find no baby." The loss affects Mary for the rest of her life: "Whenever I am left alone to my own thoughts, they always come back to the same point—that I was a mother, and am so no longer."

It comes as no surprise, then, that a little over a year later, in June, 1816, Mary begins work on a novel of life and death, *Frankenstein; or, The Modern Prometheus*. The novel famously came about because of a parlor game at the instigation of Lord Byron in Geneva. The summer of 1816 is no summer at all—snows, freezing rains, and days that seem to lose their light by noon. These darkened skies are the result of an eruption of Mount Tambora in Indonesia a year earlier. Byron leases the Villa Diodati in Coligny and invites the Shelleys to take up residence in a nearby cottage. They gather each day in this gloomy atmosphere to discuss poetry, philosophy, and the mysteries of life. Then Byron surprises them.

He suggests that each member of their party compose a ghost story. The idea is greeted with enthusiasm, but soon is cast aside for more interesting pastimes. The results are desultory. Byron produces a meager effort; Shelley nothing at all; Claire does little more than continue the romance she began with Byron in April; and John Polidori starts his short fiction, *The Vampyre*, published in 1819. But for Mary, the challenge leads to a startling book that speaks to her grief and deepest yearnings.

On June 16, between 2:00 a.m. and 3:00 a.m., she has a "waking dream . . . with shut eyes, but acute mental vision," assisted in part by the group's steady ingestion of wine and laudanum. "I saw the hideous phantasm of a man stretched out, and then, on the working of some powerful engine, show signs of life, and stir with an uneasy, half vital motion." Years later, in her introduction to a revised edition in 1831, she writes that her novel was "making only a transcript of the grim terrors of my waking dream," a vision that has striking similarities to her recurring dreams of restoring infant Clara to life. This connection between the birth of *Frankenstein* and the death of Mary's baby is not as tenuous as it may seem.

"Although Frankenstein's creation of life from dead bodies might seem far removed," says Fiona Stafford with the University of Oxford, "there is some association, I think, in Mary Shelley's mind between birth and death." Biographer Miranda Seymour sees in these dreams a direct link to the novel. "It's difficult *not* to think of that when we see her, two years later, writing the story of a creature being quickened into life," she says. Noted French author Jean-Claude Carrière agrees. "She probably thought a lot about life, about death, about why her child died," he suggests, adding that having lost a child, Mary was now carrying one born of her imagination.

Seen in this light, any morbid sentiments in *Frankenstein* are understandable and surprisingly practical: a sharp reminder of death, the varied aspects of sorrow, and the fragility of existence. "Life, although it may only be an accumulation of anguish," cries the creature, "is dear to me." Mary's monster is articulate, reasoning, and a being of deep and profound feeling. "He's by far the most eloquent person in the book," notes Seymour. "Far more so than Frankenstein."

Yet the creature's anguish soon turns to hate. Cultural historian Charles Frayling suggests this is the result of rejection by his only father, Frankenstein, without the intercession of a mother. Mary also knows paternal abandonment shorn of comforting maternal love. She dedicates the book to Godwin, but it is not clear if this is a compliment, a satirical critique, or a plea for his affection. Just as her novel is steeped in conflicting emotions, so too, is its author.

Mourners often speak of losing their illusions of control and safety. In fact, clinicians assure us that negative emotions like disillusionment, fear, and regret are characteristic of healthy grief. "When a culture no longer provides adequate forms of mourning," writes researcher Mary O'Neill on novels like *Frankenstein*, "these works can act as a means of engaging with bereavement, disenfranchised grief and ambiguous loss."

Young Mary Shelley is finding ways to express herself in a culture that condemns her. But her suffering has only begun.

On January 24, 1816, Mary gives birth to a son, William, named after her father. They call him "Willmouse." She and Shelley marry that same year, on December 30, at the church of Saint Mildred in London. Within five months she completes *Frankenstein*, and none too soon. On September 2, 1817, another daughter, Clara Everina, is born. The girl dies of dysentery shortly after her first birthday, on September 24, 1818, in Venice. Then while the grieving family is in Rome, on June 7, 1819, three-year-old Willmouse dies of malaria. They bury him in a local Protestant cemetery, but the heartbroken father insists that his son's spirit does not lie in a tomb:

> —if a thing divine
> Like thee can die, thy funeral shrine
> Is thy mother's grief and mine.
> Where art thou, my gentle child?
> Let me think thy spirit feeds,
> With its life intense and mild,
> The love of living leaves and weeds
> Among these tombs and ruins wild

Five months after William dies, on November 12, 1819, another son is born: Percy Florence. Three years later, Mary is again pregnant but miscarries on June 16, 1822—six years to the day of her waking dream that led to *Frankenstein*. Blood loss nearly kills her. Then, as she recovers, on July 8, Percy Shelley and retired army officer Edward Williams drown in the Gulf of Spezia. "Great God! No, he is not there, he is with me, about me," Mary cries when she sees the box containing her husband's ashes. "Life of my life, and soul of my soul; if his divine spirit did not penetrate mine I could not survive to weep thus."

Shelley is buried near his son Willmouse and his friend John Keats in Rome's Protestant cemetery. But like her husband, Mary does not believe her loved ones lie in the cold ground.

She senses her three children, Shelley, and his friend are still with her. She insists that in death "a wild and beautiful spirit" lives on with "a beauty of its own." She relates that once, when she dozes off, Edward's spirit comes to pass a few hours with her, though he cannot stay long.

Near the first memorial day of her husband's death, in July, 1823, Mary composes an elegiac poem of despair and hope, "The Choice." It is her most personal yet strikingly formal piece. Arnold Markley with Penn State University notes that it tackles head-on the central issue of "how to have a continuing intercourse in spirit with a man who can no longer be an earthly lover."

Mary opens the poem with a prayer to her husband, candidly recalling the struggles their relationship endured and asking forgiveness for her "cold neglect." This kind of honesty is especially helpful after a loss: Mary's lament anchors her love in reality. She also mourns their second daughter, Clara Everina, who rests in the Protestant section of the Lido Cemetery, Venice, and their son, Willmouse:

> A happy Mother first I saw this sun,
> Beneath this sky my race of joy was run.
> First my sweet girl, whose face resembled *his*,
> Slept on bleak Lido, near Venetian seas.
> Yet still my eldest-born, my loveliest, dearest,
> Clung to my side, most joyful then when nearest.
> . . .
> His spoils were strewed beneath the soil of Rome,
> Whose flowers now star the dark earth near his tomb:
> Its airs and plants received the mortal part,
> His spirit beats within his Mother's heart.
> Infant immortal! chosen for the sky!
> No grief upon thy brow's young purity
> Entrenched sad lines, or blotted with its might
> The sunshine of thy smile's celestial light;—

> The image shattered, the bright spirit fled,
> Thou shin'st the evening star among the dead.

Mary includes sorrowful lines for Shelley's friend Edward, and for Allegra, the daughter of her stepsister Claire and Lord Byron. She speaks reverently of nature, where her husband is now free to wander the vast gulf waters. "The spirit waits with this in our far home," she writes,

> The sad revolving year has not allayed
> The poison of these bleeding wounds, or made
> The anguish less of that corroding thought
> Which had with grief each single moment fraught

Modern readers may dismiss Mary's sorrow as negative or brooding, but often such moments of remembrance have a positive impact on the bereaved. Creative expressions provide a means to mourn openly. They offer meaning and gentle memory. Mary will need both.

Now Mary is alone with three-year-old Percy Florence—an ostracized widow and a bereaved mother of three dead children. But she does not give up: "I no longer enjoy, but I love. Death cannot deprive me of that living spark which feeds on all given it, and which is now triumphant in sorrow. I love, and shall enjoy happiness again. I do not doubt that; but when?"

I am struck by the similarities between Mary's question and the psalmist's lament, "How long must I wrestle with my thoughts and day after day have sorrow in my heart?" Her plea also calls to mind a poem by another nineteenth-century author who wrote about grief, Christina Rossetti:

> *Yet a little while*
> Heaven is not far, tho' far the sky
>   Overarching earth and main.
> It takes not long to live and die,
>   Die, revive, and rise again.
> Not long: how long? Oh, long re-echoing song!
> O Lord, how long?

Mary's heart is *all wounds*, she says, but she anticipates a day of reunion after death "when I forget a thousand memories and griefs that are as yet alive and burning." She keeps locks of Clara's and William's hair in her writing desk for the rest of her life. Such keepsakes are normal and can be helpful when waves of grief return over the years. "O my god—what a lot is mine," Mary mourns anew on June 7, 1836, William's seventeenth memorial day. "Tracked by disappointment & unutterable wretchedness—blow after blow—my heart dies within me."

Today much of Mary Shelley's work is acknowledged as noteworthy: *Frankenstein* is a staple in many college courses. One of her lesser-known short stories, "The Mourner," written in 1829, depicts a daughter's guilt after her father drowns. She weaves insights on family, love, hope, and death into a poignant tale on the complicated nature of grief. She touches upon similar themes in "The Dream." This too is healthy. Writing "provides us with the metaphors to experience ongoing attachment," observes psychologist and grief research pioneer Margaret Stroebe, "to help us understand and find a place for the loss." Mary does just that.

Her novels, *Frankenstein*, *Matilda*, and *The Last Man*, reflect the author's life of abandonment and grief. In each book, her characters lose loved ones and end up alone.

Mary begins *Matilda* on November 9, 1819, five months after William's death and just a few days before the birth of Percy Florence. "When I wrote *Matilda*, miserable as I was," she confesses, "the *inspiration* was sufficient to quell my wretchedness temporarily." This is also true of her 1826 book, *The Last Man*, which according to Constance Walker with Carleton College is best understood in the context of parental bereavement. Writing the novel is not easy for Mary.

Throughout 1824, she wrestles with grief and painful loneliness. "The last man!" Mary exclaims on May 14. "Yes I may well describe that solitary being's feelings, feeling myself as the last relic of a beloved race, my companions extinct before me." The next day she receives news that "dear capricious fascinating Albe [Lord Byron]," a friend of many years, particularly that summer in Geneva of 1816 when *Frankenstein* was born, has died in Greece.

Within a few weeks she is writing again, "a pleasure not a task . . . as I pour forth my soul upon paper." But *The Last Man* is not published until 1826. It takes all of Mary's powers to finish it, and even then she feels there isn't time to give the book its due. Had she known this, she admits, "I should never have had the courage to begin." And yet for many readers, this is her finest novel.

The Last Man is redolent of resignation and resolve. Mary writes of a pandemic that nearly extinguishes all life on earth. In the end, after losing everyone he loves, her titular character, Lionel Verney, sets out in a small boat with only a dog and books as companions. "Neither hope nor joy are my pilots," Mary writes in the voice of her protagonist. Under the sun, the moon, and the eyes of angels, God, and the spirits of the dead, the boat sails on, its captain longing for "some task, however slight or voluntary, for each day's fulfillment." Two hundred years later, modern therapists have a name for Mary's insight: *meaning reconstruction*.

Grief expert and psychology professor at the University of Memphis, Robert Neimeyer, suggests that authors like Mary Shelley express "the extent to which our most intimate sense of self is rooted (and uprooted) in our shifting relationships with others." Death disrupts our lives in the most fundamental way. We feel a strong need to come to terms with the sudden abyss that loss creates. This normal reaction is called *meaning reconstruction*, which includes putting the death in perspective as well as finding some purpose to our lives ahead. In this way, Mary's writing serves as both lament and adjustment.

But it's not all doom and misery, observes Thomas Bauer, a specialist in grief-related poetry at the University of Münster. Prose and verse often contain an "artistic and playful element," he writes, that facilitates healthy mourning. Many of Mary's stories have moments of whimsy that help to express pain and provide a means of coping. This in turn offers relief from passive suffering. Creation in honor of our dead allows us to give voice to our love for them through sorrow and memory. "A poem (or any other work of art)," Bauer concludes, "is a means to break the speechlessness of death."

Mary writes with gentle pathos, patience, and calm—traits common to those who have endured terrible loss. Her observations on life's many ironies offer catharsis for author and reader alike. Yet in her originality and considerable wit she is more than a pioneer of science fiction or horror. *Frankenstein* closes with Victor dead in a frozen wasteland as his creation wanders alone into darkness. But Mary's story does not end in the starless black.

HOW OFTEN IN THE INTENSITY OF GRIEF DOES ONE INSTANT SEEM TO FILL AND EMBRACE THE UNIVERSE! IT IS BETTER TO GRIEVE THAN NOT TO GRIEVE. GRIEF AT LEAST TELLS ME THAT I WAS NOT ALWAYS WHAT I AM NOW. I WAS ONCE SELECTED FOR HAPPINESS; LET THE MEMORY OF THAT ABIDE BY ME.

—MARY SHELLEY

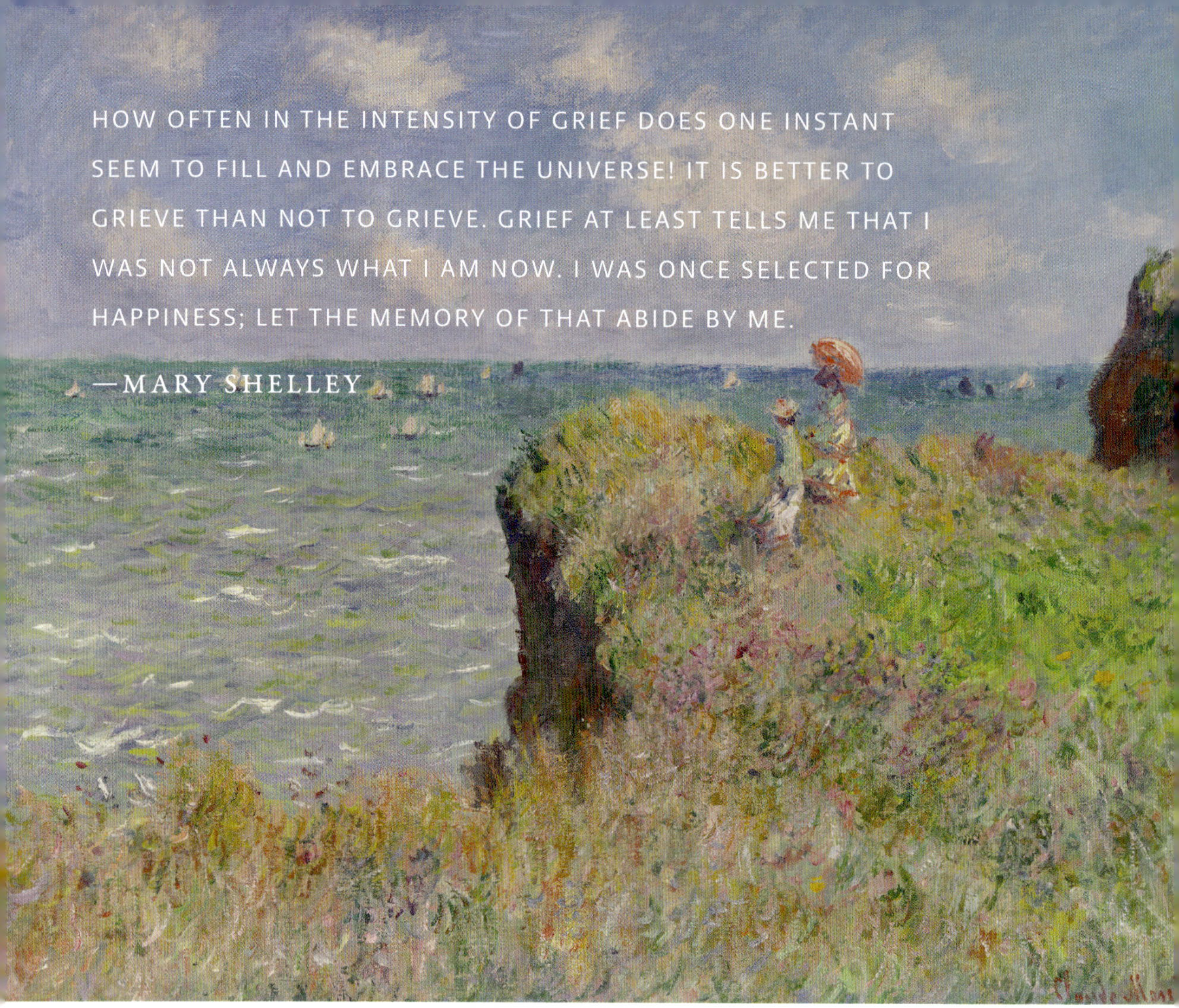

She and Percy Florence return to England after Shelley drowns. There, Mary often walks alone. Solitude is difficult, yes, but also helpful. "My grief was active, striving, expectant," she confesses. "I sounded the depths of my own nature, magnificent, deep, pathetic, wild, and exalted." She does not turn from these dark depths. Rather, her sorrows, and her words, speak to us of love across the centuries.

Claude Monet,
Cliff Walk at Pourville, 1882,
Mr. and Mrs. Lewis Larned Coburn Memorial Collection
Art Institute of Chicago

FACING LOSS WITH JOB AND *FAUST*

"Job plans to try and console himself and grieve."

> *I lie in the dust; revive me by your word. . . . I weep with sorrow; encourage me by your word.*
>
> PSALM 119:25, 28 (NLT)

We are obsessed with the *why* of things. Why did my loved one die? Why do mass shootings continue? Why is there suffering in the world? Why evil? Yet *why* can sometimes be the wrong question. "I do not want God to 'make it plain,'" wrote author and theologian Lewis Smedes on the death of his infant son. "I have given up asking why such bad things happen." Smedes had a point.

How, the close cousin of *why*, interests me even less. I know how my mother passed: cancer. I know how my father and uncle died. Age and disease, alas, are the way of the world. There is little mystery to how my niece and my wife's younger brother died. How my daughter, Jess, died is written on the death certificate: a fentanyl-laced heroin overdose. These details are crass, uninteresting, morbid.

But words like "eternal" and "afterlife" have taken on new meaning. *Is my daughter happy and safe?* I ask. *Is she near, as close as a falling leaf or the taste of an apple or a distant hawk's cry? Does she continue on?* Tell me this that I may endure the rest: *Where is she now?*

Sometimes I quip to other bereaved parents that if angels appeared today—say Michael and Gabriel—my first response would be, "Mike, Gabe, glad to know you. Where's Jess?" I have yet to meet a fellow mourner that did not nod in quiet recognition of my little joke. They, too, ask of their dead loved ones:

Where are they now?

Mourners have posed these queries for centuries, in a tradition that traces its lineage to the Book of Job. In that story, the protagonist and his visitors tackle topics of suffering and the silence of God. They observe that we have a disconnect between what we perceive with our senses—the misery in this world—and what exists beyond them. Yes, we believe the soul exists, and yet, and yet.

God permits the slaughter of Job's ten children, attacks on his health, and the loss of his belongings. Job quite reasonably insists that God's hand is heavy. Then he surprises us. Job repeatedly identifies himself with "dust and ashes." Katherine Southwood, an expert in the Hebrew Bible with the University of Oxford, explains that the words *dust* and *ashes* are frequently tied to mortality, human frailty, and mourning. "Job plans to try and console himself and grieve," she writes, "[he] is just a mere mortal of 'dust and ashes.'"

Job's awareness of "dust and ashes" progresses from the *outside in*, according to Ariel Hirschfeld, professor of Hebrew literature at the Hebrew University of Jerusalem. Job is *sitting in* dust and ashes; then he is *like* dust and ashes; until at last he *is* dust and ashes. This final revelation "is the realm of the divine," Hirschfeld concludes, when Job simultaneously inhabits the physical and invisible worlds, crossing the chasm between his skin and his soul.

Many mourners feel similar yearnings in the face of cold reality. We hope for a future reunion; at times we may even feel our loved ones near, bridging the gap between our physical and spiritual worlds. Then we blink, and like Job, are painfully reminded that here in the dust we must merely believe. "Have I enough strength to go on waiting?" Job despairs. We who have lost someone may ask the same question.

After a death, long-ignored rituals linger in our minds, often just below the surface. Without them—the funeral, music, and customs—we feel adrift. I saw this every day when I worked in a busy funeral home. People often turned to the Psalter for consolation, but not those hymns popular in Sunday services. Many believers seek psalms of lament in times of loss. These songs make up one third of the Psalter, and for good reason. They echo our sorrow from across the centuries.

For example, Job's lament influenced the unknown author of Psalm 119, an important hymn used in Western mourning rituals. German tradition holds that 119 encompasses all other psalms. This is why Heinrich Schütz set it to music in 1671. When Schütz died a year later, his setting was performed at the funeral, along with a separate motet using Psalm 119 as composed by his former student Christoph Bernhard. It was also the text for his memorial sermon:

"I lie in the dust; revive me by your word. . . . I weep with sorrow; encourage me by your word."

"I have spoken of the unspeakable and tried to grasp the infinite, but now my eyes have seen you," Job declares when God appears at the end of the book. "Therefore I will be quiet, comforted that I am dust." Rabbinical scholars and Christian theologians have wrestled with this enigmatic finale for millennia.

Semitic linguist Gustav Bickell saw relief in Job's sudden awareness that there was in fact no explanation for his unutterable suffering. Author and translator Emile Joseph Dillon went one step further, suggesting that Job's *dust and ashes* indicated complete surrender, "at once intelligible and wise." Job sees at last that life's pleasures and pains do not present themselves in easy formulae of punishment and reward. Rather, Dillon writes, "the explanation we seek, the light we so wistfully long for, will never come." A leading authority on Job, Stephen Vicchio, emeritus professor from the University of Maryland, sees the protagonist's consolation as one of finitude. This too speaks of relief. "His suffering may soon come to an end—and he is happy about that," Vicchio writes, "for we are not God."

Job's surrender resonates with me. To me as a fellow bereaved parent, questions of *why* seem suddenly and absolutely trivial. I see Job's comforting *dust and ashes* in purely practical terms. God appeared, eternity and the spiritual are real, and therefore Job's children live on. The invisible world of the soul is as tangible as my skin and my heartbreak. There is hope of reunion. As answers go, it's better than most. For Job, this may be the one comfort that matters. It certainly is for me.

The Book of Job has an unsettling mirror in Johann Wolfgang von Goethe's *Faust,* yet the play holds a fond place in my heart. On October 30, 2009, I saw Hector Berlioz's *La Damnation de Faust* at the Metropolitan Opera in New York City. The next day I called my daughter for Halloween, one of her favorite holidays. I was in Manhattan to lecture at the American Translators Association's fiftieth annual conference. That was my big news, I crowed, but Jess didn't care. "You saw *Faust* on Devil's Night?" she interrupted. "How cool is that?" My presentation is a distant memory, but Jess's enthusiasm will forever bring a gentle smile to my lips.

Like the book of Job, Goethe's *Faust* also addresses concerns of dust and eternity, approaching them from a wholly different perspective. Both stories feature a bet with God over a man's soul; each speaks to our struggle to embrace the spiritual when faced with a daunting physical world. But here the similarities take a shocking turn. Job was a bereaved parent, beset with poverty and horrifying malignancies. Misery consumed his world, as described by Emily Dickinson in 1862:

> Pain—has an Element of Blank—
> It cannot recollect
> When it begun—or if there were
> A time when it was not—

Whereas Job's abysmal condition had little to offer, in Goethe's play, Mephistopheles overwhelms Faust with transient worldly joys. He provides shallow copies of all that was taken from Job. Faust has companionship, wealth, health, and the renewed vigor of youth. Fame, fortune and excess are all his. These may prove temporary and insubstantial, but this seldom stops us from greedily consuming them as treasures of value. "Dust he will eat," chortles Mephistopheles. "And he'll like it."

Faust falls prey to a common quirk: When things go well, the spiritual world may seem uninteresting if not unimportant. Soon enough he discovers that the world's largesse is dust. Faust can tell little difference between the eternity of his soul and his gluttony of dirt.

Goethe created a vision of "an imperfect Job and an imperfect God," observes Ilana Pardes, professor of comparative literature at the Hebrew University of Jerusalem, in which "the Lord's ways are rather dubious." Mephistopheles gloated to God, who accepted the wager, that he would have Faust wallowing in the muck "like my famed relation, the snake." The tales have a similar goal: Faust and Job must betray transcendence and focus wholly on the tangible.

And yet, in the end, neither does.

Tonight questions of death and afterlife seem larger than usual. My thoughts naturally turn to my dad, dead these many years. He was a professional photographer. From him I learned that "forced perspective" is a filmic trick in which objects appear smaller than they actually are.

Grief, too, forces a new perspective. What we imagined was important recedes from view. Wealth and fame offer few lasting rewards; death and pain, surprisingly

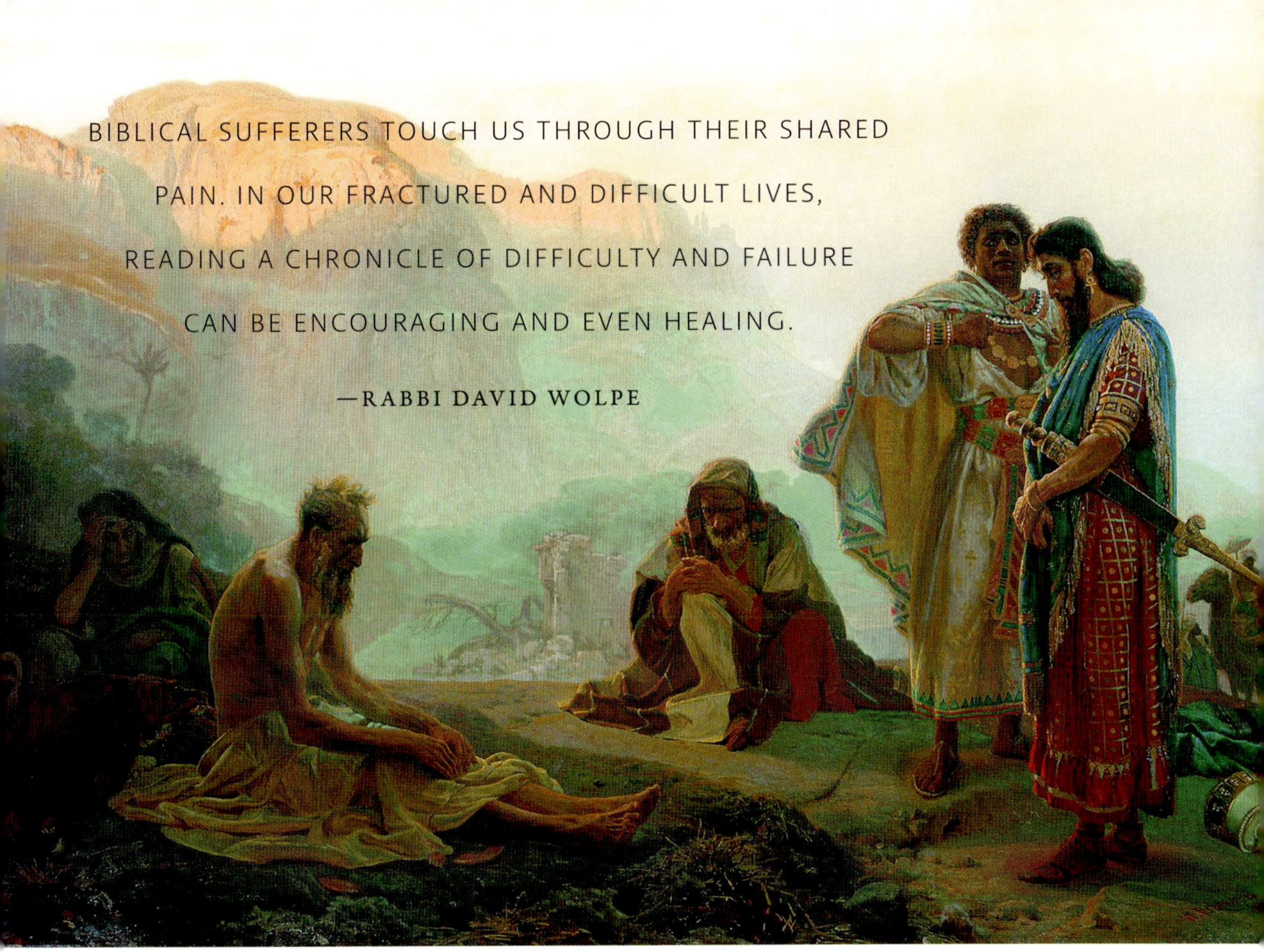

scant fear. Questions of *why* seem trivial. Suddenly we see with terrible clarity what matters most. We are desperate for any hint of our loved ones. Spare us homilies and theodicy, we may muse. We are surrounded by ashes and need to know: *Where are they now? Will we see them again?* After all, *how* they died is not nearly as important as *who* they were to us.

"Adonai has compassion," sang the psalmist, "for he understands how we are made, he remembers that we are dust." Perhaps in our dust of grief, we see clearly for the first time.

Ilya Repin,
Job and His Friends, 1869,
Russian Museum

THE LAST OF THE LION'S BROOD

"The boy in him had died."

Live a life filled with love, following the example of Christ.

EPHESIANS 5:2A (NLT)

Theodore Roosevelt led a boisterous, strenuous life. That all changed with the loss of his son Quentin in the First World War. "To feel that one has inspired a boy to conduct that has resulted in his death," the ex-President wrote, "has a pretty serious side to a father." Self-reproach and regret came to dominate his private moments. Roosevelt died in January, 1919, six months after writing those words.

Roosevelt was no stranger to death. While the real-life cowboy and explorer may have enjoyed an anticipatory nostalgia for the mythological West, he never lost sight of its harsh realities. "The men who have shared in the fast vanishing frontier life of the present feel a peculiar sympathy with the already long-vanished frontier life of the past," he wrote in his preface to *The Winning of the West* in 1889. Roosevelt spoke from experience. Terrible grief had once led him to seek solace in the Dakota plains he adored.

Roosevelt's mother and wife died the same day: February 14, 1884. His mother succumbed to typhoid fever. His wife had given birth two days earlier to a girl. Weakened, she died of Bright's disease, a kidney ailment. Later that year Theodore entrusted the infant to his sister and left for the Dakota territories, where he spent two years as a rancher and sheriff. He returned to New York in 1886 and soon after married his second wife, Edith.

These experiences shaped Roosevelt. He understood childish yearnings, accepted them for what they were, but never allowed them to overcome his good sense. A close friend of Owen Wister, Roosevelt helped edit and correct the initial manuscript of the well-known novel *The Virginian*. Wister dedicated the book to Roosevelt.

This mix of man and boy helped mold Roosevelt into what in many ways has become a symbol of the quintessential American male, a symbol vibrantly alive to his own children. "He represented the final distillation of the Western experience," observed historian Dee Brown, "and as President he did much to imprint these traits into the American ethos where they endure to this day."

Roosevelt recognized that his longing for adventure was at times a bit of boyishness. When in 1913, at age fifty-five, the ex-President undertook a leisurely cruise down the Amazon, he coyly admitted it was his "last chance to be a boy again." Later he chose to forego his scheduled trip for an arduous trailblazing trek down the River of Doubt, a man's work about which he had no childish fantasies. The difference was absolutely clear to him. "I don't in the least mind risk to my life," he wrote, "but I want to be sure that I am not doing something for which I will find my physical strength unequal." To Roosevelt, jaunts in search of masculinity were the play of boys; reasoned wariness was the province of men.

Recalling his time in the West while campaigning for vice president in 1900, Roosevelt told a crowd in Medora, North Dakota: "Here is where the romance of my life began." And so it did. "We who have felt the charm of the life, and have exulted in its abounding vigor and its bold, restless freedom," he admitted, "will not only regret its passing for our own sakes, but must also feel real sorrow that those who come after us are not to see, as we have seen, what is perhaps the pleasantest, healthiest, and most exciting phase of American existence."

This echoed a sentiment Roosevelt had nurtured his entire life, one his sons knew and took to heart. "These outrages are, as a rule, the work of the roughs and criminals who always gather on the outskirts of civilization and who infest every frontier town," wrote Roosevelt in 1888, "until the decent citizens become sufficiently murderous and determined to take the law into their own hands and drive them out." The same civilizing spirit of justice was part of Roosevelt's less-eloquent bombast during the war years, yet he was undeniably aware of the dangers involved.

The distinction between fantasy and reality is important. Later, after his son Quentin died, Roosevelt allowed grief to obscure reason. He felt certain, somehow, that he had inspired his son to the military action that led to his death.

At the outset of the First World War, Roosevelt petitioned Woodrow Wilson to raise another contingent of Rough Riders cavalry. His request was denied. His son, Quentin, on the other hand, served in the United States Army Air Service. Two of Roosevelt's sons were already in the war. Quentin was "the last of the lion's brood" to go, as Roosevelt put it. He celebrated his son's first dogfight.

On July 14, 1918, Quentin Roosevelt was shot down in his French biplane fighter aircraft, the Nieuport 28 C.1. He was "tail-end Charlie" that day—the last plane in his formation.

Quentin had spotted three German aircraft approaching. He immediately broke off and rose alone to meet them. He made "repeated attacks" until, in a duel with an experienced non-commissioned officer who had flown with Manfred von Richthofen (the Red Baron), Quentin's aircraft was downed.

His German opponents landed. Their propaganda office required that they take a photo of the body. Having dispensed with this distasteful task, they buried him with full military honors, using wire from the Nieuport to erect a wooden cross. Within days, Americans took the area and marked the grave with a cross of their own, around which French soldiers later built an enclosure of wood.

Theodore Roosevelt had already been told about his son's death before it appeared in the newspapers. He tried to go on as usual, but at a luncheon with Albert Shaw of the *Review of Reviews*, he was unusually quiet. "Don't give up hope, Colonel," Shaw said when he arrived. "The news may not be true."

"No," said Roosevelt. "Quentin's dead. Quentin's dead."

Quentin's parents dealt with their loss differently. Roosevelt had a blustery persona that is often misunderstood, but beneath it was a great breadth and depth of feeling for his children and a subtle, tactful, resolute nature that showed itself at home and while in the White House.

Quentin's mother, Edith, was adamantine in her dealings, graceful and disciplined. She had always said, "You cannot bring up boys as eagles and expect them to turn out sparrows." Such homilies were very much her way. Just as others misunderstood Theodore's bombast, few visitors perceived the grief that lay within her composed resolve.

In August, a month after Quentin died, Nicholas Roosevelt visited prior to his leaving for service in France. "When she saw me in uniform her eyes filled with tears and she turned away," he wrote. "Then she put her hand on my arm and said: 'I'm all right, Nick; I'm all right.' And she was."

Roosevelt knew his wife better than that. On August 10, 1918, he wrote to their son Kermit: "Mother will carry the wound green to her grave." That same month, Roosevelt told Edith Wharton, "There is no use writing about Quentin for I should break down if I tried."

By the end of August he managed to write a generalized eulogy for all the young men dying in Europe. "Only those are fit to live who do not fear to die; and none are fit to die who have shrunk from the joy of life and the duty of life." This tribute, "The Great Adventure," ran in newspapers on September 17, 1918, and in the October 1918 issue of *Metropolitan* magazine. Near the end, his article's tone grew weak and sentimental. The task of writing about his son so soon after the boy's death was beyond him.

No eulogies could be more eloquent than Roosevelt's cries of grief: sitting for hours in his son's room, whispering, "Quen-tee;" rocking in the chair on which he had held his children, repeating in liturgy, "Poor Quinikins;" or when he was heard sobbing into the mane of his son's pony, "Poor Quentyquee!"

Quentin's sister, Alice, quoted the Book of Job to express their family's heartbreak: "The stout lion's whelps are scattered abroad." When General Peyton C. March asked about moving Quentin's remains, Roosevelt also relied on Scripture, this time Ecclesiastes. "Where the tree falls," he wrote March, "there let it be."

Roosevelt blamed himself for his son's death. A careful reading of Roosevelt's papers and letters clearly demonstrate a father's burden of grief and guilt. He felt that his aggressive martial convictions had led all four of his sons to volunteer for military service. "It is rather awful to know that he paid with his life," Roosevelt wrote of Quentin on September 20, "and that my other sons may pay with their lives, to try to put in practice what I preached."

On October 27, 1918, Roosevelt turned sixty. Two days later, Edith wrote to their son Kermit that his apparent stoicism was a facade. "Quentin's death shook him greatly," she wrote, adding that the physical discomfort of his rheumatism was aggravated by grief. "I can see how constantly he thinks of him and not the merry happy silly recollections which I have but sad thoughts of what Quentin would have counted for in the future."

Owen Wister visited the Roosevelts in late October. On leaving, he wrote: "They stood at their hall door as I drove off, stood watching, after their words bidding me to come again soon, she quiet beside him, he waving his hand: Quentin's father and mother, carrying on."

Three months had passed since their son's death, but as was readily apparent to Wister, it might have been three days. An acquaintance who saw Roosevelt around the same time noted that the "old exuberance" was gone "and the boy in him had died."

Theodore Roosevelt died on January 6, 1919. Edith traveled to France the following month. She had a fountain and a stone marker erected for Quentin in Chamery. The memorial's engraving was taken from Percy Bysshe Shelley's elegy for John Keats, "Adonais":

He has outsoar'd the shadow of our night

In 1955, Quentin was reinterred in the Normandy American Cemetery, abroad where he fell, as his parents wished.

JOY IS A PARTNERSHIP,

GRIEF WEEPS ALONE;

MANY GUESTS HAD CANA,

GETHSEMANE HAD ONE.

—FREDERIC LAWRENCE KNOWLES,
FROM "GRIEF AND JOY"

Carl Bloch,
Christ in Gethsemane, 1873,
The Museum of National History at Frederiksborg Castle

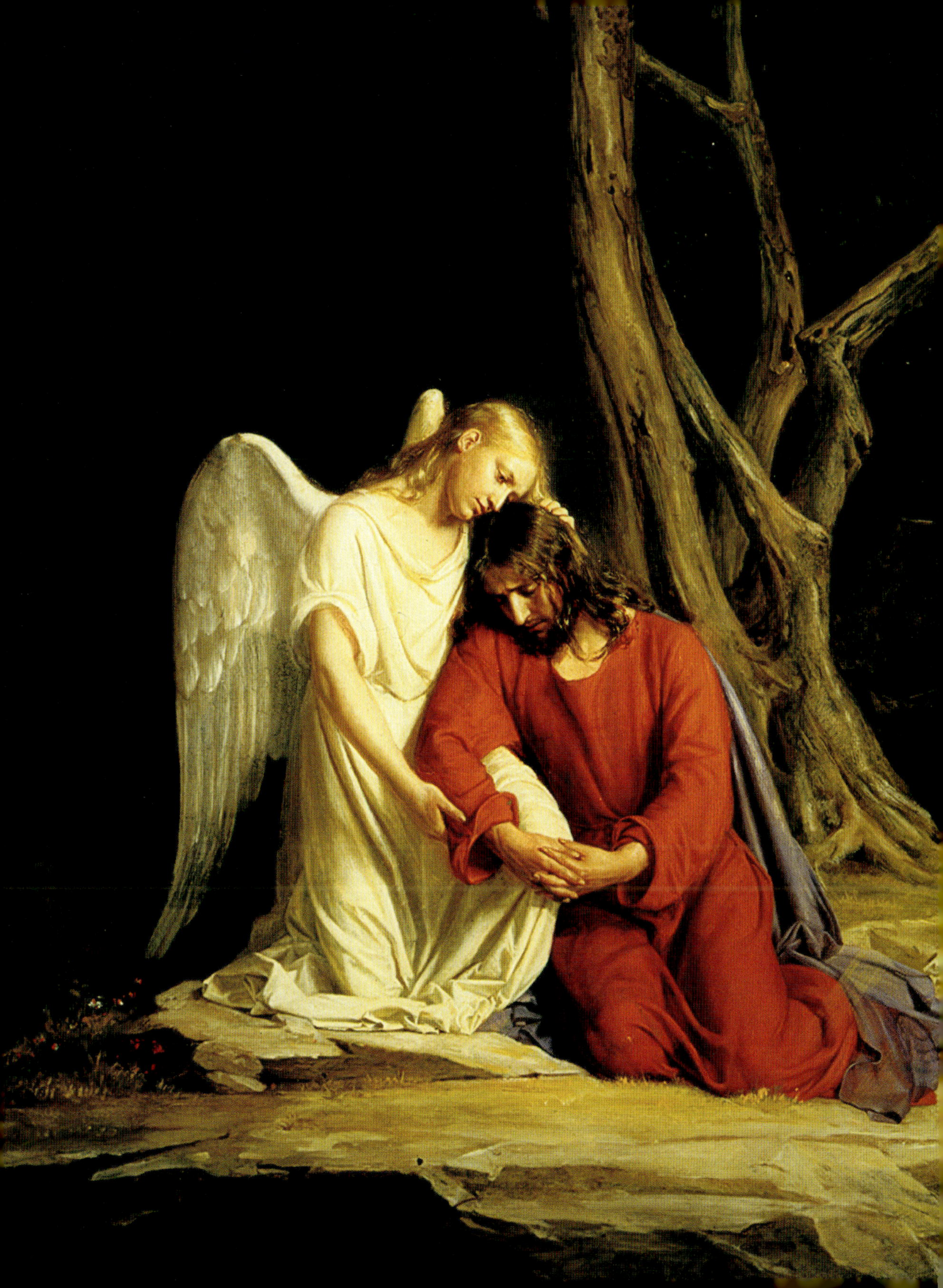

THE CONSOLATION OF SILENCE

"Faith is not a substitute for grief, but a resource."

> *"Watchman, how much longer is it night?" The watchman answers: "Morning is coming, but also the night."*
>
> ISAIAH 21:11B–012A (CJB)

Margarethe Susanna von Kuntsch lost thirteen of her fourteen children. Ten had already passed when her nine-year-old daughter, Dorothea, died on January 31, 1690. Kuntsch was devastated. Shortly afterward, she wrote a poem in response to the kind but empty platitudes of family and friends:

> Spare me your attempts at consolation:
> little wonder that they seem to shatter
> the bond between my body and my soul

Kuntsch's lament is reminiscent of Job's cry to his wrong-headed consolers: "Why offer me such meaningless comfort?" Rote condolences can seem hollow or insincere. Some may be. However, many people offer customary phrases because they do not know what else to say.

This may be one reason that the tradition of giving casseroles continues today. Supportive friends slave over their treasured recipes and present them to the house of mourning. When I worked at a busy funeral home, the bereaved sometimes scoffed, "Nothing says *I'm sorry* like a casserole," only to learn later that their derisive statement was surprisingly accurate. In the onslaught of acute grief, faced with seemingly endless tasks before and after the funeral, mourners may slip a healthy and delicious casserole into the oven. No more effort is required. Such practical help is an act of love.

Our visits to the bereaved may be welcome, but sometimes our words are not. Silence is often more meaningful than chit-chat. Much of what we say can come off as trivial or harmful. "Human beings are grieving animals," writes Christoph Jedan of the University of Groningen, "and consolation, an experiential assemblage through which grief is ameliorated or assuaged, is an age-old response to loss." Our best gift may be to sit, hush, and listen.

In the Jewish consolation tradition of sitting *shivah*, or sitting seven (days after the burial), visitors to the bereaved are advised to say nothing and answer briefly when spoken to. Mourners sit in low chairs and abstain from wearing jewelry or make up. Men do not shave. The point is to make a sacred space for the natural reaction of grief.

German-Jewish theologian and philosopher Franz Rosenzweig observed that liturgy, rites, and prayers create a shared silence of redemption: Each person becomes part of a still community that transcends the misapprehensions and failed communications of words. Faced with the sacred, he writes, we grow silent.

It is considered a special blessing to visit and comfort the bereaved during *shivah* and, by extension, to pay close attention to the needs of the grieving throughout the coming year. Irwin Kidorf, Chief Psychologist at the Cumberland County Guidance Center for many years, holds that "the almost naked expression of feeling" involved in mourning plays an important cathartic role for everyone involved in the observance of *shivah*. It presents an opportunity to weep, to speak of deep emotions, questions, and pain.

Silence may go against the grain in twenty-first-century America. As a culture we often feel driven to act, to do, to fix. Self-help books dominate nonfiction shelves, and videos with advice on how to improve are a mouse-click away. This may not be healthy in general; and it is certainly harmful for those who mourn.

A 2014 study, published in the professional journal *Death Studies*, found that among the many mourners who experience a spiritual crisis after a loss, most express resentment and doubt toward God and significant changes in their beliefs. The bereaved are beset with deep questions and crippling fears of future loss. They report that at such times church friends often rush to quote Scripture, whether with compassion, scolding, or both.

Another series of interviews with 184 grieving families revealed that many believers stopped going to church because they felt ostracized for not publicly praising God that their loved one is in heaven, or for failing to recover after a

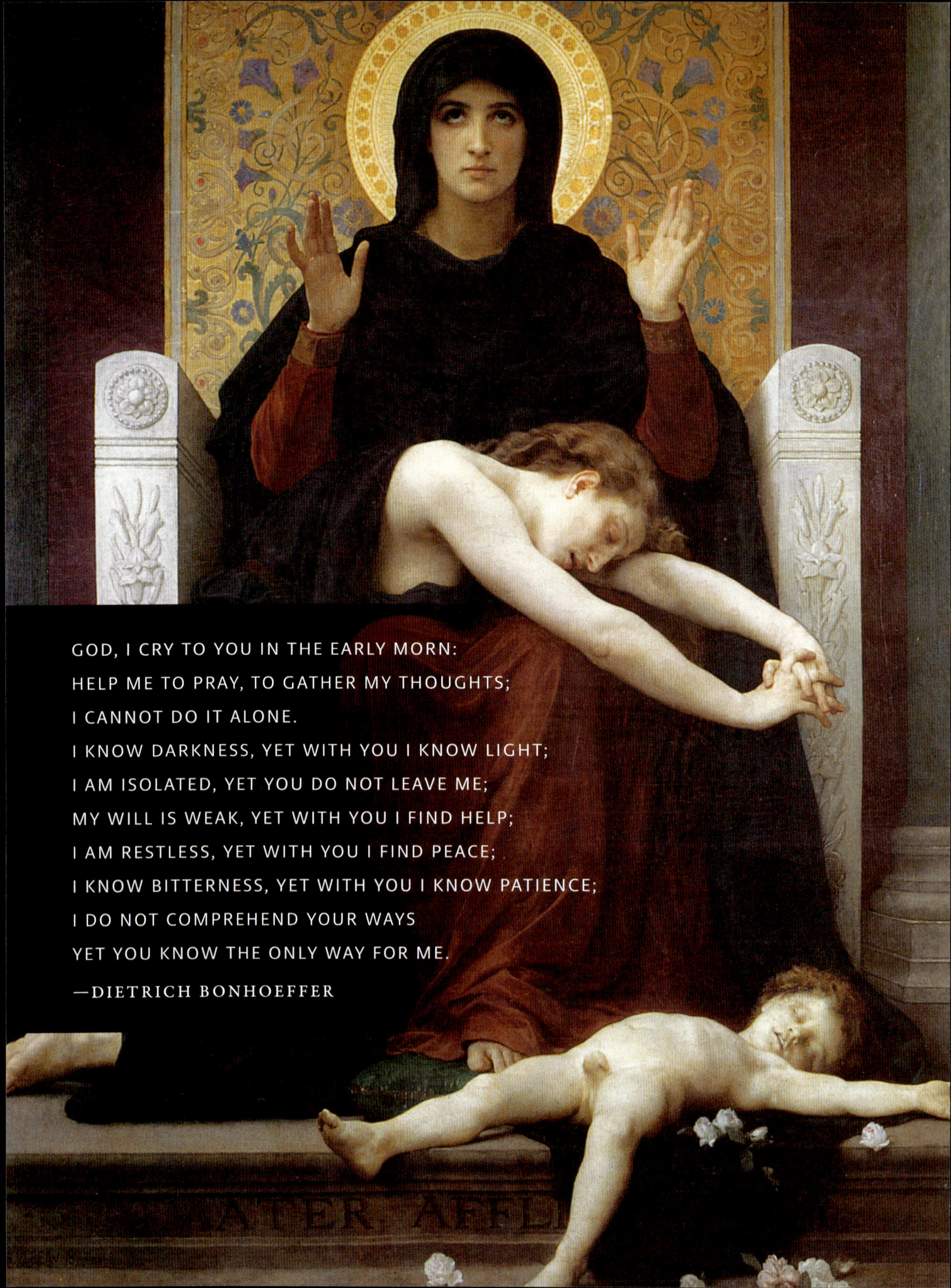

GOD, I CRY TO YOU IN THE EARLY MORN:
HELP ME TO PRAY, TO GATHER MY THOUGHTS;
I CANNOT DO IT ALONE.
I KNOW DARKNESS, YET WITH YOU I KNOW LIGHT;
I AM ISOLATED, YET YOU DO NOT LEAVE ME;
MY WILL IS WEAK, YET WITH YOU I FIND HELP;
I AM RESTLESS, YET WITH YOU I FIND PEACE;
I KNOW BITTERNESS, YET WITH YOU I KNOW PATIENCE;
I DO NOT COMPREHEND YOUR WAYS
YET YOU KNOW THE ONLY WAY FOR ME.

—DIETRICH BONHOEFFER

desirable period. Those who had been active churchgoers before the loss found little solace in their faith community.

Mourners listed three detrimental behaviors among clergy and congregations: a lack of support in general; a pressure to celebrate the death; and a tendency to ignore feelings of anger, resentment, or grief. The bereaved who "fell apart" at church were often told such a response displayed a lack of trust in God. "The faith community can sometimes be a source of re-victimization," observes Janice Harris Lord, an advocate for victims and survivors of crime and traumatic loss, "even though they do not intend to be." This in turn leads to a fear that grieving openly might set a poor example.

Mourners also speak of a struggle to find meaning in life. They sometimes feel abandoned by their dead loved ones, their church, and the divine. Such concerns can cause others to condemn the bereaved as faithless because they challenge pat answers and glib platitudes, adding to their anxiety and sense of helplessness. Death expert and hospice pioneer Paul Irion decries this approach: "In the religious community we need to be reminded often that faith is not a substitute for grief, but a resource."

The trend is not universal. Many churches host grief support groups, encouraging the bereaved to attend for as many months or years as they feel necessary. Others recognize the long-term impact of loss with such important annual rituals as "Blue Christmas" services, designed specifically for mourners who find the season difficult.

Grief is not an aberration to be mended. Rather, it is a universal, biological imperative found across all human cultures. In this respect, the myth of "letting go and moving on" is revealed as typically ineffective, uninformed, and perhaps even deleterious.

Daily reminders of joy and loss remain, as does the love that inspires them. We weep, we withdraw, and to our astonishment, we may find ourselves reaching out to others in service and communion. Such *meaning-making*, as researchers call it, helps us find ways to make sense of our loss, easing our overwhelming distress in the first few years after a death.

For example, Friedrich Rückert published the following poem in 1836, two years after his two youngest children died. In four brief lines he transforms an old platitude, "Rest in peace," into something poignant and comforting:

Nightwatch

Do they rest? a watchman's horn sounds in the west;
from the east a horn replies: *They rest.*
Do you hear, poor heart, angel whispers in the night?
Wrap yourself in peace, put out the light.

The poem so moved Johannes Brahms that he set "Nightwatch" to music in 1888, the second of his famous *Fünf Gesänge*, praising Rückert's gift for evocative words and memorable images. The centuries have not changed our need for genuine consolation. But modern societal constraints and misapprehensions regarding what to do and say can leave us feeling helpless in the face of death.

Recently in our local Bible study group, a member mentioned that he was going to call a bereaved friend who had lost a daughter. "Of course, I won't mention her at all," he said. This is a common misconception. Mourners, we think, do not want to speak of their loss. The opposite is true. I suggested that the death of his daughter was the only news that mattered. "Say her name," I said. "I suspect that in all the world, no sound could be sweeter."

Speaking of our loved ones eases the terrible solitude of sorrow. And it does something more. Mourning forces us, unwillingly but inevitably, to come to terms with our loss and all the changes it entails. In this way, grief is as much *from* one thing as *to* another.

Long silences are healthy and expected in a house of mourning. Despite this, we may feel uncomfortable when we visit. It is difficult to resist fidgeting, filling the quiet with chatter, or rushing to leave when conversation lulls. Please remember that your presence is needed. Hush. Stay. Show your love by letting them grieve.

(PAGE 52) William-Adolphe Bouguereau,
The Virgin of Consolation, 1875,
Musée des Beaux-Arts de Strasbourg

Cope

For no one is cast off by the Lord forever. Though he brings grief, he will show compassion, so great is his unfailing love.

LAMENTATIONS 3:31–32

I live in the high and holy place but also with the broken and humble, in order to revive the spirit of the humble and revive the hearts of the broken ones.

ISAIAH 57:15B (CJB)

98.6 PERCENT OF US SENSE OUR DEAD

"The stories are so consistent and so typical that they cannot be easily dismissed."

> *Won't you keep me safe in the afterlife? . . . If a human being dies, will he live again?*
>
> JOB 14:13A, 14A (ISV)

My daughter, Jess, died in 2015. I don't expect to see her again, not in this life. I know she's dead. And yet I join millions of fellow bereaved parents in sensing my child's presence. Many mourners tell me that they feel a similar connection with their lost loved ones. They are often relieved to learn that such experiences are more common than we might think.

In 1995 the University of Nottingham conducted an extensive survey in conjunction with the University of York's Institute for Research in the Social Sciences. Clinicians interviewed 1,603 bereaved persons about sensing the presence of their dead. The results were surprising: 98.6 percent reported experiencing their loved ones at home, while driving, in a dream or when ill; 1.4 percent—only 23 individuals—were uncertain if the sensations they experienced were real at that moment or merely memories.

"Why hasn't the media picked up on this?" asked journalist Philip Yancey when I shared these results with him. The answer is simple, writes Mary-Francis O'Connor with the University of Arizona: "Grief researchers have not been very successful at broadcasting what they have learned." Perhaps it's time for a hard look at what experts have discovered.

Visionary experiences such as those evaluated in the Nottingham study are "hyperreal," according to Simon Peng-Keller with the University of Zurich. Unlike dreams, he relates, they have an intense grounding in reality and a high level of clarity. The visions are not fleeting; rather, they are powerfully imprinted in our memory. Grief experts refer to them as *external dialogues*. They consist of literal interactions with the deceased, whether as a sense of presence, or as a visual or auditory expression.

Yet this ordinary experience is rarely discussed.

A vast majority of the bereaved speak nearly in a whisper of these subtle but meaningful exchanges, as though fearful that they will be perceived as irrational or deluded. "It may seem the stuff of a suspense novel," observes respected grief counselor Ashley Davis Bush, "but the stories are so consistent and so typical that they cannot be easily dismissed." Nor, perhaps, should they be.

The American Psychiatric Association considers these phenomena, when the bereaved "hears the voice of, or transiently sees the image of, the deceased person" as "characteristic of a 'normal' grief reaction." Such experiences do not indicate mental disorder. "While we would not want a person to experience hallucinations," writes bereavement therapy pioneer Lorraine Hedtke with California State University San Bernardino, "all these responses could lie well within emerging views of normalcy." Thousands of others relate similar stories. Christine Valentine with the University of Bath reports that in the Centre for Death and Society's work with mourners there have been numerous occasions when interviewers and interviewees sensed an active presence of the deceased in the room.

Roberta Dew Conant, a clinical psychologist with Outpatient Mental Health at Boston Regional Medical Center, interviewed widows who had lost their husbands to sudden, unexpected deaths. "Most of the widows also reported dramatic times that had convinced them of the husband's presence as a spirit," Conant writes. "These were highly emotional experiences that were felt to be consoling." The widows related that they were amazed at the *vividness* of their experiences. They spoke of seeing, hearing, or being touched by their husbands. "The comparison to hallucinations was voiced spontaneously five times and was always denied," Conant adds. "These were *not* hallucinations."

One finding of Conant's study was that the events were "an experience of externality or realness" that was simultaneously *acceptable* and *private* for the widows. They expressed feelings of comfort. Their husbands seemed to recognize and commiserate with their sorrow in a way that allowed their attachment to continue to grow in absence. "The intense pain of grief was an acknowledgement of the present reality, not an end to caring," Conant concludes. "The widow was often left with emotional peace, a conviction of ongoing spiritual life for the deceased and of resolution of her internal conflict over the death."

Widows, widowers, bereaved parents, siblings, orphans, close friends—these experiences are not limited to a single category of mourners. Susan Datson, director of Spiritual Care with Cornerstone Hospice, and psychologist Samuel Marwit interviewed twenty male and sixty-seven female mourners "related to the personal sensing experience." They found that such factors as the quality of support, beliefs, or specific demographics do not play a significant role in the perceived presence of their dead. The only common thread seems to be the surprising clarity and sense of *nearness* of their loved ones.

Reports of sensing the dead were commonplace among Christians in the early first century. Then as now, such experiences are not easily disregarded as pastoral hyperbole. Something more seems to be going on. "I feel very strongly (and I am not alone in this), that some great good comes from the dead to the living in the months or weeks after the death," writes C. S. Lewis. "I think I was much helped by my own father after his death. . . . Certainly, they often seem just at that time, to be very near us." Others share Lewis's belief.

Author and Bible translator J. B. Phillips swears he interacted with Lewis shortly after he died. Frederick Buechner relates a dream and tangible expression of a friend who had passed a few months earlier. After his daughter died in his arms, Martin Luther knew and approved of one story about a mother's spiritual encounter with her dead son. Norman Vincent Peale frequently told the story of seeing his father walk down the aisle at his own funeral. "Is it not at least conceivable, therefore, that around us now in this mysterious universe are those we have loved and lost for a while," Peale writes, "but that between us is a barrier through which we can see only in rare moments when for some reason the frequency in them corresponds with some higher frequency in ourselves? I think so."

Ronald Knapp with Clemson University interviewed 300 bereaved couples over the course of ten years; a surprising 298 couples (99.3 percent) reported sensing their children with them at one time or another, usually more than once and often for years. Another ten-year analysis, reported in the professional journal *Death Studies*, found that almost all bereaved parents feel that they experience their children now and will see them in heaven. This is true even with those who do not believe such a place exists.

The spiritually inclined relate that they feel the soul of their loved one was immediately accepted by God after leaving the body. Cold comfort, perhaps, but in grief the thought that our loved ones continue on, whole and happy, provides a deep and meaningful solace. "The dead are here with us, in the air that we are moving through all the time," writes poet and priest John O'Donohue. "With the refinement of your soul you can sense them. You feel that they are near."

Researchers have concluded that belief in a soul provides the bereaved with hope that they may somehow feel the deceased. This sense of presence frequently occurs within the first few weeks of a death. "Sometimes it seems to me that a special deep communication can exist between us and those we loved so much and left us," writes Henri Nouwen. "I think that anyone who we love sends us his or her spirit when they die. I am convinced that in a very deep sense [they] remain with us, not just in our memory but also in our life with each other."

Later, as months or years pass, the bereaved report that their dead remain with them. "Perhaps it was a fancy," writes Jane Goodall when she felt her husband's presence after his death, "but it comforted me, the thought that he was there." They also tell of signs from their lost loved ones: a fallen leaf, a bird, a knick-knack, a random word, an unexpected wind or scent. Isabel Allende says poignantly that her daughter Paula, who died in 1992, "is a gentle presence that is with her always, like a second skin."

Hearing, seeing, or sensing a presence is almost never associated with a belief that the dead have come back to life in any physical way, writes Christopher C. H. Cook with Durham University. Rather, our dead seem to be a source of support and comfort. These experiences often contribute to a religious belief that fosters healthy grieving as the bereaved adapt to life without their loved one.

Therapists call our ongoing connection with the deceased *continuing bonds*. These bonds facilitate acknowledgement of death while providing comfort that our loved one's influence lives on. As such, the question of whether we actually *see* our dead in a mystical vision or as part of a "personal mythology" is beside the point. Our experiences have meaning in the context of a relationship that remains important to us.

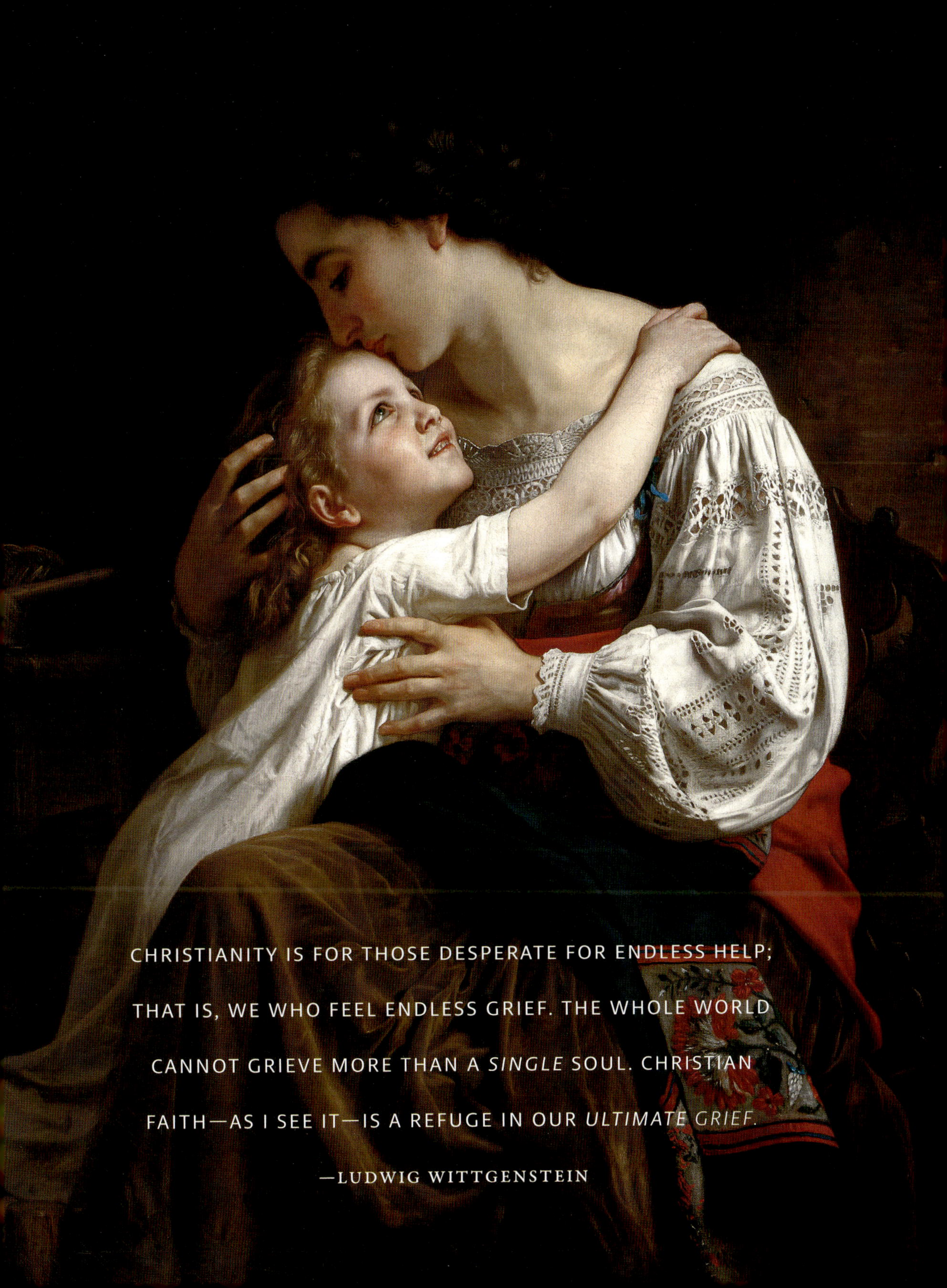

CHRISTIANITY IS FOR THOSE DESPERATE FOR ENDLESS HELP; THAT IS, WE WHO FEEL ENDLESS GRIEF. THE WHOLE WORLD CANNOT GRIEVE MORE THAN A *SINGLE* SOUL. CHRISTIAN FAITH—AS I SEE IT—IS A REFUGE IN OUR *ULTIMATE GRIEF.*

—LUDWIG WITTGENSTEIN

Continuing bonds with our dead are part of contemporary spirituality and recognized as helpful by grief experts. Yet some believers, particularly in Western Christianity, fear that such a connection is in conflict with their allegiance to God. This may be one reason that churchgoers seldom feel comfortable discussing experiences of their dead loved ones. They report hiding their grief and any anecdotes of messages or signs. Some congregations have discouraged these stories as being "demonic," citing the Levitical prohibition against spirit mediums. The dead are with God and therefore, it is suggested, cannot interact with the living.

Such *negative religious coping*, as therapists call it, is fostered externally by a lack of support in some faith communities and pressure to celebrate the death as a union with God. Mourners relate that their lived reality of sorrow is in conflict with these expectations, causing prolonged acute grief and a form of heightened reactivity. They find it even harder to adjust.

It occurs to me that perhaps we have created an impossible *either-or* choice where none needs to exist. "Since both the departed saints and we ourselves are in Christ," notes respected Bible scholar and Anglican bishop N. T. Wright, "we share with them in the 'communion of saints.' I see no reason why we should not pray for and with the dead and every reason why we should. . . . Love passes into prayer; we still love them; why not hold them, in that love, before God?"

We will always feel the absence of those we have lost, *loving in separation*, as philosopher Thomas Attig puts it. I often tell fellow mourners that we have a new relationship with our dead. They are with us still, their presence deeply felt. It's comforting to sense that my daughter will continue to inhabit and inform my life until that hoped-for day of reunion—the moment I hold her in my arms again.

(PAGE 61) William-Adolphe Bouguereau,
Le Lever, 1865,
Private collection

FALLING IS NOT FAILURE, AND GETTING UP IS NOT THE POINT

"We knew in our tears that God was with us, paying attention to us, shedding ten thousand tears for every one of ours."

> *If I say, "I'll forget my complaining, I'll put off my sad face and be cheerful," then I'm still afraid of all my pain.*
>
> JOB 9:27–28A (CJB)

Falling is not failure. Our society pushes the idea that what matters is getting up after a fall. This misses the point entirely. Gravity is not an evil; it is a reality. We all fall, literally and figuratively. Any fall can be excruciating; one may in fact be life-changing; but in this, believe it or not, gravity is our friend. Perhaps it is our fear of the inevitable that debilitates us.

Janet Simpson with St. George's Hospital Medical School and Associate Physiotherapist Halcyon Mandelstam found that of 552 potential fallers in geriatric medicine units, one third were unwilling to discuss the practical aspects of coping with a fall. "Most of those who refused or only reluctantly agreed were not facing up to their risk of falling," they conclude. And therein is the danger.

I learned to fall as a martial artist. One of the first things I was taught in that long-ago gym in South Korea was how to tumble. The lesson has served me well. I am learning it again with long COVID. But it was my daughter's death that taught me falling is as unavoidable as gravity. Both can be a grace.

In martial arts, particularly in my discipline, hapkido, I step into my opponent's circle. Defense and offense require being within reach. I face two important realities: *I will be hit; I will fall down*. In the actual event, neither may occur, but this knowledge has a pragmatic benefit. I no longer fear my fall. I judge the onrushing ground, bend my body to land on the least vulnerable spot, and roll into a fall when possible.

"Falls knock us off our feet, confusing the sense of our place in the world," writes Ann Cooper Albright, chair of the Department of Dance at Oberlin College, who frequently publishes on philosophy. Albright sees falling as a connection with gravity that helps us navigate with grace the slips and failures of life, moving from what *was* to what *will be*. She suggests that our occasional losses of balance hint at deeper knowledge. "We rarely think about where we are until we have been lost," she says. "In order to understand what orients us, we need to experience disorientation."

With long COVID I have days when my legs give out from under me. I use gravity to fall, to bend, to roll. And I lie there. Pausing on the floor, I gain a new perspective. There is no rush to get up. I fell down, that's all. It's not the end of the world.

When my daughter, Jess, died, I felt the floor give way beneath me. Suddenly my legs were unreliable. An outside force seemed to push me to my knees. In sorrow beyond words, my soul cried to God for help. To this day, in the same way that I know I am breathing, or typing these words, I know that he heard me. As with most spiritual experiences, this awareness was palpable yet ineffable. That terrible night I experienced the same loss of balance that I knew in many a sparring session, with one important difference: *I am still falling*.

Grief is unending. Jess's absence can never be resolved. No amount of "getting up" will return her to me, not until the moment of my death when I hold her in my arms again. I continue to plummet as I continue to love: ceaselessly, vulnerably, yet with an odd confidence that I need not stick the landing. I can let myself fall.

God and I may never see eye-to-eye on my daughter's death. Still, for the most part, I believe that he takes my good into account. This isn't always easy. Other bereaved parents have wrestled with the same question.

Theologian Lewis Smedes and his wife lost their child within a day of the infant's birth. "Doris and I cried a lot," Smedes writes. "We knew in our tears that God was with us, paying attention to us, shedding ten thousand tears for every one of ours." Yet he suggests that even if an angel appeared to explain why his child had to die, no answer would suffice. After years of thought, Smedes decided that the privilege of life comes at a cost: "The price is that things can go wrong, badly wrong sometimes, which should come as no surprise."

It was certainly no surprise to another bereaved father, Friedrich Rückert. Three years after the deaths of his two youngest children, the linguist and poet boldly rewrote the Gospels in rhyming verse. The more he dug into the texts, the less he cared for any apparent contradictions between them. Rückert joked that such historical critiques of the Gospels ultimately circled back on themselves:

> Where the witnesses agree
> I doubt such harmony;
> and where they contradict
> both seem to me suspect!

Rückert focused on the Gospels' moral aspects. He asked his friend, pastor and hymnist Albert Knapp, for a candid assessment: "Do you take greater exception to my presumption, or to my prudence in refraining from poetic embellishment?" Knapp had comments on both points, yet enjoyed the manuscript for its clarity, lyricism, and keen insight into the Gospels' spiritual messages. Others shared his view.

Life of Jesus: A Gospel Harmony in Verse was published in 1839. It quickly became a favorite among believers in Germany and America. Christian Hermann Weisse, a respected philosopher with the University of Leipzig, felt that Rückert had woven the four Gospels into a paraphrase that dared the heights reached by great mythic poems, "transforming the events into a true artistic epic." Twenty years later, in 1859, Franz Liszt adapted the work for his oratorio *Christus*.

Rückert's *Life of Jesus* is redolent of compassion and patience. "In the beginning was the Word, with God," reads his first gentle stanza of the Gospel of John, "then and always, God was that Word." Later, at the introduction of Simeon, we sense the poet's measured sorrow and spiritual calm:

> In the temple he waited, old Simeon,
> free of shadow, death, oblivion,
> until the Spirit's promised day
> that he would at last see Messiah
> and his eyes would rest on the Lord.

> "As he stands, many in Israel will fall
> or rise, a rock and a stone to all;
> He will be maligned in the battle ahead
> (a sword will pierce your soul with dread).
> By this sign what was hidden is made clear
> and revealed at last many secrets held dear."

Simeon was right. The death of my daughter, too, was a sword that pierced my soul. This wound is irremediable, irreparable, but not beyond redemption. I am reminded of Dallas Willard's suggestion: "Nothing irredeemable has happened to us or can happen to us on our way to our destiny in God's full world." Perhaps, but as with Lewis Smedes, I am not entirely certain that I care if any "good" can come of such a devastating loss. Rather, I join Smedes and Rückert in my struggle to find meaning in a world without my child. I am not alone.

Fellow bereaved father Donald Murray writes that he often senses his dead daughter outside the door of his office, sitting in a chair to his left, or standing beside him. Usually it is when he finds himself writing an unexpected phrase, Murray relates, "a line that suddenly runs clear, a word I have never used in quite that way before." I know the feeling. I sense my daughter near as I type. I may not be a finer writer, or a better person, but on good days I am more Jess-like: more alive, more empathetic, more present. Until I hold her in my arms again, this will have to do.

Life knocks us down. It is the price of this world, however much we may kid ourselves otherwise. In his poem "The Gift of Gravity," Kentucky farmer Wendell Berry observes that a river is shaped by its injuries. Our falls become part of us.

I fell again today. My legs betrayed me. I bent sideways, landed on a shoulder, and turned on my back. From there I saw rain outside our window, falling as I have fallen, surrounded by other drops that know their own falls: each unique, yet none entirely alone. Nor am I without companions. I have friends, family, and to my astonishment, a God who tumbles with me. I roll into each fall, and that makes all the difference.

Jean-François Millet,
Man with a Hoe, c1860-1862,
Getty Center

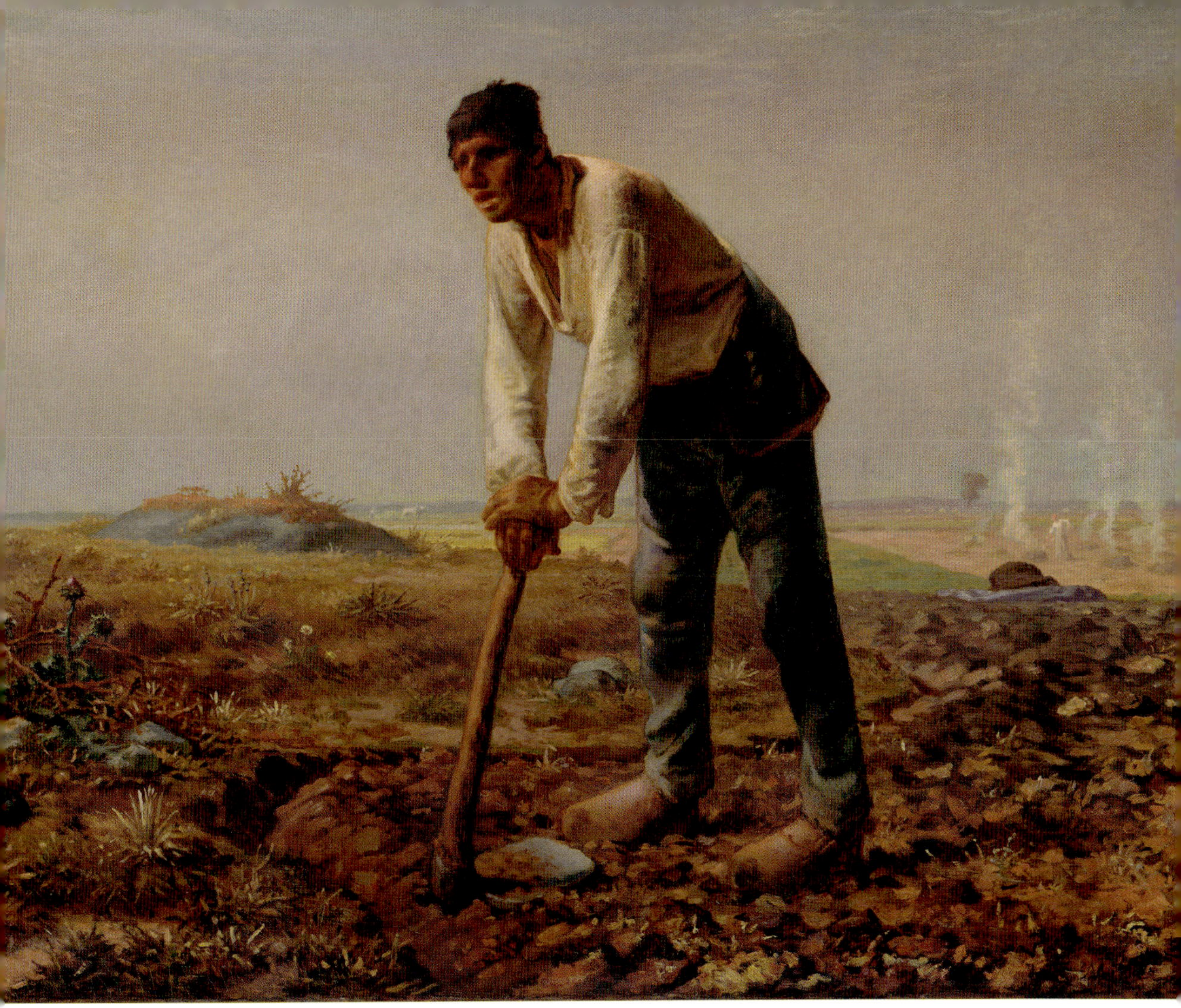

ALL THE *wonderful things* IN LIFE ARE SO SIMPLE THAT ONE IS NOT AWARE OF THEIR WONDER UNTIL THEY ARE BEYOND TOUCH. NEVER HAVE I FELT THE WONDER AND BEAUTY AND JOY OF LIFE SO KEENLY AS NOW IN MY GRIEF.

—JOHN GUNTHER, *DEATH BE NOT PROUD*

GO, DAUGHTER OF GOD, GO

"My grief would overwhelm me if I were not in God's grace."

> *This brilliance around him looked like a rainbow in a cloud on a rainy day. This was how the appearance of the glory of Adonai looked. When I saw it, I fell on my face, and I heard the voice of someone speaking.*
>
> EZEKIEL 1:28 (CJB)

Joan of Arc is in mourning the day her king is crowned. The slender seventeen-year-old stands in full armor. As commander of France's army, she bears her white standard of a field sprinkled with lilies, an angel on each side, inscribed with the words JHESUS MARIA. The banner has been with her through the blood-soaked battles that led to this day. "It shared in the pain," she says. "It's only right that it share in the honors."

The coronation of King Charles VII of France takes place in Rheims Cathedral on Sunday, July 17, 1429. For years both France and England have asserted a blood right to the throne. Burgundians may have allied with the English, but today, the dauphin asserts his claim and accepts his crown from Archbishop Regnault de Chartres. Charles could not have done it without a teenage girl from Domrémy village.

Joan, known as the Maid, stands in a place of honor, surrounded by her parents, Jacques and Isabelle, along with her older brothers, Jean and Pierre. The eldest son, Jacquemin, cannot attend. And someone else is missing.

Joan's only sister died two months ago, in May, 1429.

Catherine was a few years older than Joan. They frequented Domrémy and neighboring Greux, attended services together, and learned sewing, spinning, and shepherding from their parents. Their family lived, Joan says, "in a two-story house, with two lofts above the rooms, two small corridors in front of the house, with a small chicken coop." There is little doubt the girls shared a room and a bed, as was customary in village homes.

Life in Domrémy had improved in general due to the ravages of the Black Death a century earlier, when a decreased population presented opportunities for survivors. The village was surrounded by rivers and streams which helped the growth of wheat, rye, and oats. Neighboring hills were forested with beech and oak: ideal for building, heating, and supplying acorns for pigs, the main economic strength of Domrémy, along with cattle, horses, sheep, and fowl. Wine from the vineyards of nearby Greux was as much a staple as cheese, milk, pork, beef, and poultry.

Joan's father, Jacques, owned some fifty acres, thirty of which were pasture and farmland; the other twenty, woodland. Joan was often tasked with tending the fields, using hoe and plough, as well as guarding their livestock, she said, "until I reached the age of reason." As a comfortably affluent landowner, Jacques was a dean of Domrémy and responsible for the village's defense, taxes, and accuracy in weights and measures. He accompanied the mayors of Domrémy and Greux with seven other notables to pay tribute to the lord of Commercy in 1423. It is not surprising, then, that his first daughter, Catherine, was soon wed to Colin, the son of Greux's mayor.

But nothing prepared Jacques for the astonishing news that his other daughter, Joan, had led the French army in taking the city of Rheims from the English. French kings had always been crowned there, but Charles was unwilling to enter enemy territory. Hearing this, Joan undertook a series of battles against nearby towns to ensure the dauphin's safe passage.

Now as she rides with Charles through northern France, townspeople throw open their gates to allow the royal procession to pass. Joan herself leads the dauphin into Rheims.

The next day, as light streams through the stained glass windows of the vast Rheims Cathedral, Joan stands beside Charles as he is crowned king. Her family has traveled from Domrémy for the occasion. Jacques and his wife are in awe. Then they receive a shock.

The new king instructs Joan to name a royal favor for all that she has done. She asks nothing for herself but instead requests that the people of her village of Domrémy and Greux be freed from the burden of taxation. Two weeks later, Charles VII signs a decree to that effect, writing three words in explanation: "Nothing: the Maid."

Joan's request on behalf of her townsfolk is not as odd as it may seem. She was selfless by nature, and her concern for others is a common aspect of grief. Many people suffering from stress and acute sorrow turn outward as a means of daily survival. Robert Neimeyer, a leading authority on grief, observes that in their search for meaning, the bereaved often commiserate with fellow mourners, displaying compassion and searching for a sense of transcendence.

The regal coronation is a vindication of Joan's actions to free France and a moment of parental pride. But for the entire family, it is also a day of joy tinged with sorrow; or more accurately, sorrow tinged with joy. Joan's parents know that she has more battles ahead. They leave for Domrémy as they mourn one daughter and fear for the future of another. This is the last time her parents will see Joan until the day of her death.

France is in religious and political turmoil. Believers' faith has been badly shaken by the Papal Schism of 1378, which lasted forty years. Two men, then three, each insisted that he alone was the true pope. The question is resolved in 1417, but the ongoing Hundred Years War, which started in 1337 and will not end until 1453, has left much of France occupied by English forces.

Joan's home in Domrémy is on the Gallic side of the Vaucouleurs castellany in northeastern France. There are frequent unofficial skirmishes between village boys from across the English boundary. Orléans has been under siege by the English since October of 1428. The people of Vaucouleurs, Mont-Saint-Michel, and Tournai are the last remaining bastion of support north of the Loire for the Dauphin Charles.

But the dauphin, once brave and reckless in his youth, now seems unwilling to act. For his people, papal supremacy and royal status are not political debates: they are questions of faith, just rule, and divine right. This series of disasters creates a vacuum.

People yearn for a sign, a prophet, a mystic.

One summer afternoon in 1424, Joan, a village girl of Domrémy, senses herself "surrounded on all sides by a great light," she says. The thirteen-year-old cannot speak or move out of sheer terror. This, her first vision, is in keeping with well-known angelic visitations, including biblical accounts, in which heavenly messengers often announce: "Fear not!"

More spiritual manifestations follow.

Over time Joan experiences Michael the Archangel, Catherine of Alexandria, Margaret of Antioch, Gabriel, and a large number of angels. "Were I in a wood, the voices would still come to me," she insists. "A day does not pass when I do not hear it; I need them so." Her visitors speak with her plainly and in clear, concise terms, each with a unique personality, she relates. When asked if the voice is that of an angel or a saint, Joan replies, "It is from God."

Her response is not surprising. Mystics frequently have difficulty putting their experiences into words. Joan uses voice and voices interchangeably, sometimes in the same sentence. The best she can do, she explains, is to say that her visions are extremely real. "Joan's 'problem', like that of religious visionaries throughout history," observes biographer Donald Spoto, "was to report an ineffable experience, to find some sort of expression within the currency of her own religious and cultural norms."

Joan is not the only member of her family to have visions.

Throughout Joan's childhood, her father, Jacques, occasionally wakes his wife in the night to relate a recurring dream of their daughter "going off with men-at-arms." He fears that she might become a camp follower—a euphemism for prostitutes that inevitably make themselves available near military encampments. "If what I fear will happen with Joan, does happen," he tells Isabelle, "I'd rather you drowned her, and if you don't, I'll drown her myself." Before we berate Jacques for an impious interpretation of his dreams, we need look no further than Ezekiel or John of Patmos to find evidence of other men who struggled to understand visions that were far outside their usual frame of reference.

Still, his explanation seems at odds with what we know about young Joan. Some 115 witnesses who knew her from infancy, including a number of priests, described her repeatedly as good, sweet-natured, devout, simple, pious, and pure. It was well known that she was a regular attendee at the local parish. But parental fears, alas, seldom jibe with reality.

His dreams lead Jacques to keep Joan close at home. He also attempts to marry her off quickly. But Joan rejects potential suitors, including one man in the city of Toul who is so incensed that he brings Joan before the court of justice to force her to be his bride. The court finds in Joan's favor. "From the first time I heard the voice," Joan explains, "I vowed to remain a virgin for as long as God so pleased."

Jacques's prescient visions of his daughter in the company of soldiers ultimately become reality—but not in the way he fears. While in Domrémy, Joan's voices continuously urge her, "Go, daughter of God, go." Where she goes and what she does are unique in the history of the world.

Joan approaches the Dauphin Charles in March of 1429 and boldly announces her divine mission to deliver Orléans and save France. The dauphin is dubious. He has an ecclesiastical commission question this audacious seventeen-year-old. Joan's examiners tell him they are convinced that her visions are genuine. This is not without precedent. Since the time of the Black Death, a tradition has arisen of young peasants leaving their flocks to perform sacred tasks. Charles sees in Joan a leader to rally his people. She proves him right.

Joan is given command of some 7,000 men, including the most famous captains of the day, as the army's *chef de guerre* (war chief). On March 22, 1429, she dictates a letter to the King of England, ordering his forces to surrender and withdraw. If they do not, she warns, "I will order them killed, to the last man, for I am sent by God, Lord of Heaven, to throw you out of France, body by body."

Joan does not shirk from her responsibility, or the suffering she feels for the deaths that result from her orders. "Sent by God, she, normally a gentle, pious country girl," writes Nadia Margolis with Mount Holyoke College, "would kill as often as necessary and without hesitation to achieve her goal." Joan sees her mission as an incarnation of divine will.

Joan's detractors in the twenty-first century often dismiss her visions and voices as the result of a mental pathology, such as bipolar disorder or schizophrenia. Others, like Larissa Juliet Taylor with Colby College, think that Joan lied to break free of societal constraints and to pursue her aims. "Was she doing so at the behest of God?" Taylor asks. "It is impossible to know." These modern explanations seem reasonable on the surface, but they may be asking the wrong questions.

Gwendolyn Morgan with Montana State University notes that we have left the real Joan far behind in our rush to apply modern psychiatric terms. "All these recreations," writes Morgan, "ignore the fundamental medieval reality of Joan as a woman of unshakable faith in her personal and profound experience of Christianity." Respected medievalist Juliet Barker agrees, adding that what matters is Joan's belief in her visions.

Attempting to diagnose Joan with a physical or psychological disorder serves no purpose, says Helen Castor, a Fellow of Sidney Sussex College. Societal and religious views in fifteenth-century France were vastly different from our modern world. Visions were considered commonplace. Men and women of sound mind frequently had spiritual encounters that were taken at face value. There was no question at the time as to whether Joan's experiences were real. "The problem was how to tell whether her voices came to her from heaven or hell," Castor concludes.

Such mystical experiences have striking parallels with many aspects of grief, such as the sorrow caused by Joan's loss of her sister, writes David Aberbach with McGill University. Both display withdrawal, searching, keening, despair, communion, and the realization of a new identity. Mysticism and grief are not equal, but each may lead to transformation and a previously undiscovered spirituality. This was true of another mystic, Thérèse of Lisieux.

While reading about Joan's life, Thérèse received what she considered the core revelation that led to her own vocation as a Carmelite. At that moment, writes the nineteenth-century nun, "I received a grace which I have always looked upon as one of the greatest of my life." Though the two women were separated by four centuries, observes Randall Rosenberg with Fontbonne University, Thérèse is still thought of today as Joan's spiritual younger sister.

Skeptical simplifications of Joan's life are not entirely convincing. She did not seek power, wealth, or fame. "I ask for no final reward," she tells critics in her own time, "other than the salvation of my soul." A close examination of the historical record provides more evidence of the miraculous than the pathological.

Orléans is "the boulevard to invasion," writes historian Régine Pernoud with the Museum of the History of France. The town's bridge over the Loire is seen by the English as a key military location. They assign an experienced captain, Thomas Montague, to lay siege to Orléans on October 12, 1428. Montague's blockade and war of attrition nearly works. The town fathers send a delegation to discuss terms with the Duke of Burgundy.

Then the unexpected happens.

Joan's convoy of 500 men arrives outside Orléans on April 28, 1429. She enters the city the next day. Soon reinforcements appear. The following week sees the bloodiest fighting of the siege.

Twice Joan writes to the English, demanding that they leave. The last letter is delivered by her herald, Guienne, who is promptly taken prisoner. When, on May 5, hostilities cease to honor the Feast of the Ascension, Joan writes a third and final warning to her enemies. She sends for an archer and instructs him to fasten the missive to an arrow and fire it into the English camp: "Men of England, who have no right to be in France, the Lord of Heaven commands you through me, Joan the Maid, to abandon your garrison and return to your own land. Leave now or I will raise a war cry that will echo through eternity."

Two days later, during a skirmish on May 7, an arrow pierces Joan's armor, driving several inches between her neck and shoulder. That night Joan weeps to the point of exhaustion at the sight of the slain on both sides. The next day, on May 8, 1429, after 6 months 3 weeks and 5 days, the English forces leave Orléans. Joan has ended the siege in a little over a week.

"No miracle was ever so clear," writes prominent fifteenth-century author Christine de Pizan of the events at Orléans. "A girl of sixteen (I ask you, is that natural?)." Pizan's "Hymn to Joan of Arc" is the only tribute written during Joan's lifetime. It is a lyrical verse of sixty-one stanzas that focuses on heroism, the dignity of women, peace, and the ultimate victory of good over evil. Pizan begins her poem just after the coronation in Rheims, casting the story in a scriptural light. She compares Joan to giants of faith like Esther, Ruth, Gideon, Deborah, and others:

> Sacred, profound, in her
> life we see God's grace;
> in all things she looks to Him,
> calls Him, serves Him,
> in words, in deeds; in all places,
> devout, relentless.

During or shortly after the fighting at Orléans, Joan's sister, Catherine, dies in childbirth at the age of twenty-four. Before Catherine's death, Joan has always been fearless, dreading only the dark shadow of betrayal. Experiences both spiritual and martial have honed her survival instincts while increasing her dependence on the voices of God's messengers. But this is a blow Joan cannot prevent, a battle that cannot be won through belligerence, cunning, or miracle.

Siblings feel a tremendous sense of failure at the death of a brother or sister, says Albert Cain with the University of Michigan. For those who lose a family member to an accident, 78 percent feel persistent guilt. If Joan was like so many sisters before and since, she may have felt responsible for the loss: She failed to keep Catherine safe; she should have been there. Respected grief researcher Ronald Knapp of Clemson University suggests that this sense of shame and remorse seems to be inescapable. Joan may have felt that her own shortcomings somehow contributed to Catherine's death.

Then as now, the death of a sibling has marked similarities to losing a child. Yet despite the striking parallels between these types of grief, mourning for a sister or brother receives scant social recognition. Psychotherapist Julia Samuel, an expert in sibling loss, observes that "although 80 percent of the population has a sibling, we as a society give it less acknowledgement than it deserves." Debora Davidson with York University goes a step further, calling siblings the "forgotten mourners."

Many siblings report pressure to cope well and appear normal. Yet they frequently experience existential chaos and trauma. "Internally the bereaved sibling struggles with intense emotions," says clinical psychologist Eleferia Woodrow, adding that an unspoken conspiracy of silence surrounds sibling grief and increases their sense of isolation. The initial shock of losing a brother or sister may last for months; the grief endures for years. Little wonder, then, that when Joan's cousin Jeanne has a daughter that same year, she asks that the girl be named Catherine Robert in honor of Joan's sister.

A month after the coronation of Charles VII, in August, Joan's hectic, heart-breaking, victorious spring and summer begin to take their toll. In five short months she has returned to France its rightful territories. Her mission is fulfilled. By now her brothers, Jean and Pierre, are part of the company, but still she yearns for Domrémy. "If only it would please God, my creator, that I might leave," Joan says, "that I might set aside my armor and return in service to my parents, tending their flocks; how they would rejoice to have me home."

This is not wistful nostalgia. Rather, it is a desperate plea of grief and exhaustion, suggests English poet Robert Southey. He frequently returns to the theme of

Joan's sorrow in his 1853 epic poem about the Maid. "Her mind's eye beheld Domrémy and the fields of Arc," he writes. "Her burden'd heart was full; such grief she felt."

Yet Joan perseveres. She is a bold and gifted tactician, albeit a mediocre strategist. At times clever, at others cagey, she takes advantage of opportunities as they arise. But the complexities of international and court relations are beyond her.

King Charles VII is hoping to bargain a peace with Burgundy; negotiations with the English are under way. When Joan's attack on Paris in September, 1429, meets with failure and retreat, her usefulness to the court is at an end. Suddenly Joan's acumen and popularity become a liability. Charles has her watched throughout the winter. Then he makes a cruelly savvy move.

On Christmas Day, 1429, the king decrees that Joan, her family, and their descendants are ennobled. Joan is now a *comtesse*, though she never uses the title, referring to herself as simply Jeanne la Pucelle—Joan the Maid. Charles VII has given Joan a dubious compliment: As a noble she can raise her own troops, yet any actions are solely her responsibility. The crown is distancing itself from the new countess.

Joan's skirmishes that winter are largely unsuccessful. Between sorties in the lower Loire area, she stays at the Trémoïlle family castle in Sully-sur-Loire. Her host, Georges de la Trémoïlle, is a favorite of the king and one of Joan's main detractors. He is unwelcoming and spiteful. Rumors that he tries to have her killed are unfounded but easy to believe nonetheless.

Joan is separated from her comrades for much of January and February, 1430. Forced inactivity and lack of support weigh on her. Her sister is dead; many comrades have perished in battle; and now her voices have inexplicably fallen silent. Joan is alone physically, emotionally, and spiritually.

Then, with the arrival of spring, in April, Catherine, Margaret, and Michael return to guide her. Joan describes a light that illuminates them, at times with clarity, at others as though in a haze. These impressions echo long centuries of mystical experience. "What matters is not what one feels," Thomas Merton explains, "but what really takes place beyond the level of feeling or experience." This seems to be the case with Joan. But suddenly her visitations are redolent of unease and foreboding.

Joan is standing near a moat sometime during the Holy Week of April 16 when her voices tell her she will soon be captured. "I begged my voices to spare me the long torments of prison," she says, "and that I should die immediately if I were taken." It is not to be.

That spring the enemy overruns her forces. She refuses to swear their ritual oath of loyalty, insisting her faith belongs to another. Joan is taken prisoner by the Burgundians on the afternoon of Tuesday, May 23, 1430. They promptly sell her to the English. King Charles VII does nothing.

Joan languishes in a tower cell in Beaurevoir throughout the hot summer. By the fall, she hears rumors of Burgundian forces slaughtering innocents in Compiègne along the river Oise. Children as young as seven years old are being put to death by fire and sword. She is desperate to go to their aid.

"Angels often come without being called," Joan insists. "I have never needed them and they were not there." So it is now. Saint Catherine appears, but forbids Joan to escape by jumping from the window. For the first time in her young life, the Maid of Orléans expresses concern about a God that allows such massacres. But Saint Catherine is adamant: Joan is to remain in her cell and God will deal with Compiègne.

It's all too much. Witnesses and those who know Joan say she has an unofficial maxim when faced with inaction: "Go boldly!" She leaps from the tower.

The seventy-foot drop leaves her painfully bruised and unable to eat or drink for days. "After my fall," Joan says, "Saint Catherine comforted me. She said the people of Compiègne would have succor without fail. It was then that my health returned." Joan insists that the messengers, her voices, prevented the fall from killing her. As Saint Catherine promised, Joan quickly heals from her injuries.

That same month French forces rout the enemy and free Compiègne. Joan's faith in the wisdom of her voices is renewed; yet the nature and purposes of her God remain a mystery.

Joan's trial by the Inquisition begins on January 9, 1431, in Rouen, Normandy, and continues into the spring. She stands accused of sorcery, heresy, and wearing men's clothing. She is chained and subjected to taunts and physical threats from the guards that are stationed inside her cell. Strangers are allowed to jeer at her day and night.

IF I AM NOT IN GOD'S GRACE, MAY HE SO PLACE ME;

IF I AM, MAY HE SO PRESERVE ME.

MY GRIEF WOULD OVERWHELM ME IF I WERE NOT IN GOD'S GRACE.

—JOAN OF ARC, FEBRUARY 24, 1431

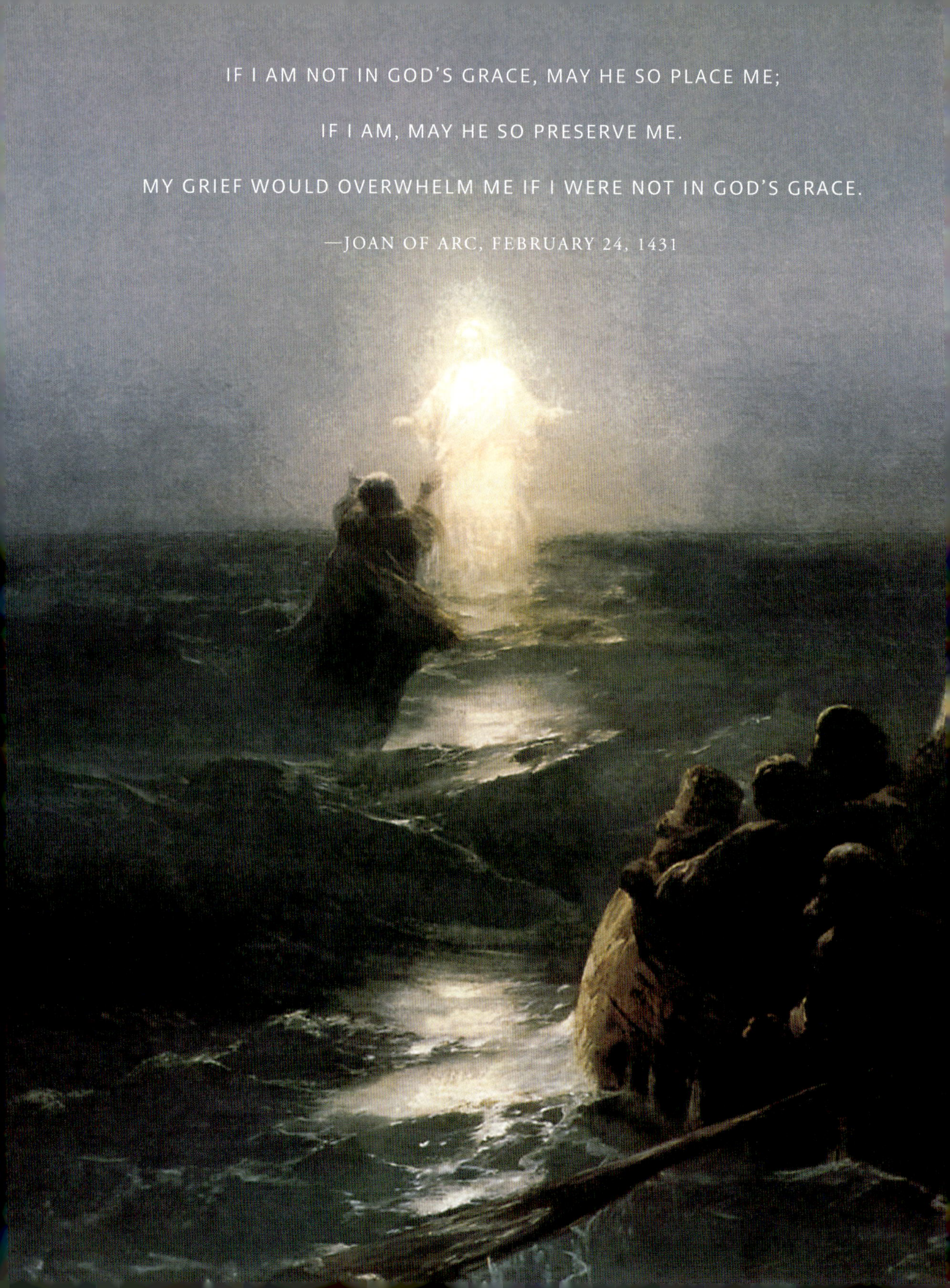

Joan is grieving and betrayed but never broken. "It would be impossible for me to revoke these visions and revelations from God or to denounce what I have said and done," she tells her accusers. "Nothing will make me do so. Nothing can stop me from obeying what God commands and will command. I am the servant of all—but Our Lord's first."

Bishop Pierre Cauchon, a well-known English partisan from Compiègne, presides over the tribunal. Though Joan is being tried by the Church, the English are paying for every part of the proceedings: court costs, fees from judges to clerks, even the meager rations Joan is fed from scraps off the judges' tables. The outcome is inevitable. Joan is found guilty of heresy.

"It is true that God sent me," she cries. "Alas! To be so horribly and cruelly treated!" On May 30, 1431, Joan's family watches helplessly as their only living daughter is burned at the stake. Joan shouts from the pyre, "Jesus, Jesus!" These are the last words her parents hear her say. Joan is nineteen.

Joan's father, Jacques, dies that same year. Friends and neighbors say it is from ailments brought on by sorrow. They may be right. Janet Lord with the School of Immunity and Infection, University of Birmingham, and her colleagues, relate that the stress of acute grief affects the autoimmune system and leaves the body susceptible to disease or the advancement of preexisting conditions, especially among older adults.

Joan's mother, Isabelle Romée, moves to Orléans in 1440, a widow who has lost two daughters. When her eldest son dies ten years later, the city fathers provide Isabelle with a modest income and pay for medical expenses as she grows older.

But Isabelle is not yet done with France.

She fights tirelessly to restore Joan's good name. This is not out of concern for the family reputation. Therapist Harriet Schiff notes that bereaved parents care little for such things. Rather, they frequently give priority to moments of peace, communion, transformation, and a new sense of meaning, according to leading grief expert Dennis Klass. It is also likely that Isabelle acts out of motherly devotion, a desire for justice, and some sense of balance. Most of all, perhaps, she wants to honor the memory of her daughter.

Twenty-four years after Joan was killed, on November 7, 1455, seventy-eight-year-old Isabelle enters the Notre-Dame de Paris Cathedral and approaches a cadre of papal commissioners. Supported by her two remaining children, Jean and Pierre, as well as priests and friends from Orléans, Isabelle states her official request in a plaintive, sorrowful voice. "Joan was my daughter; I reared her in the faith," Isabelle begins. "She grew up in our fields and our pastures, fasting and praying for the torments of our people."

The grieving mother's sighs and groans are frequently interrupted by cries from spectators. Demonstrations in support of Joan grow so violent that the officials are forced to take refuge with Isabelle in the sacristy until order is restored.

Isabelle's efforts are not in vain. She dies two years later at the age of eighty-one, but not before seeing Joan's conviction overturned on July 7, 1456.

(PAGE 78) Ivan Aivazovsky,
Walking on Water, 1890s,
Private collection

CONFESSION

"I'd have said you're innocent the whole time, whatever they had on you."

> *I, yes I, am the one who blots out your offenses for my own sake; I will not remember your sins.*
>
> ISAIAH 43:25 (CJB)

"I don't roll on nobody," I said, abysmal grammar and all, but a jail cell is no place for linguistic niceties. My voice was rough, as much scared as aggressive. My bunkmate, or *cellie*, looked across our 7 x 10 room. He paused a moment. "No," he nodded. "I don't believe you do."

We had been talking over how we got locked up. Danny admitted freely that he and his sister did pretty well stealing supplies from construction sites. The night before, Danny told me, he had been *lifting* some copper wire when the owner spotted him and chased Danny's truck through downtown Denver all the way to Golden. Apparently a 911 call was made and soon he was in custody.

"I don't know why he had to chase me down and call the cops," he said. "I mean, a man's got to make a living, right?" Danny was a multiple offender, having done time before, so he expected to go down *all day*—that is, serve his full sentence.

Suddenly he asked if I was a law officer. He had heard that I would have to admit it. "I don't think that's right, actually," I laughed. "But they love for us to think so!"

I had been picked up for criminal impersonation. Suddenly I was telling my cellie everything, not out of moral propriety, but because I knew there was no getting around the facts. The movies have that part wrong. Claims of innocence do nothing for your *street cred* inside.

I had made a living out of presenting myself as something I was not. I started with small deceptions that grew into cons, or *grifts*, which then escalated to a point where I was being interviewed on national television and radio. I was even getting calls from screenwriters and film stars about a movie of my life—an autobiography that was pure fabrication and nonsense.

"You're famous!" Danny chuckled when I finished. He passed me half an orange that he had filched from the food cart. He knew the inmate distributing the lunches and snagged us extras. "See, David? You got to make a living." His eyes got deadly serious. "Now don't roll on me, brother." By that, he meant don't tell; more to the point, don't *roll over* and give information about him to anyone.

We had both been arrested that night. The others in processing were first-timers like me. But I hit luck. I double-bunked with a frequent visitor. My cellie told me how things are inside, how to avoid trouble, and how to find a crew. "Don't be a loner, don't be a loud mouth, just go with the flow," he said. Then he looked me up and down. "People think you're a doctor, right?"

"Well, a PhD, yeah," I shrugged.

"So you're smart," Danny said. "You learn law inside, help write letters to lawyers or whatever, and you're protected." Good advice, but that day Danny couldn't stop staring out the window.

"I hope my sister comes through," he muttered over and over. They had a standing agreement to bail each other out.

The next day, Danny and I swapped numbers: If I was released first, I would call his sister; if it was him, he was to phone my wife. They announced his name and Danny walked out. He rang my wife that afternoon.

I was alone in my cell. I bit into the orange he had left me. It tasted sweeter than any orange I've had before or since. I have an idea why.

For the first time in over ten years, I had been *completely* honest with another human being.

That night, restless and desperate, I turned to God. I was out of practice, to be sure. I had been baptized at fifteen, but in my thirties I went through a paradoxical *there-is-no-God-and-I-hate-him* phase. Now I faced the reality that I needed help. "It was inevitable, I suppose," I whispered. "You knew this would happen, if you're there, and here I am." I tried bargaining. "If you help me out, Lord, I'll tell the truth. To everyone."

My wife posted bail via wire transfer. I caught a cab at the detention center. "I'm broke," I said. "I got enough for the fare but no tip. Sorry, man."

"My brother's doing time," the driver said. Then he smiled, surprisingly warm and calm. "Forget it. Lots of guys I pick up here have the same problem."

A compassionate cabbie, I thought to myself. *Who knew?*

When I got home, my wife was sitting on the front porch. I thanked the cabbie and ran to her. The moment we walked inside, I knelt—next to our cat's litter box, as it happened. She knelt with me. And I told her the truth.

The next day, I drove to see my teenage daughter, Jess.

And I confessed.

"I'd have said you're innocent the whole time, whatever they had on you," Jess said defiantly. Her eyes were steeped in hurt and betrayal.

"I know, sweetie," I said. "That's why I told you first thing."

The next week at the arraignment, I spotted my cellie. "I saw you on TV, brother!" Danny laughed, shaking my hand. Then he lowered his voice. "Some reporters are outside waiting for your perp walk."

"Did they ask you anything?"

"Sure, *Doc*." He winked. "But I don't roll on nobody."

Confession is not an easy thing for our loved ones to live with. I didn't necessarily feel better; and they definitely felt worse. Most of my family ignored me. The last time I spoke with my parents for several years was the day of my arrest.

I pleaded guilty at my trial. CNN captured every word. My last appearance on television was the most excruciating for my family. I was sentenced to five years: time served plus probation. I did three.

After my release, my aunt called. She was a woman of plain talk and deep beliefs. In her view, I had confessed my crime, did my time, and paid what was due. "That was *then*," she said. "What are you doing *now?*"

My parents remained silent until seven years after my arrest. It took my mother's funeral for my father to speak to me. Over time, he and I found a way to face our wounds and ended up friends at last. On one visit, he asked about my crime.

"It's pretty simple," I said, standing in his kitchen. "I thought I was Mister Clever Boots and they caught me—"

"Fine, if you don't want to tell me, forget it," he said and stomped away.

That was our only moment of acrimony in the last years of his life. For whatever reason, my father seemed to *want to know* and *not want to know* at the same time. I understood. I wanted to tell but was relieved not to.

I had held up my end of that jail-cell prayer. Still, I wasn't sure if God had done much of anything. *Perhaps it was just the normal progress of the legal system,* I mused. Then, a few years later, my daughter spoke with me in another kitchen. This time her eyes held no recrimination as she said four of the gentlest words I will ever hear: "I forgive you, Dad."

My confession doesn't stop here.

Jess died of a heroin overdose in 2015. She was twenty-six. The night I learned she was gone I collapsed, buried my head in open hands, and groaned between tears, "*Oh Lord, help!*"

For the first time in my life, I knew God heard me. I could feel his presence. As with many spiritual experiences, my sense of *knowing* was beyond words, but palpable nonetheless. I was not alone.

God heard me in my jail cell. When I doubt, I need only recall a cabbie's compassion or my daughter's forgiveness. God heard me when Jess died. Now I share one last confession: I feel Jess near as I type these words. I wanted to know that she continues on, that we will be together again. And I do.

Today I write and speak on loss and facilitate bereavement support groups. Each week I correspond with other mourners, or meet them in the most unexpected circumstances. In sorrow they, too, confess alarming guilt and pain. Some of their stories are personal, to be shared only among fellow sufferers. They needn't worry.

I do not roll on anyone.

WHEN WE GO TO CONFESS OUR WEAKNESSES, OUR SINS, WE GO TO ASK THE PARDON OF JESUS, BUT WE ALSO GO TO RENEW OUR BAPTISM THROUGH HIS FORGIVENESS. JESUS IS THERE, JESUS RECEIVES YOU, HE RECEIVES YOU WITH SO MUCH LOVE.

—POPE FRANCIS

Franz Ejsmond,
Hermit, 1881,
National Museum in Warsaw

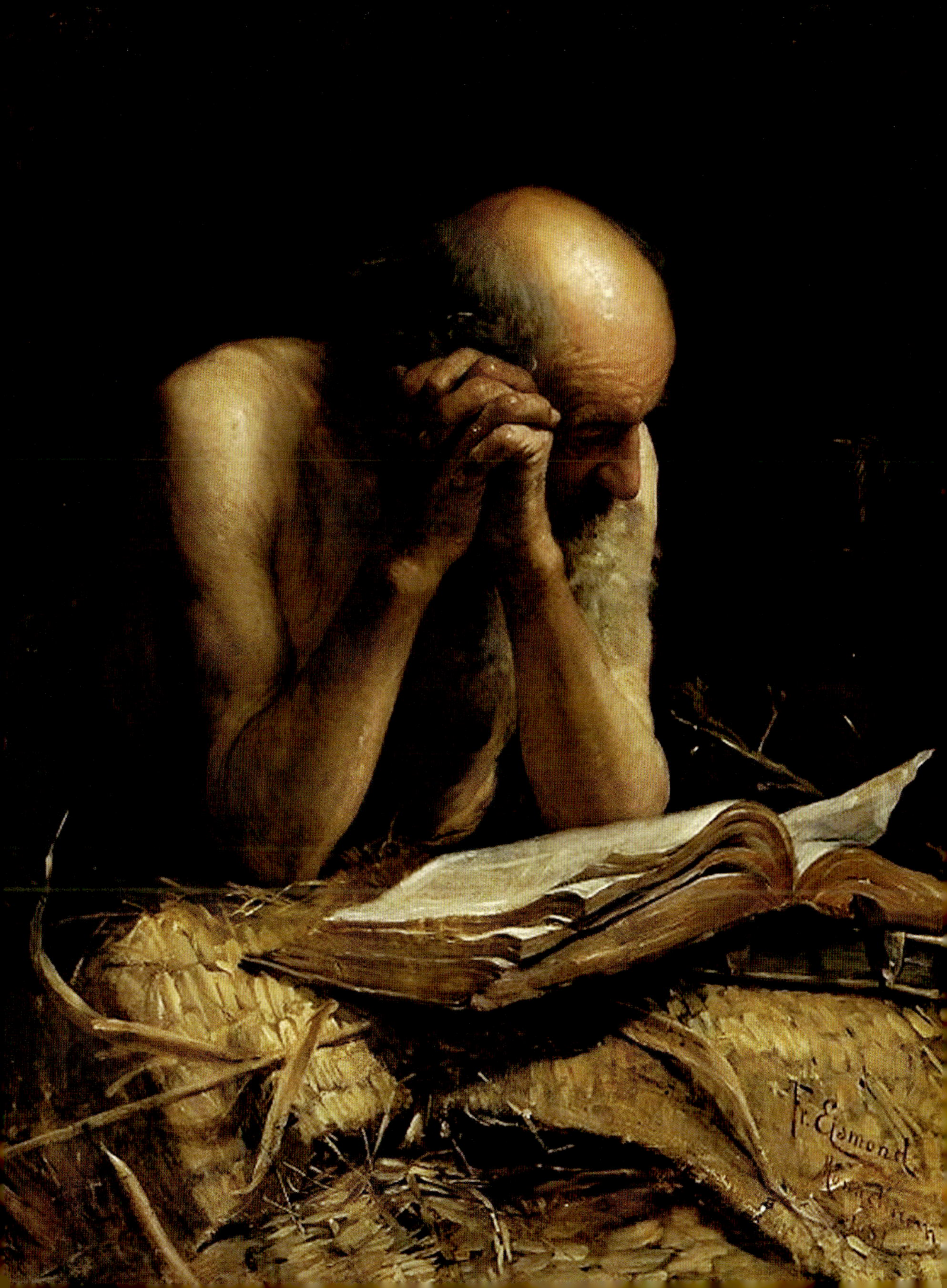

HOW IT SHOULD BE

"We know that we will remain inconsolable."

My grief is beyond healing; my heart is broken.

JEREMIAH 8:18 (NLT)

We never truly know someone until we know their grief.

Consider Martin Luther, so fond of quoting Job to bereaved parents: *The Lord gave and the Lord has taken away; may the name of the Lord be praised.* "Joyfully give God his own," he advises. Then the unthinkable happens. "My little girl, my tiny Elisabeth, has died," Luther writes a friend in August of 1528. "My spirit is left strangely broken, moved by this heartache, shocked that a father could love his child so much." Never again would Luther offer callous bromides to fellow mourners.

William James makes a similar mistake. Grief is only heightened by tears and sobs, he insists. Succumbing to waves of sorrow does not provide relief. Then his son dies. Suddenly the pain of loss is all too real. Today James's search for spiritual meaning in the face of loss is a comfort to millions.

I'm no better. I work for years at a busy funeral home, seeking to emulate the compassion I see in directors and staff. Yet grieving couples leave me helpless. *This way to the viewing room*, I say in calm, polite tones—before scampering to my office in shock and fear of what I cannot comprehend. Now when I meet fellow bereaved parents, I pause in silent communion and ask their child's name.

Even old atheist Sigmund Freud puts my past actions to shame. At least he *tries* to speak for mourners. His initial reflections on grief are based on helping those in pain. As W. H. Auden writes in his poem "In Memory of Sigmund Freud," the psychiatrist goes down among lost people living in their own hells, among the injured and the rejected. He faces what we often ignore, reminds us that the night, too, needs our love. In directing a light on our personal darkness, Auden writes, Freud endures our cry of "Judas." His focus is on the broken people he serves.

Yet Freud, like Luther and James, like me, learns that he does not understand loss until he faces his own. The passing of his younger brother, Julius, aged six months, three weeks before Freud's second birthday, contributes to years of remorse. When Freud is forty, his father, Jacob, dies in 1896 at the age of eighty-one. This leads to a lifelong engagement with self-analysis: evaluating and re-evaluating the impact of death.

By 1917 the psychologist writes his influential paper *Mourning and Melancholia.* He defines mourning as a severing from an object (our loved one) that no longer exists. An inability to detach, he suggests at the time, is pathological grief.

But loss changes us.

On January 25, 1920, Freud's daughter Sophie dies from pneumonia after a bout with the Spanish flu, one day before her seventh wedding anniversary. She is twenty-six, a mother of two, with a third child on the way. "Our dear Sophie in Hamburg has been taken from us, as if she never existed," Freud tells a friend. "Our poor Sunday child!" Shortly after Sophie's death, on February 4, he writes, "The loss of a child is a terrible blow. Deep within me I can trace feelings of a profound hurt that will never heal."

Freud decries to his daughter's husband, Max, the senselessness and brutality of a fate that took Sophie, adding, "We must bow our heads under such a blow: helpless, poor humans, playthings of a higher power." Later, he confides to a friend that now Max must pay dearly for the happiness they shared for seven years. Such statements are quite common in the first onslaught of acute grief, when mourners flail about, seeking explanations, often blaming the divine.

Freud also discovers that his previous paper on mourning is unequal to the reality of grief. "No sooner did he formulate this conception, than he put it into question," observes L. Scott Lerner of Franklin & Marshall College. It is seldom reported, but after losing Sophie the heartbroken doctor completely changes his views on sorrow. He soon dismisses any thought of getting over a death. Tammy Clewel of Kent State University notes that Freud now redefines *melancholia*, insisting it is not something to work through, but rather an integral part of bereavement. "Freud's later work registers the endlessness of normal grieving," Clewel says, "to suggest the affirmative and ethical aspects of mourning."

In *The Ego and the Id* (1923), written three years after Sophie's death, Freud resists his initial idea that we must separate ourselves from those we have lost. In mourning, he writes, our mind readjusts to a new reality. Our sense of identity, or ego, is structurally altered to continue an equally important identification with our loved one. He adds that this is "the sole condition" under which we can accept the death.

Modern research confirms that our brains are hard-wired this way, suggests neurologist Mary-Francis O'Connor of the University of Arizona. While our loved ones are alive, our brains devote tremendous energy to mapping their locations so we can find them in times of need. "Grieving requires the difficult task of throwing out the map we have used to navigate our lives together," O'Connor says, "and transforming our relationship with this person who has died."

One way to do this, Freud learns, is through service to others in honor of our dead. A month after Sophie's death, on February 24, 1920, he launches the first free psychoanalytic outpatient clinic in Berlin. The idea is suggested to him by Max Eitingon and Ernst Simmel. Opening the hospital at such a crucial point in his life, Freud says, is "at just this time the most gratifying thing I could do."

All too soon Sophie's son, Heinz, called Heinele, also takes ill. Freud adores the boy, calling him "the cleverest, sweetest child I have ever known," and noting in 1922 that although Heinele is physically fragile, he is especially bright and endearing.

Heinele is staying with his aunt Mathilde (Math) and uncle Robert Hollitscher when he dies after three weeks' illness of miliary tuberculosis on June 19, 1923. The loving grandfather is shocked at this loss and also by Heinele's peculiar prescience. "He too possessed high intelligence and ineffable grace of the spirit," Freud writes in 1928. "He often spoke of dying young. How do children know?"

Freud has placed much of his love for Sophie in Heinele, perhaps as a way to honor his daughter, and even more for Heinele himself. "He was the best of all my children and other grandchildren," he says. "When little Heinele died, I tired irreparably of life." This leads to three weeks of near-constant weeping and "the darkest days of my life," he tells the boy's father, Max.

Freud's subsequent letters during this period reveal an astonishing litany of lament.

"He was my future," Freud writes Oscar Rei. "And so he took the future with him." Ernest Jones, his lifelong colleague, observes that Heinele's death is the only time his friend has shed tears. Freud tells him that the loss affects him differently from others he has known. "They had brought about sheer pain," Jones recalls. "But this one had killed something in him for good." Freud relates to Marie Bonaparte that now he feels incapable of loving anyone again. He confides to his friend Sándor Ferenczi that though he had never suffered from depression, this must be what it feels like. He sees only darkness ahead. "This loss is excruciating," he writes to Kata and Lajos Lévy on June 11, 1923. "I have never known such overwhelming grief. . . . I work because I must; but in the end everything has lost meaning."

These emotions are expected, normal, and a natural reaction to death. Freud loves Sophie and Heinele. In expressing his love through epistolary lament, it may be that he discovers the precise meaning he feels has been lost. Ten years after Heinele's death, he remains a doting grandfather. When poet and novelist Hilda Doolittle begins therapy with Freud, now seventy-seven, she despairs that he is forever wondering aloud, "What will become of my grandchildren?"

In July, 1925, Freud pens one of his most influential works, *Inhibitions, Symptoms, and Anxiety* (1926). The first section is titled "Modification of Earlier Views," a theme that runs throughout the book. In his final chapter, "Anxiety, Pain, and Mourning," the bereaved father and grandfather asks a question that never seems to be far from his mind: "When does separation cause anxiety, when does it cause grief, and when, perhaps, only pain?"

Perhaps not *only* pain. Freud also expresses love. On Sophie's birthday, April 11, 1929, nine years after her death, he offers this advice to a friend who has recently lost a son:

> My daughter, now dead, would have been thirty-six years old today. Anything that fills this emptiness, even filling it completely, will forever be something *else*. Our acute grief may pass, but we know that we will remain inconsolable, never finding a substitute. And this is how it should be. It is the only way to continue a love that we would never forsake.

Freud doesn't wake up one day to a belief in God. Rather, his certainties are considerably less certain. In 1928 he asks his longtime friend and correspondent Swiss Lutheran minister Oskar Pfister how morality and order may be reconciled with the miseries of this world. "I really want to know," he writes, adding that he "deeply regrets" his inability to accept the idea of a loving God who looks over us all. This has left him without recourse. "I am unbelieving, profoundly so, and have no one to blame, nowhere to lodge my complaint."

He suggests without irony that though he has no direct mystical experience, he may well be mistaken and envies Pfister's confidence. "It is not a question of which belief is more pleasant or comforting or advantageous, but which veers closest to the mysterious reality that is outside us. . . . You know the more glorious the prospect, the less the certainty, and the greater the passion."

Freud's doubts and questions make him like many of us who mourn. We may ask ourselves: *How much do I dare believe? Can I live without the hope that I will see my loved ones again?* His example is of a flawed man, broken with sorrow yet still serving others, who sought answers, as we are seeking, and who is not shy about telling the world when he is wrong.

Briton Rivière,
The Temptation in the Wilderness, 1898,
Guildhall Art Gallery

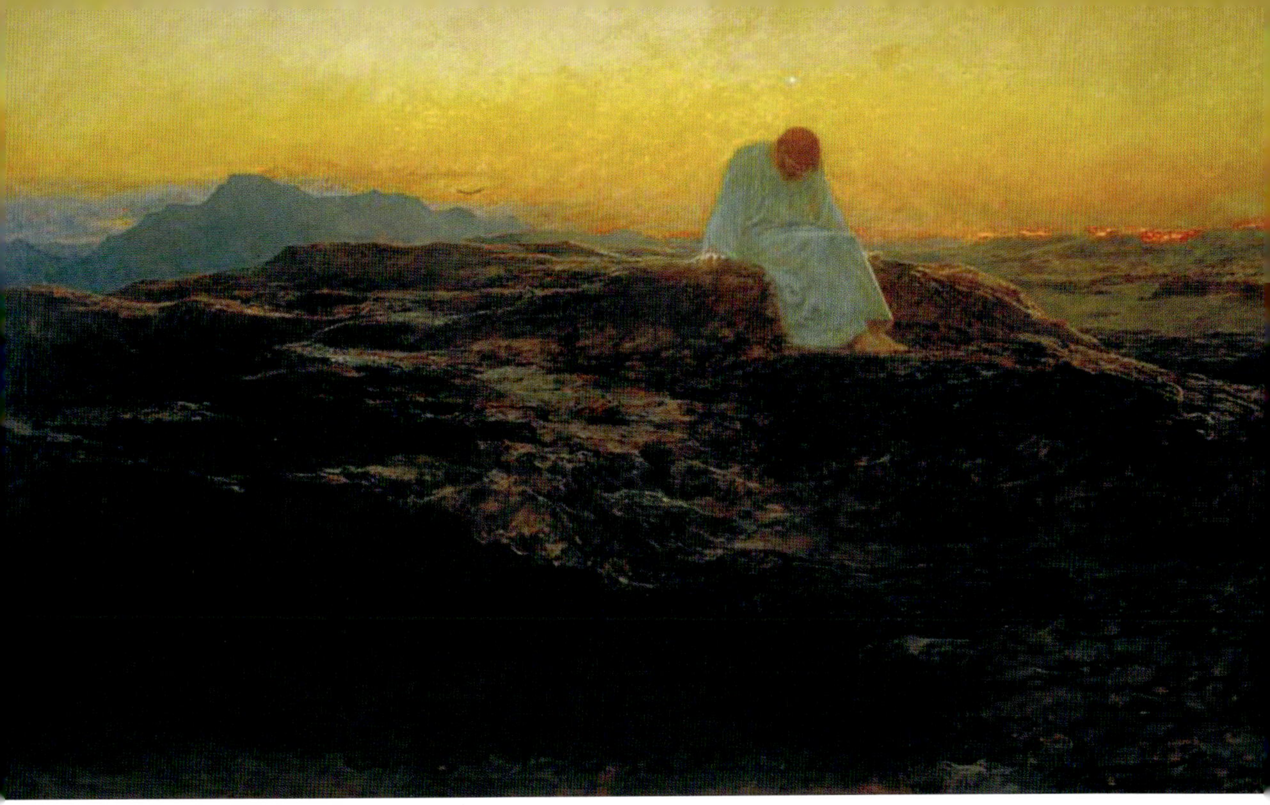

WHAT I TRY TO DO IS SPEAK TO GOD. EVEN WHEN I SPEAK AGAINST GOD, I SPEAK TO GOD. AND EVEN IF I AM ANGRY AT GOD, I TRY TO SHOW GOD MY ANGER. BUT EVEN THAT IS A PROFESSION, NOT A DENIAL OF GOD.

One of the most serious questions I have confronted over the years is whether one can still believe in God after Auschwitz.

It was not easy to keep faith. Nevertheless, I can say that, despite all the difficulties and obstacles, I have never abandoned God.

I had tremendous problems with God, and still do.

Therefore, I protest against God. Sometimes I bring God before the bench. Nevertheless, everything I do is done from within faith and not from outside. If one believes in God one can say anything to God.

—ELIE WIESEL, NOBEL LAUREATE AND HOLOCAUST SURVIVOR

THE PRICE WE PAY FOR LOVE

"I grieve that grief can teach me nothing."

> *I will give them singleness of heart*
> *and put a new spirit within them.*
>
> EZEKIEL 11:19A (NLT)

Ralph Waldo Emerson's five-year-old son, Waldo, called "Wallie," died of scarlet fever on January 27, 1842. "Shall I ever dare to love any thing again," he wrote the next day. "Farewell and Farewell, O my Boy!" That spring Emerson composed one of America's finest laments. But the poet's grief had only begun.

All too soon, the spring harvest demanded Emerson's attention. He begrudged its attendant duties and the new fields of thought that called to him. "An eye fastened on the past unsuns nature," he wrote in March, "bereaves me of hope, and ruins me with a squalid indigence which nothing but death can adequately symbolize."

His reaction is characteristic of *acute grief*: an inability to initiate and maintain organized activity in the first onslaught of loss. Then Emerson surprises us. The poet spent the early months of 1842 writing a memorial poem entitled "Threnody," or lament. In it, he honors Wallie while mourning nature's implacable advance:

> Not mine — I never called thee mine,
> But Nature's heir, — if I repine,
> And seeing rashly torn and moved
> Not what I made, but what I loved,
> Grow early old with grief that thou
> Must to the wastes of Nature go, —
> . . .
> The eager fate which carried thee
> Took the largest part of me:
> For this losing is true dying

Two years later, in 1844, Emerson penned an essay on his inability to find meaning in Wallie's death. "Souls never touch their objects," he observes. "Something which I fancied was a part of me, which could not be torn away without tearing me nor enlarged without enriching me, falls off from me and leaves no scar. . . . I grieve that grief can teach me nothing, nor carry me one step into real nature."

Many Emerson scholars wrestle with this last sentence. One suggests it indicates indifference. Another posits that the poet is acknowledging his own limitations. Others maintain that he is expressing an awareness of the uselessness of grief. Harvard philosopher Stanley Cavell spots the desperation in Emerson's tone, interpreting the passage "to mean the ground of the world falling away, the bottom of things dropping out, ourselves foundered, sunk on a stair."

Poet Linda Pastan also compares sorrow to a circular staircase. In her 1977 poem "The Five Stages of Grief," she relates her struggle with the titular phases until she victoriously reaches final ACCEPTANCE (her capitalization), only to realize that it was all for nothing. "But something is wrong," she concludes. "I have lost you."

The following year, Pastan used this piece as the title for her third poetry collection. The poem has since been anthologized in grief books and medical texts. "If I remember correctly," Pastan said in 1996, "the poem seemed to write itself." Yet neither Pastan nor Emerson, for all their hard-bitten fatalism, is dismissing the role of healthy mourning.

Emerson's essay on grief was written two years after Wallie's death—no time at all in the calendar of mourning. Common knowledge among support groups and therapists holds that the second year is especially difficult. With each birthday, anniversary, special occasion, or holiday, the death's finality is brought home anew. Such finitude is a devastating aspect of loss. As the years continue, we may learn to live with waves of sorrow, occasional moments of regret, and even unending loneliness. George Bonanno with Columbia University observes that these *anniversary reactions* are a permanent part of loss. They may last only a few hours, he says, but they will not change much over time. Death and its accompanying grief remain a constant in our lives.

Here I pause. I too am a bereaved father. I too know the relentlessness of grief. I too feel painful anguish that leaves no outward wound. And yet my soul *touches* and *is touched*. I did not stop being a father the moment my daughter died. Jess will forever be my child: Our love, our relationship, continues on in separation. In this Emerson and I differ, as well we might. "*We each have to find our own personal pathway as we deal with loss*," writes death expert Kenneth Doka. "Grief is as individual as fingerprints or snowflakes."

Emerson's essay speaks with determination and resolve. It occurs to me that his intent requires no convoluted explanations. Perhaps we should take him at his word. *I grieve that grief can teach me nothing* may mean exactly what it says. Wallie is gone; no visible scar remains. Mourning provides no lesson, no answers, no closure. The poet is not decrying grief for its lack of utility. He does not insist that some benefit be derived from his son's death. Instead, it seems that the irrevocable fact of Wallie's absence presses upon him.

Emerson forcibly illustrates that his wishes are not taken into account. He need not chase a chimera of resolution. "Grief is the price you pay for love," observes Doka, "but how you grieve is not necessarily a measure of that love." Emerson has no control over his grief—his love—for Wallie, however much he might hope otherwise. Sorrow and death do not benefit us, he suggests; they do not bother with us at all. They are simply part of life, inextricably linked and absolute, carrying him not "one step into real nature."

Emerson acknowledges a debt to nature, without which there would be no creation at all, but his loss proves to be ineffable. "The world of poetry is boundless and endless," observed Friedrich Schlegel, who, along with Goethe and Rückert, was an important influence on Emerson. "But how can it compare to the unstructured and unconscious poetry that stirs in a plant, that lights a child's smile, that shimmers in the bloom of youth?" There is no comparison, as Emerson knew. This may be why he selected these four lines from "Threnody" for the inscription on Wallie's gravestone in Sleepy Hollow Cemetery, Concord, Massachusetts:

THE HYACINTHINE BOY, FOR WHOM

MORN WELL MIGHT BREAK AND APRIL BLOOM, —

THE GRACIOUS BOY, WHO DID ADORN

THE WORLD WHEREINTO HE WAS BORN

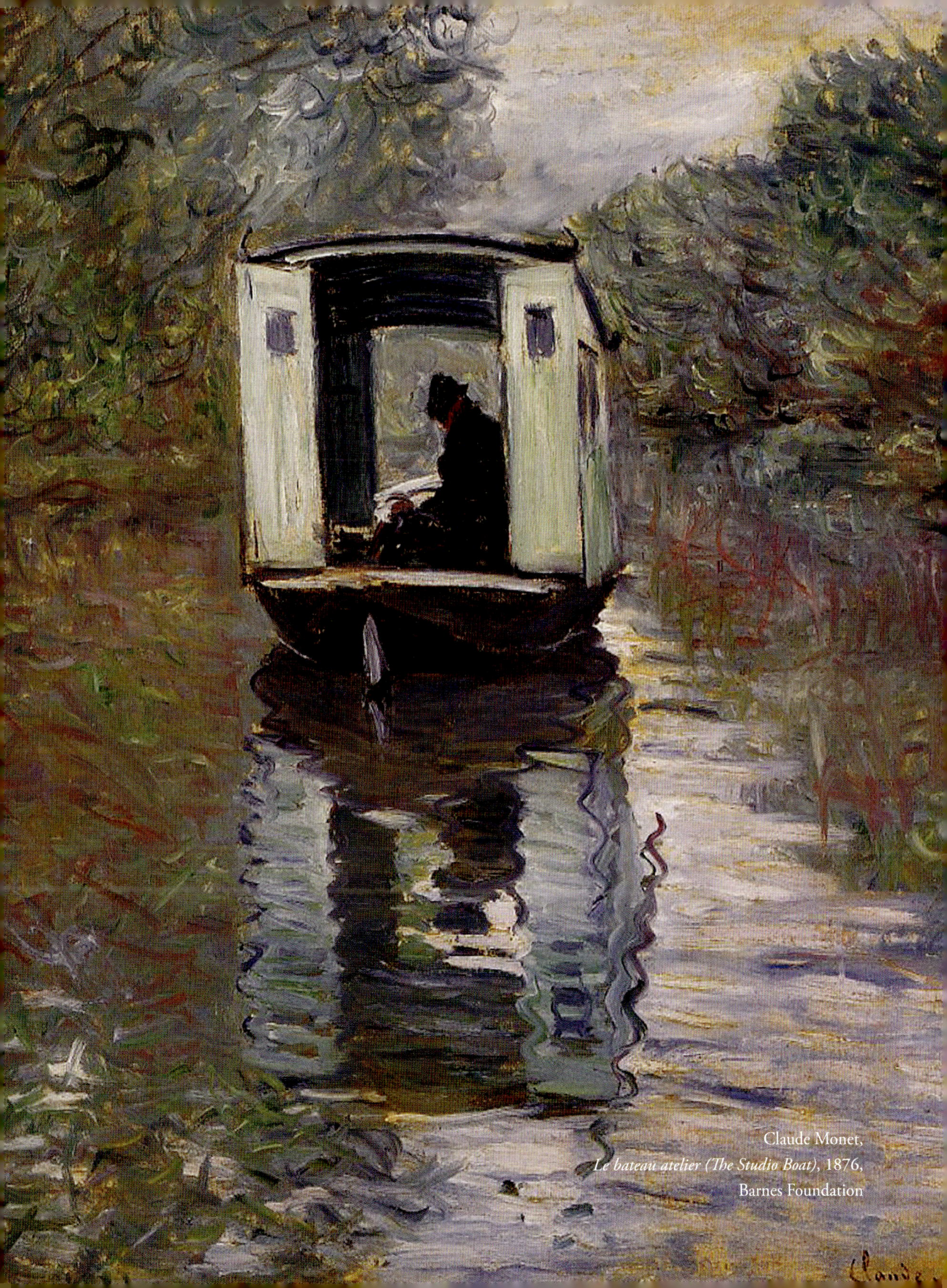

Claude Monet,
Le bateau atelier (The Studio Boat), 1876,
Barnes Foundation

A COMMUNION OF GRIEF

"I asked myself, 'Why did this have to happen to me?'"

> *Our mouths were filled with laughter, our tongues with songs of joy.*
>
> PSALM 126:2A

I watched *Abbott and Costello Meet Frankenstein* the night I learned my daughter died. All through that evening I had keened to the point of exhaustion. My voice was hoarse, body numb, restless and unable to sleep. I turned instead to a favorite from childhood, steeped in nostalgia for better days and comforting familiarity. It was January 18, 2015. Jess had died two days earlier. She was twenty-six.

In the wake of my only child's passing, clear thoughts proved disturbingly rare; concentration, a chimera. I revisited my Abbott and Costello collection: films, TV shows, and old radio programs. A friend assured me that this was healthy and worthwhile. "They minister to you," he said. It occurs to me that the form such solace takes is not nearly as important as that it exists at all.

While writing about mummy movies recently, I gave *Abbott and Costello Meet the Mummy* (1955) a quick spin. I once told Jess that the film wasn't very good compared to their others. But Jess loved ancient Egypt as much as I do. "It's not *that* bad, Dad," she said. "Cuz Mummies!"

We may dismiss Bud Abbott and Lou Costello as Saturday morning fare, but it wasn't always that way. In the 1940s, they were the most popular comedy team in film and radio. Their extraordinary wordplay was delivered with such exquisite timing that even now stars like Jerry Seinfeld hold them up as exemplars for aspiring comics. Carol Burnett says Abbott was the best straight man in the business.

Buck Privates, *In the Navy*, and *Hold that Ghost*, all released in 1941, were massive hits. The receipts from these three films alone bailed the nearly bankrupt Universal Pictures out of the red. Those of us reared on a TV diet of Abbott and Costello monster movies may not know what we missed, with the exception of . . . *Meet Frankenstein* (1948), which returns to the brilliance of their earlier features.

Costello didn't care for the . . . *Meet Frankenstein* script, but his family and audiences loved it. *Variety* praised it on June 25, 1948, as "a rambunctious fracas that is funny and, at the same time, spine-tingling." It was the third largest-grossing film in the world that year and is today listed in the American Film Institute's The 100 Funniest American Movies of All Time. It has withstood the passing years, an "all-time great horror comedy [that] still works beautifully," Leonard Maltin tells us. Filmmaker John Landis insists it "is just as funny today as it was then." Author and pop culture historian Roy Thomas, perhaps best known for the Avengers, X-Men, and Conan series, simply calls it "one of my favorite films—period!"

Shortly after my daughter died, I came across Costello's biography, *Lou's on First*, written in 1981 by the comedian's daughter, Chris. Happenstance? Perhaps, but as Frederick Buechner observes, at what point does it take more effort to believe in coincidence than to accept the obvious? For me, holding this book in my hands, I sense another reminder that God—and Jess—are looking out for me. In its pages I learn something surprising.

Costello also lost a child. This is his story.

Lou Costello was in a good mood as he prepared for his evening broadcast on November 4, 1943. He had recently recovered from a long bout with rheumatic fever. This was his first appearance in many months. Also, in two days the family had plans to celebrate his son Lou Jr.'s first birthday. They called the boy Little Butch.

"Keep Butch up tonight," Lou told his wife, Anne, as he left for the NBC studios in Hollywood. "I want to see if he'll recognize my voice over the air." He planned on making some of the quirky comic sounds that his son so loved.

Later that day, Little Butch drowned in the Costello family pool.

Lou's long-time manager, Eddie Sherman, took the solemn phone call. He immediately drove Costello home. "Lou was terribly heartbroken," Sherman recalls. "He felt the whole world tumbled from under him."

When word spread, calls came in from stars Mickey Rooney, Lana Turner, and many others offering to fill in for Lou during the broadcast. But the grieving father refused. "I promised Little Butch that he would hear me tonight," Lou told Sherman. "Wherever God has taken him, I know he will hear me, and I want to keep my promise."

The show was standard Abbott and Costello fare, though perhaps a bit more strained than usual. Lou wound down near the end of the program, collapsing into a chair on stage. The studio audience had only a moment to notice before Bud stepped out of character to inform radio listeners of the death. "In the face of the greatest tragedy which can come to any man, Lou Costello went on tonight," he said, choking back tears. "I would like to take a moment to pay tribute to my best friend and to a man who has more courage than I have ever seen."

The next few days were a torment to the bereaved father. He wasn't home when his son needed him, Lou told himself. He was riddled with feelings of self-doubt, blame, and recrimination.

Little Butch's funeral was held on what would have been the boy's birthday, November 6. Silent tears streamed down Lou's face. Platitudes offered by well-meaning friends had had no effect. During the service, the priest assured them that Butch was now with God. Somehow this spoke to Lou in ways that other words of comfort had not. He lifted his head, sat erect in the pew, and felt for the first time that he was not to blame for his son's death.

This moment is not the end of Lou's story. Grief lasts a lifetime. His marriage suffered but survived. It wasn't until a year after Little Butch's passing, over the Christmas holidays, that their family felt a small return to laughter and love, though now tempered with a sense of shared endurance and sorrow.

Lou carried his grief all of his days. Friends noticed that he was a changed man: at times impatient and temperamental, but also surprisingly sensitive, caring, and private. For years, Lou wore a bracelet with his son's name on it, welded together so he could not take it off. Studio makeup artists were forced to camouflage it. "Butch's death," says Lou's daughter Chris, "clouded everything else he did for the rest of his life."

Others also sensed the change in Costello.

Carol Burnett, herself a bereaved parent, sees pathos in Lou's performances in the late 40s and early 50s. "I had a particular love for Costello," she says, not only because he so often portrayed an underdog, but also for his natural ability to combine comedy and tragedy. "Heartbreak and howls may seem far apart, but actually they are not," she adds. "Beneath it all was this subtle layer of tragedy." Lou may have agreed.

"I asked myself, 'Why did this have to happen to me?'" Costello admitted years after Little Butch's death. His son was constantly on his mind; every little boy he saw reminded him of a future he and Butch would never share. "There was sadness in my heart," Lou wrote. "How I managed to be a funny man in pictures and on the radio, I will never know."

When the popular television program *This is Your Life* featured Costello on November 21, 1956, ten minutes of their twenty-four minute running time were devoted to Little Butch's passing—nearly half of the episode. "With a heart that came near to breaking, Lou, you've gone on to make the world laugh," said host Ralph Edwards. "The more you suffered, the more you wanted to bring healing to others."

In 1946, Lou and Bud, who was Little Butch's godfather, founded the Lou Costello Jr. Youth Foundation. Later, on May 3, 1947, they opened a recreation center in Butch's name. "All who come here have been created equal," they wrote in a mission statement that was remarkable for the 1940s. "And will be given equal privileges regardless of race, color or creed."

Within two years the foundation had provided 10,280 youngsters with free access to sports facilities, a library, workshops, and classrooms. Doctors and dentists provided free vitamins, food, and healthcare to the needy. There was also a full-sized pool. "In memory of Little Butch," observed the host on *This is Your Life*, "many hundreds of boys and girls have had their lives protected by learning to swim." In the same program, seven young recreation center members presented Lou with a watch they had all chipped in to buy. The inscription read: "Thanks for sharing your life with ours."

The Lou Costello Jr. Recreation Center continues to serve young people in Los Angeles to this day. Little Butch's portrait hangs in the main foyer.

Sometime after his son's death, Costello invented a commercial ice cube maker, the first of its kind. By the late 1950s it was a common accessory in American households. The profits from Lou's patent were an important source of income for his family. This aspect of the comedian's personality may surprise film buffs, but not his daughter Chris. "My father loved electronics, he loved technology," she says, adding that if he saw a modern DVD player, his first response would be: *I have to have one of those.*

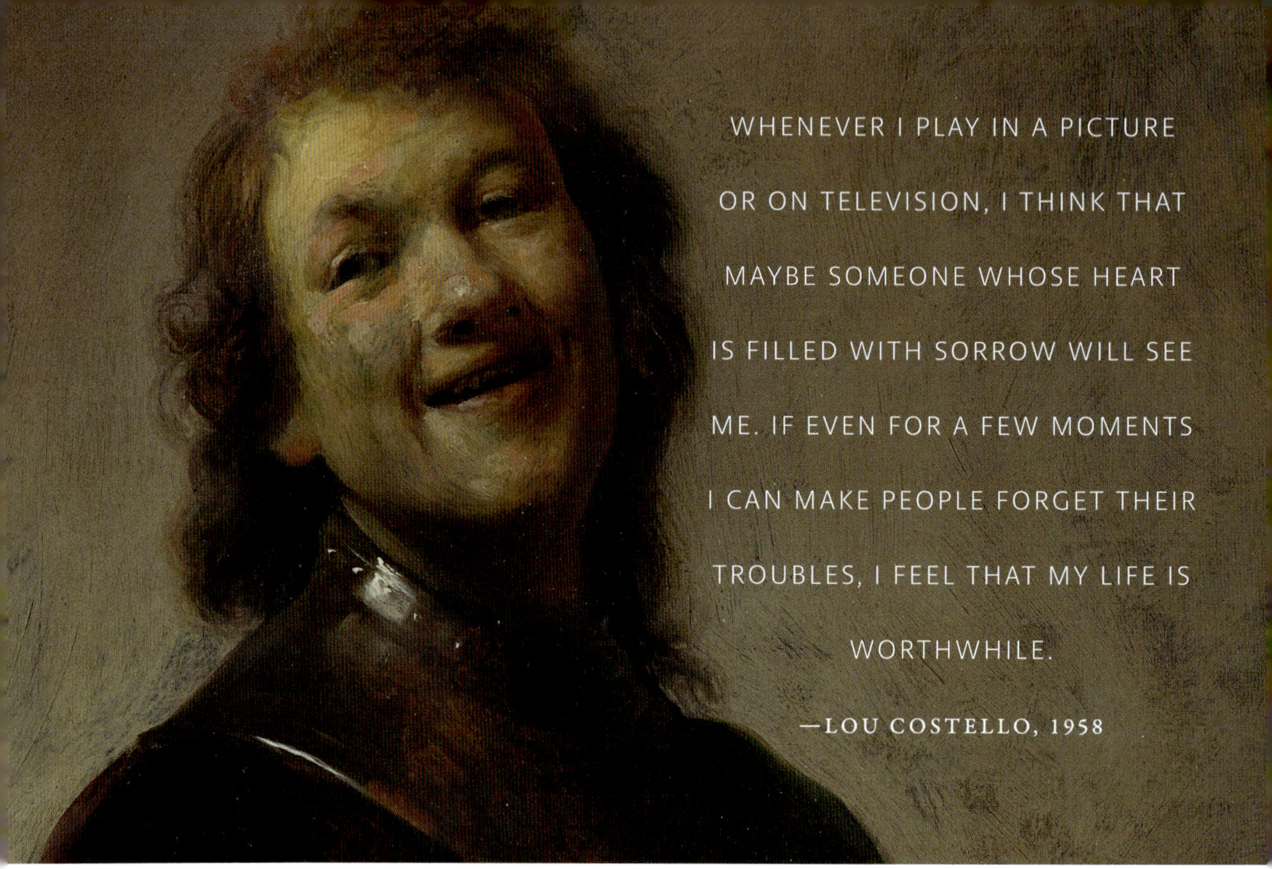

Costello suffered a heart attack on February 26, 1959. A few days later, on March 3, Eddie Sherman stopped in for a round of jokes and quiet laughter. Later, minutes after Anne left his room, Lou was struck by a second attack. He died that afternoon, three days before his fifty-third birthday. “My God, what can I say?” sobbed Bud when he heard the news. “My heart is broken. I’ve lost the best pal anyone ever had.”

A requiem mass was held for Lou on March 7. Nine months later, on December 5, Anne died at the age of forty-seven. Today they rest near Little Butch in the Los Angeles Calvary Cemetery.

I’m watching *Abbott and Costello Meet Frankenstein* again. It’s funny, and silly, and I’m enjoying it. But amidst the clever wordplay, slapstick gags, and gentle humor, I spot an undercurrent of sadness in Lou’s eyes. I didn’t know about Little Butch the night I learned my daughter died, but even then I may have sensed something more than comforting nostalgia when I selected this particular film. Perhaps I also felt a communion of grief.

Rembrandt van Rijn,
Rembrandt Laughing, c 1628,
Getty Center

Hope

Blessed are those who mourn, for they will be comforted.

MATTHEW 5:4

And if I go and prepare a place for you, I will come back and take you to be with me that you also may be where I am.

JOHN 14:3

THE GRACE OF PHANTOM PAIN

"My sorrows are too dark for day to know."

> *I am sad and hurting. God, lift me up and save me!*
>
> PSALM 69:29 (ERV)

I dread mornings. I wake to a world without my daughter in it. Jess died nine years ago. She was twenty-six.

Many bereaved parents know this particular pain. Throughout the day, we may not consciously *think* of our children. There is no need. They inhabit our minds the same way our brains tell us to breathe or blink. They are always here.

Barbara Eden lost her 35-year-old son, Matthew, to a heroin overdose in 2001. Ten years later, she wrote that although she still finds joy in life, part of her will always be missing. "Matthew is never out of my mind," she says, "and the pain of losing him and of missing him doesn't get less. I still think of him every day and dream of him every night."

Naps are slightly different. A short doze may leave me a tad hazy for a few seconds when I wake. That is when the full impact of my loss slams into me. My first reaction, my most frequent lament, is torn out of me in a torrent of pain: *Dear Lord, I want to hold her in my arms again!*

Her absence is my cry.

In a similar gasp of sudden anguish, Friedrich Rückert wrote the poem "Once I held the reality of you" after the deaths of his two youngest children, Luise and Ernst. It is a rough sketch, unfinished and raw. He holds in his hands two pastel portraits of his three-year-old daughter and five-year-old son. Each word is redolent of loss. The paintings are a poignant reminder of when they were alive, within arm's reach, and a bitter confirmation that he can no longer hold them, save in a pair of two-dimensional images.

> Once I held the reality of you,
> young and alive;
> unforgettable, a dream swept
> away too soon.
> We need irony to endure the
> dictates of heaven:
> these will have to do for now,
> portraits of you.

Portraits (or photographs) may provide much-needed testimony of our loved ones' lives. Visiting a grave offers a similar sense of solace and communion in our difficult adjustment to a world in which they no longer exist. For this reason, the seemingly jarring and morbid sentiment of irony in Rückert's poem is actually quite useful.

I learned on January 18, 2015, that my daughter had died two days earlier. One year later, to the day, German pop star Madeline Juno recorded her own cry of desperation and sorrow, "Phantom Pain (*Phantomschmerz*)." In her lyrics I find a precious gift: the peace only communion of grief offers. Her loved one's face lingers, Juno sings. Her heart has phantom pain.

Comparing the continuing presence of a dead loved one to a phantom limb is more than metaphor or analogy, writes philosopher Matthew Ratcliffe with the University of York. He says that the two types of experiences are structurally similar in significant ways. Those close to us are part of our physical and emotional spheres. They help shape how we engage with the world just as our bodies interact with our physical surroundings. In this way, he adds, "the boundaries between bodily and interpersonal experience are indistinct."

Catherine Fullarton with Emory University builds on this idea, adding that once our situations change, our bodies are stymied, unable to execute habits and expected functions. Our loved ones are not there. Grief and phantom limbs, she says, are not part of a *process of recuperation*, but a *transformative experience* as we adjust to our new relationship in absence. But this doesn't make it any easier.

Studies over the past two decades demonstrate that phantom pain sensations represent measurable nerve activity that can be positive or excruciating. For example, *phantom limb sensation*, as it is called, is helpful in controlling a prosthesis; *phantom limb pain*, on the other hand, is debilitating. Neither is psychosomatic. They require "neuronal network reorganization," according to Kassondra Collins with the University of Tennessee Health Science Center.

"Phantom limb pain is horrible," says Paul Cederna, chief of plastic surgery with the University of Michigan. Our brains are wired that way. When we were whole, our brains mapped the limbs or other parts of our bodies; now there is no limb to correspond with the nerves. Our nerve fibers are looking for something that no longer exists. When they find nothing, Cederna explains, a neuroma forms, or a ball of raw nerve endings. Our brains don't know to ignore those sensations.

My parents are gone. With them, I lost my past. The moment I learned Jess was dead, I felt our future together slip away. The joys and sorrows of shared memories: birthday dinners at our favorite restaurant; movies yet unseen (or unmade) that we will never talk about; a wedding day with a beaming Jess and a proud father; her first child; the heartache of disease and uncertainty; phone calls that now, alas, will never come. Today my life is steeped in moments that were once *we* and are now *I*.

Madeline Juno smiles as she thinks of her loved one's jokes, of how they played games that Juno inevitably lost. I smile with her. Jess never once lost a game of *Sorry*. I too can hear Jess's laugh. At times my hands convulse, my arms quiver, as though I might turn sideways into a future where my daughter is alive. The experts are right. My nerves seek her and she is not there. This pain is no phantom.

I facilitate bereavement support groups. Participants relate that they still reach out for their loved ones, even after many years. Then reality returns. Their pain is not lessened or dulled, merely familiar, an old companion. "It wasn't just you that died," cries Rückert in another lament. "The joy woven into my world died with you."

Such feelings are normal and expected, according to Mary-Francis O'Connor with the University of Arizona. She relates that when she asks mourners if they sense a part of themselves died with their loved ones, they reply with wide-eyed astonishment, *That's exactly how I feel.* O'Connor explains that in life we develop a keen sense of psychological closeness with our loved ones. Our brains process this shared interaction, or overlap, over the course of many years.

"We might think it is simply a metaphor to say that we have lost a part of ourselves when a loved one dies," O'Connor writes, adding that this simply isn't so. Our brains code representations of our bodies in our neurons. When an amputee experiences phantom pain, the brain is recording real pain. It is mapped into our nerves. "The process of grieving is not just about psychological or metaphorical change," O'Connor says. "Grieving requires neural rewiring as well."

James Krasner with the University of New Hampshire refers to this phenomenon as *embodied grief*, "a literally embodied, neurological response to loss." As with a phantom limb, mourners are accustomed to certain interactions with another person that now have no physical expression, causing acute and long-lasting pain. This in turn leads to a disruption of reality.

Juno sings that she still talks about her loved one, says what they used to say, even argues a little, until memory returns. It's true: I often recall some of Jess's favorite expressions. And more, I have included a few of them in my personal dialogue. Thomas Fuchs, University of Heidelberg, calls this experience "a fundamental ambiguity between presence and absence of the deceased, between the present and the past, indeed between two worlds." We are living in two strands of time, he writes, a continuing past and a present without our loved one.

One healthy way to reconcile these strands of time may be to *externalize our relationship*, says Julia Samuel, a psychotherapist and pediatric counselor. For example, we may wear things that confirm a sense of connection, such as clothes that our loved one admired, a watch or hat that they favored. One of Jess's belts still hangs on the wall next to her portrait, and I have no problem using one of her messenger bags when the mood strikes.

Just over my desk is a photo with Jess, taken on a neighborhood swing set when she was very young. On a whim, I presented the picture to her as a young adult and suggested that we both sign it. *You're the best thing in my life!* I wrote, scrawling *Dad.* "I love you!" she scribbled in reply, signing her name with an image she often used in her art. Today I thank God, on my knees I thank him, for these two whimsical moments: on a swing and years later, with a black permanent marker.

After my daughter's memorial service, I invited friends to write notes to her in a blank book, with my promise (which I have kept) that I will read selections at her graveside. "Finding an external expression for the continuation of the relationship through regular rituals is not only important," concludes Samuel, "but has been shown to reduce negative emotions and increase positive ones." This has certainly been true for me.

Each line in the book is precious: scribbled notes, misspelled words, even the spaces and dashes. I linger over thoughts scratched out and rewritten. These entries are my idea of music, as Juno sings. Their gaps and scrawls, lovingly penned or barely legible, remind me of an insight from Durham University's Mark Sandy that "the final silence of death challenges poetry's eloquent capacity for meaning." I am also reminded of John Milton's unfinished elegy for the crucified Jesus, "The Passion." When he wrote the piece in 1630, funeral notices were engraved with white inscriptions on black paper—symbolism not lost on the poet:

> My sorrows are too dark for day to know:
> The leaves should all be black whereon I write,
> And letters where my tears have washt, a wannish white.

Such elegies can seem odd to casual observers. *Not getting over it*, they may whisper. *Complicated grief.* Well-meaning friends might suggest that prominent photos or beloved treasures are counterproductive. *A shrine*, they call it, implying that we're not moving on. But let's take a look at the illogic of these assertions. Shall we then remove the tombstone from our loved one's grave? Or forgo visits to their resting place? This is nonsense, of course. Memorials are millennia old and for good reason.

Consider Abraham's burial of his wife near Mamre's grove. The story takes up the entirety of Genesis 23. When Sarah died, Abraham was living in an oak grove that belonged to a man named Mamre. Nearby was a tract of land known as *The Makhpela*, something of a catch-all term that had the same intent as "the fells" or "the downs." The Makhpela contained a field and a cave, both owned by Ephron. (Adding to the confusion, Mamre was also a term for Hebron.)

As tombs and caves were nearly always in the side of a hill, it seems likely that Abraham wanted the cave to be "facing Mamre" so that Sarah's resting place would be within sight of an oak grove on the opposite side of the valley. His selection of Sarah's tomb was important for many reasons. Soon all the patriarchs and matriarchs, save Rachel, would be buried alongside her.

But this is not what resonates with me. In Genesis 23, after her death, the Torah repeatedly uses the word *l'Sarah* for Sarah. That term, Rabbi Ephraim Buchwald tells us, implies that Abraham weeps for the loss of Sarah, for herself as part of this world, rather than simply the impact of her death on him. In a prelude that seems ideally suited to Abraham's grief, the widower is consoled by neighbors who are eager for him to procure the cave and *bury his dead*—a refrain that is repeated six times in twenty verses.

Jesus provides a clue to the profound nature of this act when he tells a grieving son, "Let the dead bury their dead." This well-known and enigmatic saying is so famous that it is nearly a parable, according to proverb expert Wolfgang Mieder, adding that most speakers are unaware of its biblical origins. The phrase comes from the Gospels of Matthew and Luke.

At the time of Jesus, burial was a private affair. Remains were interred in a family tomb, usually a cave carved out of limestone rock, with shelves for their dead. A full year later, the family would return to collect the bones and place them in an ossuary. This had a pragmatic purpose: the shelves could be used again and again for the dead, allowing a family to remain together in a single tomb, literally gathered to their ancestors.

Eric Meyers, professor emeritus and founder of the Center for Jewish Studies at Duke University, describes this later *second burial* in the ossuary as both internment and symbolic expiation of death: when "the dead bury their dead," redeeming body and spirit from its decomposed state. The Gospel reference seems to have been to this traditional Palestinian practice; in other words, Christ tells the young man to let the atonement of death in the *second burial* tend to itself. Or as New Testament scholar John Dominic Crossan translates the passage, "A follower to Jesus 'I must stay to rebury my father.' Jesus to follower 'Let the dead rebury their dead.'"

While it may be a bit much to ask that mourners bear the whole load of this biblical meaning, the words of Abraham's consolers, and Jesus, offer sentiments we can understand. The bodies of our loved ones are gone; their spirits are free. As with Abraham, we do not grieve that we are inconvenienced: We mourn that they are missing from this world.

Grief is the natural reaction to death. It is also universal, death and dying counselors Stephen and Ondrea Levine observe. "We are all in grief," write the Levines. "Most display the old scars and rope burns of having one object or another pulled beyond their grasp." Abraham's healthy desire to have Sarah's grave nearby serves not only to provide a sacred place of sorrow, but also hallowed ground where he may express his love for her. Modern mourners might follow his example.

I sing along with Juno, trying to match her exquisite diction and natural lyricism. She tells her loved one to watch her—she'll hold onto what she has left. Keepsakes of my daughter do indeed help me to hold on. They are normal and healthy. There is no time limit to how long such items remain in the home: months, years, or for the rest of our lives. One vital difference seems to lie with the emotions invested in these inanimate items.

A *transitional object*, for example, is a comfort as we adjust to life without our loved one, such as a favorite stuffed toy, a blanket, or treasured clothing. A *linking object*, on the other hand, may veer dangerously close to imagining that our dead loved one is the object itself, with resulting anxiety and emotional breakdown when the object is removed. Healthy mementos may be put away when the time is right, which might in fact be never.

Photos, treasures, and creative expressions such as art or poetry may remind us of those many happy moments that are all the more precious in our loved one's absence, suggests psychologist Shanee Stepakoff, a specialist in loss and depression. Deeply felt love may lead to honest hurt, which in turn facilitates voicing of emotions that, if not faced, may fester and canker. Acceptance of pain can be liberating, or as Juno sings, bandages don't help, it still hurts. Such awareness has an honorable pedigree.

"My eyes are dim with grief," sing the Sons of Korah, crying that they are *numb* from terror. They speak of the desperation, fear, and hope that so often mingle with love and grief. "I call to you, Lord, every day; I spread out my hands to you," they weep. "You have taken from me friend and neighbor—darkness is my closest friend." For many of us, darkness is an inevitable part of grief, but it is not *all* of grief.

While my daughter was alive, our home was festooned with Jess things: artwork, certificates, newspapers and magazines with her model shoots, handwritten notes, doodles, and photos, photos, photos. There is no reason for this to change now that our relationship is one of loving in separation. In fact, to take reminders of Jess down from my shelves would be odd—as though with her death I would sponge away her life as well.

Removing our treasured memorabilia is not only peculiar, it can also be damaging. It is easy to dwell too much on negative or unpleasant memories that we wish we could change. Such ruminations may lead to brooding, self-recrimination, and remorse. However, guilt offers no solutions and no hope. Here I take the words of Jesus to heart. I too let my dead bury my dead. Her spirit is free.

Thinking of this enigmatic saying, and phantom pain, I realize that our perception of death's finality does not jibe with our secret selves, more certain and powerful than the physical world. Our souls rebel: We seem certain that there is more in this universe than what we see each day. Despite all evidence to the contrary, we sense that our loved ones continue on.

Perhaps the teacher in Ecclesiastes was onto something. It occurs to me that God touched human hearts with eternity in more ways than we may know. I believe that when we are faced with excruciating loss, this eternity within assures us that we are never alone.

Writing is my creative expression of love and grief, as it was for Barbara Eden, Rückert, and Milton. *Are you watching?* Madeline Juno weeps in refrain. I echo her resolve: *Me too, I swear, I'm watching 'til we're together.* I still wake from naps reaching for Jess. I continue to wonder how it will feel to hold her in my arms again. My phantom pain hurts, but it is also a grace. It gives me assurance of our continuing bond in this life, and hope for reunion in the next. This may be the only consolation that lasts.

Eugène Carrière,
Her Mother's Kiss, 1899
Pushkin Museum

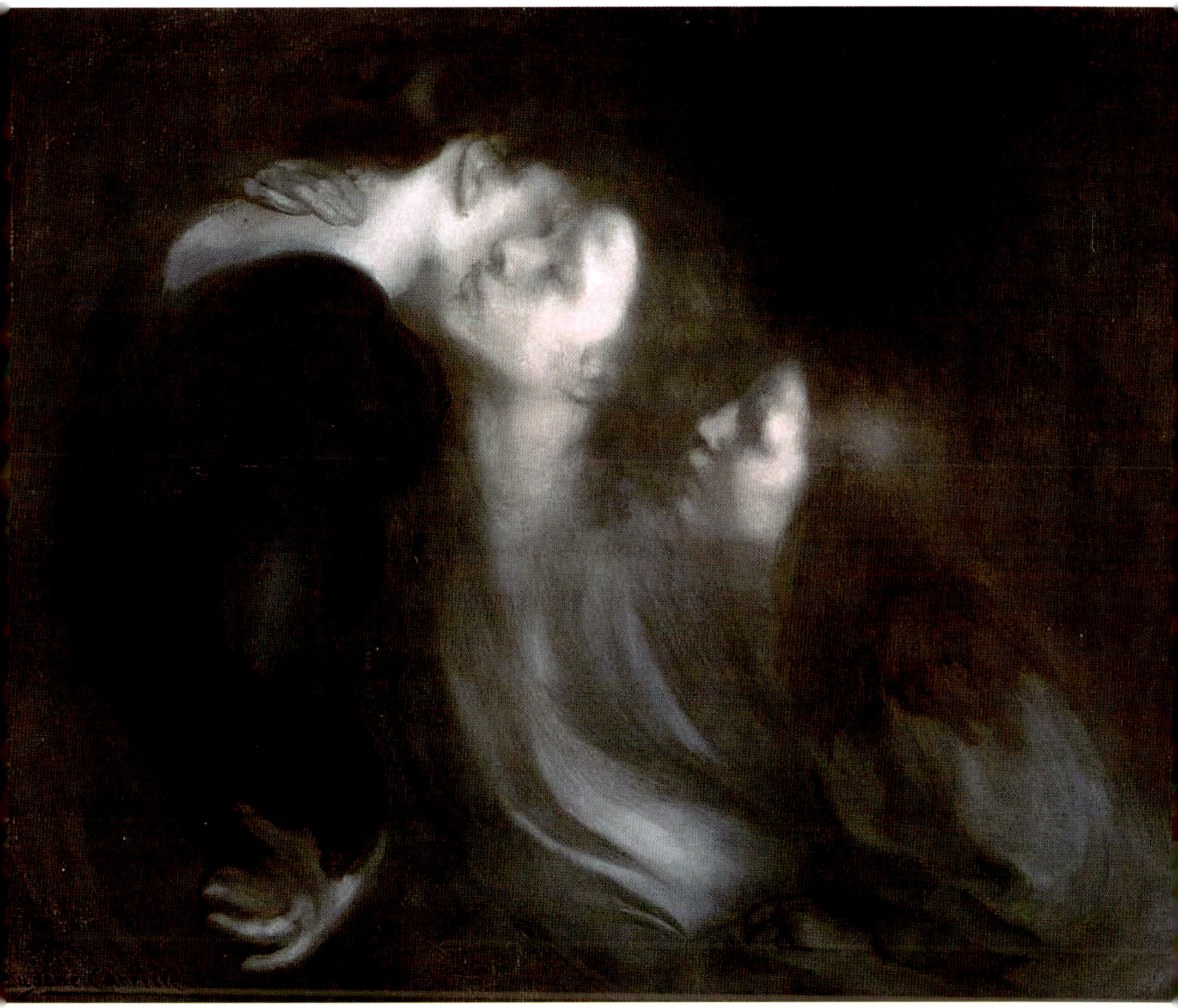

THE BRAIN IS JUST THE WEIGHT OF GOD—
FOR—HEFT THEM—POUND FOR POUND—
AND THEY WILL DIFFER—IF THEY DO—
AS SYLLABLE FROM SOUND—

—EMILY DICKINSON

BELIEF IN IMMORTALITY

"We and God have business with each other."

> *God himself will be with them. He will wipe every tear from their eyes, and there will be no more death or sorrow or crying or pain. All these things are gone forever.*
>
> REVELATION 21:3B-4 (NLT)

William and Alice James set out at 6:00 a.m. from their Massachusetts home. A small wicker basket sits on Alice's lap, wrapped in a white flannel blanket. They stop to gather pine, oak, and birch leaves, along with wild flowers, ferns, and grasses. Soon they arrive at the James family plot. They set tree sprigs, flowers, and ferns in the basket—now revealed as a casket holding their baby boy, eighteen months old, known in the family as Humster. He died two days ago. They bury Humster under a young pine tree next to James's father, Henry James Sr. "It was as lovely and touching a little sight as you ever looked on," James says. It is July 11, 1885.

The next month, on an unusually hot August night, James returns to the Cambridge home on Appian Way where his young family had once lived. He stands in the street and "looks at our old empty house under a clouded moon," staring up at one window on the second floor. Behind its shutters lies the room where Humster was born. "It *must* be now," James writes his cousin the next day, "that he is reserved for some still better chance than that, and that we shall in some way come into his presence again."

Interactions with the hereafter come to dominate James's research. "Immortality is one of the great spiritual needs of man," he says. "The surest warrant for immortality is the yearning of our bowels for our dear ones." The heartbroken father seeks confirmation and assurance, leading him to declare in 1897, twelve years after Humster's death: "Religion is the great interest of my life."

But it was a long time coming.

Thirteen years before his son's passing, in 1872, James is recruited by Harvard president Charles Eliot to lecture on vertebrate physiology. By 1875 he is teaching one of the university's first psychology courses, "The Relations between Physiology and Psychology," strongly influenced by his trip to Germany in 1867–68. James's trimmed beard, intelligent blue eyes, and incisive lectures are well known to his students, who include Theodore Roosevelt, W. E. B. Dubois, E. L. Thorndike, and Walter Lippmann. He also advises Gertrude Stein on her automatic writing project.

The popular instructor is not easily pigeonholed. He is excited about the accuracy of Charles Darwin's findings, for example, but agrees with the English biologist that it is naïve to dismiss God out of hand. Rather, James holds with Augustine's assertion that if scriptural interpretations contradict facts, the interpretations must change, not the facts. Psychiatrist Howard Feinstein notices other paradoxes in James: He studies medicine but does not practice; speaks German and French fluently but is no linguist; appears calm and positive but has a hint of sadness in his demeanor; thinks deeply on religion but is no theologian; applies strict scientific method but is no materialist. "Yes, Dr. James was a brilliant, complex man," concludes Feinstein, "but there were many things one wanted to know about him."

James is a rising star in his profession, and as the eldest son he enjoys the approbation of his father, Henry James Sr, a philosopher, theologian, and deep believer in a utopian path to grace. Henry Sr has impressed on his family a sense that the eternal is reality and religion is not folly. James is close to his father, but frequently distant from his mother, Mary.

Only in his adult years, at age thirty-eight in July 1880, did his "heart flow over with a new kind of sympathy" for all that his mother had endured in life. Fortunately, this realization did not come too late. Two years after James wrote those words, Mary died of bronchitis on January 29, 1882. She was seventy-two. James feels her loss all the more keenly for what he sees as his lack of warmth toward her.

Henry Sr falls ill that autumn. His prognosis is poor. A year younger than his wife, Mary, Henry faces the idea of death "with contentment," his doctor observes. On December 18, Henry proclaims, "I am going with great joy," truly pleased that he has "such good boys," meaning William, Henry Jr, Wilkie, and his youngest son, Bob. His last words are filled with quiet wonder: "There is my Mary!" He dies a few hours later.

James is surprised at the grief he feels for his father. He did not expect to be affected so deeply. The death leaves him dizzy with a new thought. "The tremendousness of the idea of immortality," he tells his wife. "*If only he could be joined to mother.*"

Three days later, after the funeral, James stands over his parents' graves. "Darling old Father," he says, "on the other side, let us hope and pray, dear, dear old Mother is waiting for you to join her." James is not certain if he will see them in the afterlife, but "more than ever at this moment do I feel that if that were true, all would be solved and justified." He stays in the cemetery for hours, sensing that his father can hear him, his brother Henry Jr observes, "somewhere out of the depths of the still, bright winter air."

The loss of his parents has a galvanizing effect on William James's writing. Mourners frequently find ways to express their grief through creativity, as a means of survival and an act of love to honor their dead. James later admits that he did more writing in the spring and summer of 1883 than at any time before. "The gap left by Father is even greater than I supposed it would be," he says. "Life can never again seem solid to me as it did a year and a half ago."

The resulting landmark work, "What is an Emotion?" was published in the April 1884 issue of *Mind.* Much of the essay is anecdotal. James observes a corollary between emotion and action: That is, if we feel a certain way, our bodies react accordingly; therefore, if we simulate that reaction, the original emotion will return. Mind and body seem inextricably linked. James does not suggest that merely acting the part will engender genuine feeling; rather, actions may cause us to revisit powerful emotions, such as hearing a beloved song or catching a fondly remembered scent.

In the same paper, James asks what grief would be "without its tears, its sobs, its suffocations of the heart, its pang of the breast-bone?" Waves of weeping only serve to make sorrow more acute, he posits, rather than providing relief. Tears make it worse. Modern research demonstrates that this view is untenable; many mourners (myself included) feel a small sense of relief after a good cry. It is also an interesting position to take after his dual losses, but not a surprising one for James, well known for a cool attitude toward deep passions. His early letters reveal greater concern for harmful mood disorders than healthy grief.

Once, years earlier at age twenty-four, James had berated a friend for giving himself over to melancholy. This is understandable. James too suffered from depression and lethargy, as he put it. Four years after writing that letter, in 1870, James had a nervous breakdown. He was twenty-eight. The ensuing emotional, intellectual, and spiritual crisis led to his conviction that faith is not the result of an imposition of divine will; rather, we choose our beliefs with the freedom God has granted us, what James would ultimately call "the will to believe."

Much has been written to refute James's early stance on emotions, but in fairness, it was strikingly original for its time. And his views were about to change. Within two years, his thoughts on grief, the afterlife, and his life's work would take a dramatic turn.

On November 15, 1883, less than a year after their parents' deaths, James's younger brother Wilkie passes. Alternately known as Wilky, Wilk, and Wilkums, he is thirty-eight when his heart condition and a long struggle with Bright's disease finally take him. Wilkie was a legitimate Civil War hero, commander of one of the first Black regiments, the 54th Massachusetts Infantry. His leg was wounded in combat and continued to trouble him to the point that he considered having it amputated. Two months earlier he had written to James, "It looks as if it would not be long before I shall peg out."

The death of a younger sibling bears many similarities to the loss of a child. *Meaning-making*, as modern experts call it, often takes on new importance after the passing of a brother or sister. This search may have led James to redouble his efforts to complete a collection of his father's writings, *The Literary Remains of the Late Henry James*. The act simultaneously honors father, mother, and brother: "not only a filial but a philosophic duty."

James's seemingly sideways approach is familiar to Christine Valentine of the Centre for Death and Society, University of Bath. Grief causes us to see the mundane in different, even *strange* ways, she says, as we "gain an appreciation of how 'common sense' experiences are not as self-evident as they may seem." Cultural meaning plays an important role in how we deal with loss, such as when James puts pen to paper. "I beseech the reader from now onwards," he writes in an unusually plaintive and vulnerable introduction, "to listen to my stammering exposition in a very uncritical mood of mind."

The same month his father's anthology is published, James's third son, Herman, is born on January 31, 1884. At the time, he and Alice have two children: Henry III, called Harry (age 6), and William, called Billy (age 3). Neither boy seems to mind that the baby is the apple of his father's eye, "the flower of the flock." James takes to calling the chubby and irresistibly jovial toddler Humster.

In June of 1885, Humster falls ill with whooping cough. Within a few weeks Alice also contracts it. With his son and wife suffering each day, James dreams "that poor little Humster had a hooked nose and was moribund!" Their condition is soon diagnosed as scarlet fever.

Doctors referred to the malady as "pestilential," "insidious and deceptive." At a time when about half of all deaths were children below the age of six, the pandemic made matters worse. Scarlet fever's mortality rate ranged from 16.7 percent to 33.3 percent, with most deaths occurring among the very young. Treatments were often as horrifying as the disease.

Samuel Hahnemann, founder of homeopathy, introduced belladonna as a curative that was much in vogue. Other methods included leeches, bleeding, cold and hot effusions, and a host of drugs of an emetic, purgative, diaphoretic, tonic, or narcotic nature. Every three hours, parents were instructed to force medicine down a child's throat with a mixture that likely included an infusion of roses, with an excess of acid, made palatable with an additional quantity of syrup, one of the customary prescriptions of the day.

Coughing was treated with mustard or pepper poultices applied to the chest and neck, causing terrible blistering. It was customary to subject a suffering child to mild purging with castor oil or citrate of magnesia—misguided attempts to rid the body of infection. These remedies were worse than useless; they were often cruel.

By June 28, Humster's condition was "precarious," James writes a friend, with "constant bronchitis which is apt to be fatal." By the first week of July, "Our poor little baby is in very critical condition."

On Thursday night, July 9, 1885, after battling convulsions, colic, and pneumonia, Humster dies at about nine o'clock. He is eighteen months old. Years later, the heartbroken father observes, "Every individual existence goes out in a lonely spasm of helpless agony."

Many parents blame themselves for causing their sick child needless suffering and failing to comfort them near the end. In the first year after a loss, the bereaved often obsessively reconstruct events and replay the death in their minds. This blend of regret, self-recrimination, and sorrow may be particularly acute for fathers like James, who frequently show the highest level of grief for men in every bereavement category except guilt.

Watching his wife during Humster's illness, James says, "made me for the first time understand what the word 'mother' means." Here he pauses and adds, "We get these retrospective illuminations pretty late." His revelation calls to mind another aspect of grief that is frequently ignored.

Some parents, seeing the daily suffering of their terminally ill child, secretly hope for some type of alleviation. This may take the form of prayers for healing or, unconsciously, ambivalent emotions and seldom acknowledged desires for the misery to end in *any* way possible. The child's death may then be followed by a sense of relief. This *grief-relief phenomenon*, as it is known, is often accompanied by guilt for harboring such natural feelings. "Though relief appears soon," Michael Bullock with the University of Southern California observes, "the period of bereavement may be long and painful."

Two days after Humster's death, on July 11, the grieving parents bury him in their family plot. Prior to losing his son, James had dismissed such rituals as sentimental. Later, he confesses to an aunt that the ceremony meant a great deal to them: "There is usefully a human need embodied in any old human custom and we both felt this." Well over a century later, modern researchers have found that such funerary traditions facilitate adjustment in powerful and positive ways.

James does not write in detail about his grief, but his interest in the invisible world increases in the aftermath of Humster's passing. "It brings one closer to all mankind, this world old experience," he writes of death. "It makes the world seem smaller and deeper and more continuous with the next."

Such belief is often essential to survival, suggests grief expert Ronald Knapp of Clemson University. He observes that the pain is long-lasting and acute, and requires an act of courage to face each day, even years after the death. There is only one way to ease the suffering: "The loss of a child is such a monumental ordeal for most families to deal with that reaching beyond the scope of the rational world seems the only sensible way of coping."

James would have agreed.

In 1890 William James publishes what will become a standard work, his two-volume *Principles of Psychology*. The book is praised across America and Europe by such influential colleagues as Sigmund Freud and Carl Jung. When James becomes a professor of philosophy at Harvard in 1897, he grows fascinated with the diversity of religion and humanity's deep-seated appetite for spiritual involvement. He is "in love with variety and experience as he finds it," historian Jacques Barzun observes.

By May–June of 1901, James is asked to deliver the University of Edinburgh's Gifford Lectures, one of the highest honors in a philosopher's career. The discussions are compiled in a book, *The Varieties of Religious Experience*, in which James coins such well-known phrases as *tender-hearted*, *tough-minded*, *sick soul*, and *stream of consciousness*.

Respected biographer Richard Anderson notes that the lectures demonstrate how institutions, books, Bibles, or church leaders do not hold inherent authority, which instead resides "in the actual religious experiences of individuals." These vary between cultures and persons, James observes, but a connecting thread is the *reality* of each person's conversion. Surprisingly, this insight led to the establishment of Alcoholics Anonymous (AA).

The cofounder of AA, William Griffith Wilson, known as Bill W., wrote to Jung on January 23, 1961, that *Varieties* "gave me the realization that most conversion experiences, whatever their variety, do have a common denominator of ego collapse at depth." AA responds to such collapse on an almost wholesale basis, Bill W. says, adding that "James, though long in his grave, had been a founder of Alcoholics Anonymous."

For his part, Jung, who met James in 1909, wrote four decades later that he "was tremendously impressed by the clearness of his [James's] mind and the complete absence of intellectual prejudices." *Varieties* remains one of the leading texts on religion from a viewpoint of philosophy and experimental psychology.

"We and God have business with each other; and in opening ourselves to his influence our deepest destiny is fulfilled," James informs listeners in Edinburgh.

"God is real since he produces real effects." Religious faith may not be easily dismissed as glandular secretion, nervous disorder, or the result of mental imbalance. Such observations are more than exercises in reason, James says. They are also acts of solace. "To anyone who has ever looked on the face of a dead child or parent, the mere fact that matter could have taken for a time that precious form, ought to make matter sacred ever after." His belief leads to hope—and a search that shocks his colleagues.

In 1884, after the deaths of his parents and his younger brother, James had become a member of the English Society of Psychical Research. With Humster's death, James grows more interested in questions of eternity and immortality. He helps to found the society's American branch in 1885 with Alexander Graham Bell and Edward Charles Pickering.

The American Society of Psychical Research (ASPR) has a modest goal: to study psychic phenomena under strict scientific conditions. The work is nearly chimerical, and at times frustrating for the researchers, though they manage to expose a number of frauds, whom James typifies with disgust as degenerative congeners. "I disbelieve in the substitution of 'audiences' for investigators," he writes, "'popular interest' for investigation and newspaper tattle for facts." However, there are a few psychics whom the ASPR identifies as legitimate, possessing "supernormal knowledge." This gives James hope that human consciousness may exist beyond biological life.

James continues his ASPR work for many years. "I believe in psychical research and its endowment," he says. He remains unconvinced that empirical evidence will ever be forthcoming. James is struck, however, by one startling discovery: A vast majority of mourners, perfectly sane and reasonable people, speak of spiritual experiences with their dead. Modern experts have confirmed his findings.

Medical clinicians Nadine Nowatzki, University of Manitoba, and Ruth Grant Kalischuk, University of Lethbridge, interviewed twenty-three bereaved persons who had reported seeing, hearing, or feeling their deceased loved ones. They then compared these findings with previous research and numerous historical accounts. Their results, published in 2009 with the professional journal *Omega*, found that "the encounters profoundly affected the participants' beliefs in an afterlife and attitudes toward life and death, and had a significant impact on their grief." Such experiences provide a healthy sense of connection with the dead. This would not have surprised James, who views inquiries into immortality as essential to "fruitful relations with reality."

By 1904, growing older and "just getting fit to live," as he wryly puts it, William James is even more convinced that personal immortality is not fantasy. "There is *something* back there that shows that minds communicate," he concedes. "The world that our 'normal' consciousness makes use of is only a fraction of the whole world in which we have our being."

James admits that demonstrative proof is fleeting but remains as committed to the work as his wife and his brother, Henry Jr, now a famed novelist. James asserts that orthodox science should not ignore clinical evidence. ASPR researchers have often recorded incidents, free of chicanery, when questions were answered, allusions understood, and thoughts met in ways that defied scientific explanation: "It is difficult not to take away an impression of having encountered something sincere in the way of social phenomenon."

James retires from Harvard in 1907. His next two books, *Pragmatism* (1907) and *A Pluralistic Universe* (1909), suggest that philosophy transcends empirically based science in the exploration of truth, reality, and "free wild Nature." His reference to natural scenery is not mere hyperbole: "I have often been surprised to find what a predominant part in my own spiritual experience it has played, and how it stands out as almost the only thing the memory of which I should like to carry over with me beyond the veil, unamended and unaltered." James expands on this thought in *The Meaning of Truth* (1909), asking that if we feel something that lasts eternally, such as love, "What atom of logical or psychological argument is there to prove that it would *not* be felt as long as it lasted, and felt for just what it is, all that time?"

In the fall of 1909 *American Magazine* publishes "The Confidences of a Psychical Researcher," a summation of James's hopeful, and often disappointing, work to methodically prove communication with the afterlife. After twenty-five years, he says, "I am theoretically no further than I was at the beginning." Yet he also asserts that for there to be frauds, there must be something that they are replicating, borrowing in their deceit from legitimate experiences. Supernatural

Pierre-Auguste Renoir,
Meeting in the Garden, 1911–15,
Musée d'Orsay

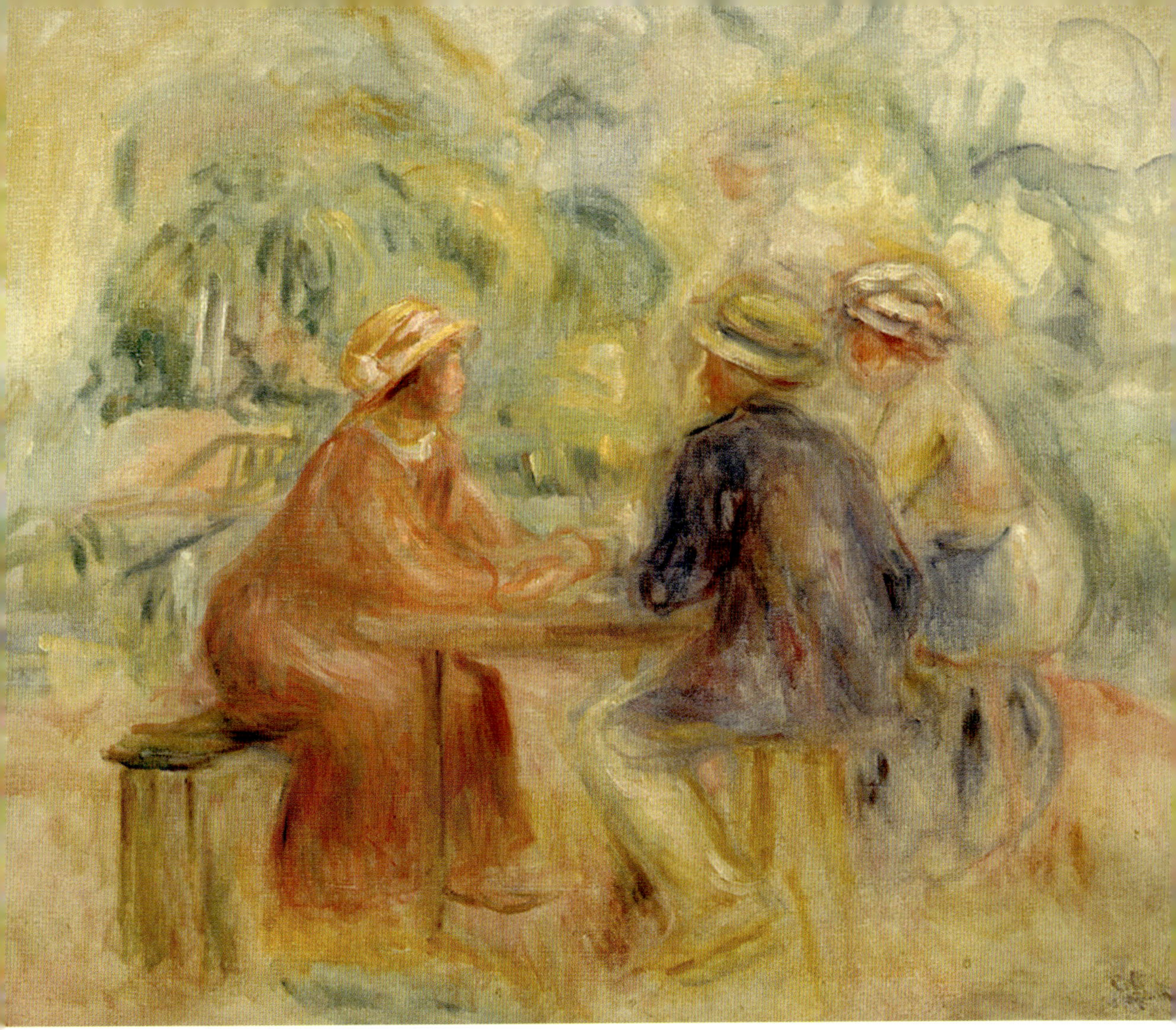

HELP ME, LOVING FATHER, TO BEAR BRAVELY THE BURDEN OF BEREAVEMENT WHICH WEIGHS UPON MY HEART. MAY THE GRIEF OVER THE DEATH OF MY LOVED ONE NOT SUFFOCATE THE GRATITUDE I OWE FOR THE YEARS OF LIFE WE SHARED TOGETHER. ABIDE WITH ME IN THE VALLEY OF SHADOW. KEEP AGLOW MY CANDLE OF HOPE UNTIL I REACH THE OPEN MEADOWS OF HEALING AND SUNSHINE THAT LIE BEYOND.

—RABBI SIDNEY GREENBERG

phenomena and spiritual interactions are far more common than we suppose, he suggests. Coincidence fails to touch the root of the matter. This thought may resign him to posterity's pit of judgment, he says in a verbal shrug, but he is writing the truth as he sees it:

> I confess that at times I have been tempted to believe that the Creator has eternally intended this department of nature to remain *baffling*, to prompt our curiosities and hopes and suspicions, all in equal measure, so that, although ghosts and clairvoyances, and raps and messages from spirits, are always seeming to exist and can never be fully explained away, they also can never be susceptible to full collaboration.

Scoffers of James's association with the ASPR seldom mention his lifetime commitment to rigorous scholarship and scientific skepticism. He is no fool, nor does he behave foolishly in grief or dotage, as some suggest. Rather, his paper displays the same keen reasoning that has been a hallmark of his career. Decades of sorrow and searching for clinical evidence have strengthened his resolve, tempered now by experiences that add up to more than disparate bits of empirical data. "There is a continuum of cosmic consciousness," he concludes, "against which our individuality builds but accidental fences, and into which our several minds plunge as into a mother-sea or reservoir."

A year later, in late August of 1910, he falls ill in England and returns with his wife to their home in Chocorua. He is immediately bedridden for what his doctor says is a failing heart. "Death has come to seem a very trifling incident," he frequently tells his wife during his convalescence. Then, on the afternoon of August 26, Alice finds him unconscious in his sickroom. She climbs into bed with him and holds him in her arms until his breathing stops. William James is sixty-eight years old.

"I believe in immortality," Alice writes. She admires her husband's assurance that what he called the will to believe is by far the most vital part of living in a spiritual world. William's body is dead, she tells a friend, but she knows he is "safe and living, loving and working, never to be wholly gone from us."

LOVE AND LOSS WITH METALCORE

"I still have the grief, loss and pain, but I also have metal."

> *Deep is calling to deep at the thunder of your waterfalls; all your surging rapids and waves are sweeping over me. By day Adonai commands his grace, and at night his song is with me as a prayer to the God of my life.*
>
> PSALM 42:7–8 (CJB)

My daughter Jess loved metalcore. I'm not a fan. My tastes lean toward Verdi, The Blind Boys of Alabama, Johnny Cash, prog rock, and Dave Brubeck. But I listened with her anyway, because, well, *Dad*. I still put on her CDs now and then. They are a bridge of sorts, conciliatory and consoling. In such moments our bond continues. Jess died in 2015, yet through music, she feels less *absent* somehow.

Metalcore has meaning that cannot be denied, whatever our personal tastes. When I resist my daughter's love for the genre, I recall her patient enthusiasm for my opera CDs, singing along with Pavarotti as we drove the busy streets of Columbia, South Carolina. "Turn it up," Jess cried with delight. "Luciano-o-o!" We wore ourselves out trying (and failing) to match the tenor's thrilling high C's. Pavarotti died on September 6, 2007. Jess called me the moment she read the news: "Oh, Dad, I'm so sorry."

The leap from classical to metal is shorter than we might think. Metalcore has a surprising place with Evangelical Christians. In Finland, for example, hundreds of Metal Masses have been conducted in Lutheran churches since 2006. Each Mass presents the conventional liturgy, including communion, with a heavy metal band instead of a cantor at the organ. Robert Walser with Case Western Reserve University insists that the power cords of metal music serve a purpose that runs parallel with the volume and force produced by pipe organs "to display and enact overwhelming power—usually, in that context, for the greater glory of God."

I still prefer Bach, but I'm not sure Pavarotti would agree. "Some say the word 'pop' is a derogatory word to say 'not important'—I do not accept that," the tenor said. "If the word 'classic' is the word to say 'boring,' I do not accept. There is good and bad music."

Recently I discovered the well-known German metalcore band Maroon. In 2009, André Moraweck, the group's lead singer, used one of Friedrich Rückert's most beloved laments as the lyric for his song "Shadows" (*Schatten*). Rückert wrote the poem in 1834 after his two youngest children died of scarlet fever. His verse is honest, tender, and steeped in desperate grief:

> You are a shadow in the day
> and a light in the night;
> you live in my sorrow,
> you do not die in my heart.
>
> Here I pitch my tent,
> here you are with me;
> you are my shadow in the day
> and in the night, my light.
>
> Here I ask after you,
> here I find you,
> you live in my sorrow,
> you do not die in my heart.
>
> You are a shadow in the day,
> but at night, a light;
> you live in my sorrow,
> you do not die in my heart.

"'Shadows' is probably the darkest, most captivating and emotional song on *Order*," Maroon's record label notes of the group's final release, "and a great climax to the most ambitious and intense album in the band's career." Moraweck's reading of Rückert is, in one metal fan's words, "loud, dark, violent, meditative, powerful." For genre fans, Maroon's choice of "Shadows" makes perfect sense.

Metal enthusiasts have a keen interest in the "genealogy" of their preferred genre. Jess certainly did. Influences range from religion, myth, and literature to horror films and graphic novels, but for the most part, listeners are eager to uncover the innumerable musical references from previous groups (Iron Butterfly is a worldwide favorite).

As with my daughter, the personalities and backgrounds of devotees may surprise us. Ethnologists have found that the majority of metal fans are predominately in their mid-thirties, educated, employed, Caucasian, middle class, and well-adjusted: "bourgeoisified," as one researcher puts it. Most avid female fans are neither subordinate nor groupies.

Germany lays claim to nearly one-tenth of the world's metal bands. In this milieu, it is not surprising that Maroon, one of the most sought-after acts in metalcore, dipped into their country's history for a song that fans would recognize and appreciate.

Moraweck was following a long line of composers who have set Rückert's work to music over the last 150 years. Some 500 of the poet's pieces have been used in over 2,000 compositions, including settings by Schubert, Brahms, Mahler, Strauss, Robert and Clara Schumann, Bartók, and many others. The popular verse "From Days of Youth," for example, has at least sixty separate musical interpretations from as many composers. Yet another sixty settings were created for Rückert's "I Love You."

A preexisting text like "Shadows" is often the stimulus for a composer's inspiration. The result is an art song, or lied, that is as much literary work as musical structure. Durham University's Mark Sandy comments on the appeal: "Romantic poetry about grief acts as a defense against, and encounter with, the final silence of death that challenges poetry's eloquent capacity for meaning."

Music styles have changed in our century, but the catharses they provide have not. "Metal saved my life," writes the pseudonymous Nachthexe in her academic essay for Emerald Publishing. "The death of my mother when I was twenty-one meant that I was alone, and if it had not been for metal, my grieving process may have been the end of my story."

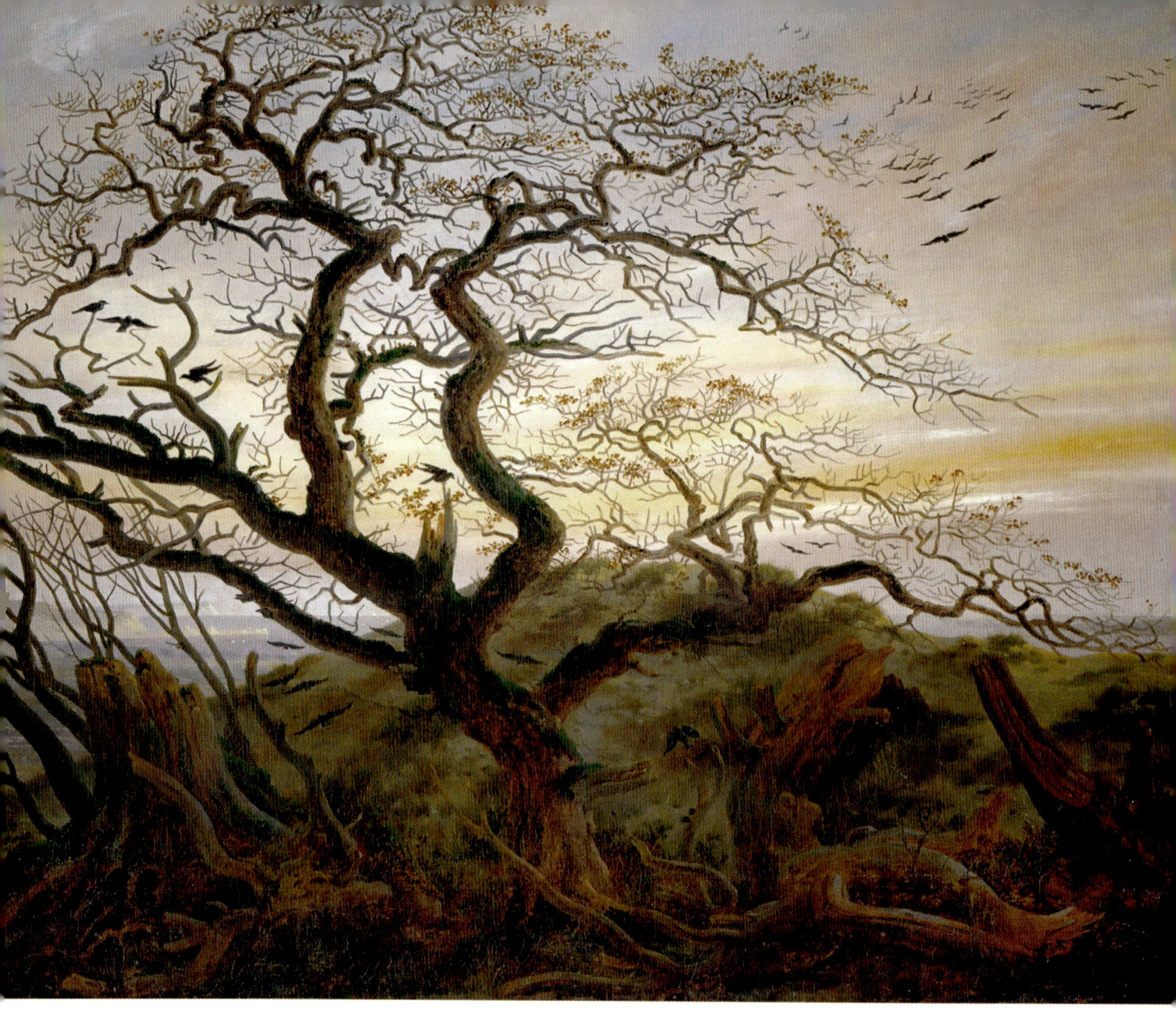

A SHADOW FLITS BEFORE ME,

NOT THOU, BUT LIKE TO THEE:

. . . THAT IT WERE POSSIBLE

FOR ONE SHORT HOUR TO SEE

THE SOULS WE LOVED, THAT THEY MIGHT TELL US

WHAT AND WHERE THEY BE!

—ALFRED LORD TENNYSON, FROM "MAUD"

Nachthexe relates that she bought her first guitar after her mother died at age forty-five. Through metal she dealt with the trauma of domestic abuse, suicidal thoughts, and her own *journey through the abyss*, as she calls it. "I still have the grief, loss and pain," she admits, "but I also have metal." Devotees are not all thugs, Nachthexe continues, nor does the music necessarily cause anger. Instead, she cites research that states metal can be liberating. "Extreme music matches and helps to process anger," she writes. "It matched my pain, sonically, texturally, musically and aesthetically."

The lead singer of Maroon might agree. "Shadows" remains one of the most popular of Rückert's laments because it resonates with mourners. Respected poet and translator Karl Krolow admires its simplicity. He considers it the "most delicate piece" of Rückert's songs and the "most artistic" German poem of the nineteenth century. Ralf Georg Czapla, an expert in literary studies, gives special attention to its repetitions and refrains. "The poet's wish that his children live on in poetry," Czapla observes, "is realized in the memorable wording."

I have listened to Maroon's interpretation of "Shadows" a number of times. Their cover, as with music created by Jess's other beloved metal bands, does not speak to me. But focusing on that fact would miss the point. We swapped her favorite discs while she was alive. The tradition continues to comfort me. "If you find an abundance of people that like that kind of music," observes Ray Charles, "you can be sure it has some kind of meaning for them, it may not be your type of music, but if you really stop and analyze it, really listen to it, you can understand."

Maroon's choice makes sense for its pedigree—and also for its revelations. At first the themes sound like standard consolation poetry: "in the light," "do not die," etc. But here Rückert surprises us. We anticipate that the comforting light of his evenings will also accompany him during the day. Instead, we find shadow. This has led to a certain amount of debate.

Biographer Annemarie Schimmel holds that the song progresses from mourning to remembrance. "This simple poem seems artless," she writes, "but that impression is deceptive." She suggests that the piece begins with a plaintive

Caspar David Friedrich,
Tree of Crows, c1822,
Louvre Museum

tone that soon turns to trust. The shadow in the day comes unbidden at first, a seeming shade or the darkness of grief. As the poem continues, Rückert realizes that the shadow is his own, linked to him in the blazing sun, a tent protecting him from the heat. The light is a guide at night. "If the final verse seems to repeat the first, the tone has changed," Schimmel concludes. "Lament has become consolation."

Another Rückert scholar, Sascha Monhoff, notes that this poem breaks free from traditional consolations that use light to represent God as an image of hope. "The fact that 'you' is only addressed as 'shadow' and 'light' emphasizes the absence of a living body—or rather: its non-existence—all the more clearly," Monhoff writes. "Here there is no body to cast a 'shadow.' In no way does the body emit a 'light.'" Commenting on Rückert's religious beliefs, Monhoff draws a parallel between this piece and the Book of Exodus, in which God's disembodied but visible presence corresponds to a primal, shadowy memory of the poet's children in his heart. "Rückert's poems are interesting," Monhoff concludes, "precisely because they ultimately undermine superficial metaphysical references."

My interpretation of Rückert's lament takes a direct approach that seems to echo the raw emotions evoked by Maroon. While we may sense that our children live on—the light of solace—this never completely eases the shadow of grief cast daily in their absence.

I take to heart the lessons of Pavarotti and Nachthexe. As I write these words, I am singing along in German to Maroon's "Shadows." Metalcore is harder on the voice than opera, but I keep at it. "You live in my sorrow," Moraweck growls. "You do not die in my heart." He repeats the last line lower, slower, coarser, hoarser: *Not die . . . in my . . . heart.*

Something unexpected happens. During Maroon's long prog rock-inspired guitar riff, my emotions overwhelm me. I am weeping, and laughing, to metalcore: for Jess, for Rückert's children, for myself. Ray Charles was right. I really *listened.*

I may never fully understand my daughter's love of metal. But today, in music, I sense Jess is near. Our love triumphs over absence; we defy separation; death is no longer absolute.

A PRESIDENT'S YELLOW ROSES

"I have never known such a blow."

> *Remember, Lord, your great mercy and love, for they are from of old.*
>
> PSALM 25:6

"This was the greatest disappointment and disaster in my life," wrote Dwight "Ike" Eisenhower in 1967, two years before his death, "the one I have never been able to forget completely. Today when I think of it, even now as I write about it, the terrible keenness of our loss comes back to me as fresh and terrible as it was in that long dark day soon after Christmas, 1920."

Forty-seven years had not dimmed the pain of losing a child. Eisenhower and his wife, Mamie, enjoyed a rich relationship filled with impressive accomplishments. What meaning they found in life, they said, ended and began anew that long-ago December.

Their first son, Doud Dwight, took ill just before Christmas in 1920. A new maid had recently recovered from scarlet fever and still carried the bacteria. The three-year-old boy, known as "little Ike," a nickname ultimately shortened to Ikey then Ikky and Icky, contracted the disease and was quarantined. It turned to meningitis.

"I haunted the halls of the hospital," Eisenhower recalled. "The doctors did not allow me into the room. But there was a porch on which I was allowed to sit and I could look into the room and wave to him. Occasionally, they would let me come to the door just to speak to Ikey. . . . Hour after hour, Mamie and I could only hope and pray."

Ikey lasted ten days. He died in his father's arms on January 2, 1921. That particular moment was to remain taboo in conversation for the rest of Eisenhower's life. "We never talked about it," Mamie told her granddaughter. "I never asked him because it was something that hurt so badly."

In this Mamie displayed prescient wisdom. Since the 1990s, top therapists across the globe have confirmed that our popular perception of *grief work* may be unhelpful and inaccurate. "Does 'grief work' work?," asked three of the world's leading grief researchers, Wolfgang Stroebe, Margaret Stroebe, and Henk Schut. Their answers were surprising and changed the course of twenty-first-century therapy.

They observed that in the current way of thinking, "we must confront and speak of our feelings and reactions to the death of a loved one. But what evidence do we have that this is so?" Not much, they discovered. The Stroebes and Schut learned that there was *no measurable difference in depression* between those who *worked through* their grief and those who did not. "Grief work," the respected experts concluded, "is not always as essential for adjustment to bereavement as theorists and clinicians have claimed."

Two other renowned experts, Terry Martin and Kenneth Doka, maintain that we as a society are wrong to hold to the traditional view that sharing emotions is the *only* mark of healthy grieving. "Another, equally sound pattern . . . tends to be private," they write, suggesting that in silence many mourners, particularly men, find the solace and meaning they seek. "We must respect individual needs and differences," Martin and Doka observe.

Guilt over Ikey's death did not debilitate the Eisenhowers, but it took a heavy toll.

Mamie was not present when her son passed. She was battling a cold so severe there was concern of pneumonia. She never forgave herself for failing to be there.

Eisenhower also felt the burden of remorse. He brooded for years over time missed with his son due to the demands of military life. "I have never known such a blow," he wrote in 1967. "I didn't know what to do. I blamed myself because I had often taken his presence for granted."

Eisenhower and Mamie also felt guilt for hiring the maid and for trusting the Army doctors, who were ill-equipped at that time to deal with children's diseases.

Such feelings are nearly universal among bereaved parents. Self-recrimination often leads to a sense of shame and guilt. Mourners report revisiting the death in their minds and the roles they played in helping, or failing to help, their child. Parents often feel that they were inadequate protectors and providers, according to grief experts Margaret Miles and Alice Demi, and condemn themselves for having survived.

Thirty years later Eisenhower confided to his friend John Gunther that he was "on the ragged edges of a breakdown" for months after his son's passing. Stephen Ambrose, who held numerous conversations with Eisenhower while editing the general's military papers, observed: "He found it difficult to concentrate for a long time after Icky's death or get interested in anything. He did his job without enthusiasm." Biographer Kevin McCann noted something similar. "Talking to him about that saddest of events in later years, I got the clear impression that he was in a very bad way emotionally for a time."

Mamie would refer to the boy now and then, as many bereaved parents do. But her husband tended to keep the pain to himself, according to Reverend MacAskill of the Gettysburg Presbyterian Church, where the Eisenhowers were members during their retirement years. For both parents, the shadow of their son's death never completely lifted.

Researchers have found that the loss of a child significantly shapes and alters the worldview of bereaved parents. This was true with the Eisenhowers. "The loss of his first son changed Ike's character," wrote McCann.

Mamie also saw this difference in her husband. "For a long time, it was as if a shining light had gone out of Ike's life," she said. "Throughout all the years that followed, the memory of those bleak days was a deep inner pain that never seemed to diminish." Decades afterward, she told family friends, "That sad, sad event had a lasting effect on the General."

Ikey's death affected the couple in other ways. Bereaved parents relate that their most devastating challenge is the relentless loneliness they feel. One study of fifty-two parents who had lost a child to an unexpected death by illness, such as the meningitis that took Ikey, found that grief and loneliness tend to *rise* over time.

Eisenhower and Mamie's relationship remained solid, though troubled. "Half a century later," wrote Julie Nixon Eisenhower, "Mamie was still unwilling to say much about how Ikey's death changed her relationship with Ike. The pain is too deep. But there is no doubt the loss of their beloved son closed a chapter in the marriage. It could never again be unblemished first love."

This observation is not quite as forbidding as it may seem. Unblemished first love may pass as trust, appreciation, acceptance, and understanding mature. The chapter of their early years and their first son being with them was closed by Ikey's death. But it did not end their marriage or their lives.

The couple's second son, John, was born on August 3, 1922. Eisenhower had been given three weeks' leave. They welcomed the child as a blessing. "John did much to fill the gap that we felt so poignantly and so deeply every day of our lives since the death of our first son," Eisenhower wrote. "While his arrival did not, of course, eliminate the grief we still felt, he was precious in his own right and he did much to take our minds off the tragedy. Living in the present with a healthy, bouncing baby boy can take parents' minds off almost anything."

In the winter of 1922 Eisenhower was ordered to Panama. They were moving to an exotic locale after months of constant reminders of Ikey. The new surroundings did not alter their grief in any way, but Panama provided the first steps into their future without him.

Over the years, Eisenhower and Mamie honored Ikey's memory in their own ways. "John is the only son I have," Mamie said years later. "That's the way I've thought of it after Icky." This method of coping carried its own challenges for the grieving mother. "It took me many years to get over my 'smother love,'" Mamie related later. "It wasn't until Johnny had children of his own that I was able to stop." Yet she continued to fuss over her husband's health and safety well into his presidency and after.

Eisenhower dealt with Ikey's death differently.

"Only once did Ike ever talk about his first son," wrote Maxwell Rabb, secretary to the Eisenhower Cabinet from 1953 to 1958. "'That was a very difficult moment for us,' he said, passing over it very quickly. I think his silence on the subject is significant." Eisenhower may not have mentioned Ikey to his colleagues in the White House, but the boy was never far from his mind.

Yellow had been Ikey's favorite color. Ann Thomas, who served as Eisenhower's secretary during his presidency, from 1953 to 1961, recalled: "I came into the Oval Office one day and found him staring off into space. He turned to me and said, very simply, that he was thinking of the little boy. Upstairs, in the family living quarters, there would always be fresh flowers. Once he pointed to some—I can't remember what kind it was—and said: 'Icky always liked those flowers.' Imagine, remembering a detail like that."

Charles Ethan Porter,
Yellow Roses in a Vase, 1890,
New Britain Museum

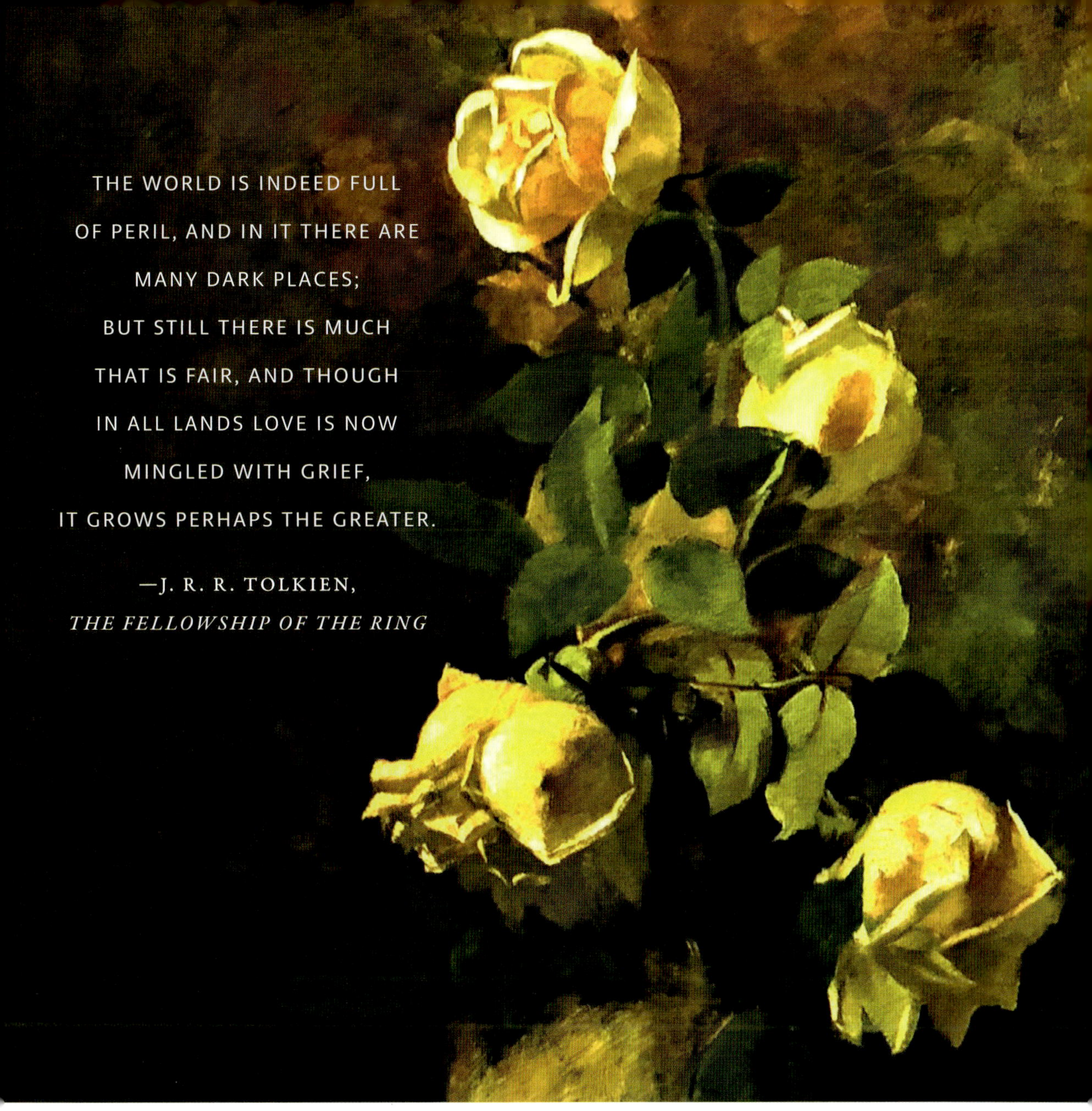

THE WORLD IS INDEED FULL OF PERIL, AND IN IT THERE ARE MANY DARK PLACES; BUT STILL THERE IS MUCH THAT IS FAIR, AND THOUGH IN ALL LANDS LOVE IS NOW MINGLED WITH GRIEF, IT GROWS PERHAPS THE GREATER.

—J. R. R. TOLKIEN,
THE FELLOWSHIP OF THE RING

Eisenhower and Mamie walked through the valley of grief together. Their relationship was rewarding, despite and perhaps in some ways because of Ikey's passing. They came to value the transience of life and found meaning along the dark path of loss they shared.

For the rest of his life, Eisenhower sent Mamie yellow roses on Ikey's birthday.

THE HEARTBREAK BEHIND THE EEG

"God has taken a piece of you."

> *He has made everything suited to its time; also, he has given human beings an awareness of eternity; but in such a way that they can't fully comprehend, from beginning to end, the things God does.*
>
> ECCLESIASTES 3:11 (CJB)

Army officer Hans Berger could handle a horse. But even the best animal may rear in the face of a careening team-drawn cannon. Berger was thrown and barely escaped the trampling hooves and grinding wheels. His injuries were severe.

Within hours, Berger received a telegram from his father, physician Paul Berger, and his mother, Anna Berger (née Rückert). It was the first cable his parents had ever sent to their son. The message related that his older sister had felt an ominous premonition, and they were checking up on him.

The telegram astounded Berger. "It was a case of spontaneous telepathy in which at a time of mortal danger, and as I contemplated certain death," he wrote, "I transmitted my thoughts, while my sister, who was particularly close to me, acted as the receiver." Such ideas were not unheard of in 1892, but the nineteen-year-old's next decision was something new. *Do our brains somehow interact with the external world,* he wondered? He committed his life to investigating the electrical activity of the cerebrum.

In 1924, Berger was the first to record electrical impulses generated by the human brain. But the method behind his invention, the electroencephalogram (EEG), remains something of a mystery. "One hundred years of research have passed by and still the human electroencephalogram (EEG) remains a puzzle to be solved," suggests a team of neurologists with the Federal University of Parana, adding that it is difficult to overstate Berger's "contribution to the field of modern neurophysiology." Unlocking the enigma of the EEG's creation reveals surprising clues about its inventor's despair, obsessions, family, and fascination with the invisible world.

A native of Neuses near Coburg, Berger completed his military service and went to the University of Jena, in the German state of Thuringia. He earned a degree in medicine in 1897 and soon joined the university psychiatric clinic. By 1906 he was a senior lecturer; by 1912, physician-in-chief; by 1919, chair of psychiatry and neurology; and in 1927 he was elected rector of the university hospital.

During this time, he never stopped his intensive study of the human brain.

Berger published his findings on the EEG in 1929, suggesting that his technique could be used for psychiatric diagnosis and research. "The continuous nerve processes which take place in the brain," he wrote, "represent . . . the contractions of the individual segments of the heart." Because of this, he proposed, the psychological and the physiological are intrinsically linked: One cannot exist without the other, nor should one be reduced in favor of the other. His paper also touched upon a plethora of EEG phenomena, such as changes associated with attention and mental effort, or those related to cerebral trauma, particularly prefrontal cortex injury.

Berger's electrical measurements and conclusions were startling. His research drew mockery from the scientific community. The instruments were dismissed as quackery. The hook-up (the electroencephalograph) was too complicated, they sniffed, the EEG record produced on film was pure gibberish.

Despite this initial resistance from his peers, Berger persisted. Twenty-three more papers on the subject would follow over the years. By 1934, independent testing established his discoveries as irrefutable fact. "The Berger rhythm is a reality," declared *Scientific American* in 1938, "and immensely important."

But long-term success eluded Berger. He was by nature a social conformist, reserved, reliable, and conservative in his views; the human brain was his main concern. However, he seems to have run afoul of the Nazi Party. In October, 1938, he was obliged to retire from his position as hospital director. This cruel blow was delivered via telephone.

Devastated, Berger accepted a position as head of a private sanatorium near Jena, in Bad Blankenburg. There he continued his work on what he considered

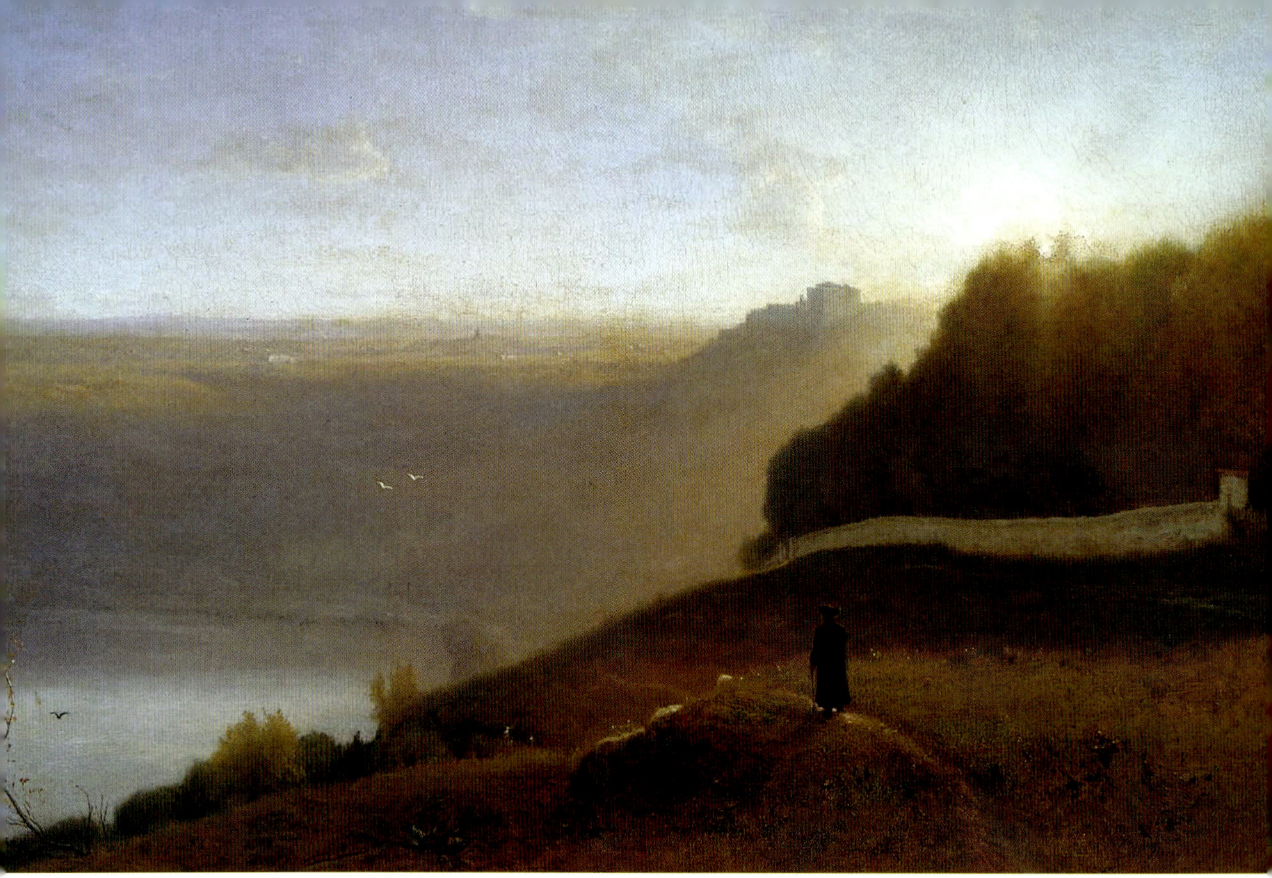

IN THAT TERRIFIC TALE OF THE PASSION THERE IS A DISTINCT EMOTIONAL SUGGESTION THAT THE AUTHOR OF ALL THINGS (IN SOME UNTHINKABLE WAY) WENT NOT ONLY THROUGH AGONY, BUT THROUGH DOUBT. IT IS WRITTEN, "THOU SHALT NOT TEMPT THE LORD THY GOD." NO; BUT THE LORD THY GOD MAY TEMPT HIMSELF; AND IT SEEMS AS IF THIS WAS WHAT HAPPENED IN GETHSEMANE.

—G. K. CHESTERTON

George Inness,
Lake Nemi, 1872,
Museum of Fine Arts, Boston

to be the central problem of psychiatry: the physical basis of psychic function, or as he wrote, "the search for the correlation between objective activity in the brain and subjective psychic phenomena."

Berger's commitment to research alienated his associates even as they admired him. His rich private life of introspection, poetry, and impassioned journal entries was entirely separate from the driven professional seen in public. "He let nobody into the secret of his investigation," wrote Berger's colleague, Raphael Ginzberg. "What he achieved, he achieved by his individual effort." Those efforts were dominated by a compulsion to perfect and establish the EEG. Yet he struggled under the shadow of his forebears: His garrulous father was a popular and respected doctor; his grandfather was one of the most revered poets in Germany.

Berger never met his mother's famous father, Friedrich Rückert, who died in 1866, but he felt the poet's influence all of his life. Rückert also knew heartbreak and hardship. He lost his two youngest children to scarlet fever in 1833–34. "God has taken a piece of you," the broken father wrote that spring. "Still, a part remains, left behind: may you prove worthy of it." Berger saw in Rückert's poetry the same connection to an invisible world that he felt. For decades, he kept a copy of one of his grandfather's early quatrains on the wall in his study:

> We each face an image:
> who we are meant to be.
> True peace eludes us
> until it is reality.

These four lines may be read as reprimand or comfort: a choice between *I'll never measure up*; or, as the teacher of Ecclesiastes sees it, God has given human beings *an awareness of eternity*. Commenting on this passage, Søren Kierkegaard observed that this sense of the eternal assures us that immortality is not a future change occurring at the moment of death. "On the contrary," he wrote, "it is a changelessness that is not altered by the passage of the years." Put another way, peace is not found in pursuit of an image of ourselves as we think we *ought* to be, but in an awareness of the eternal present that is within us each moment. Berger, too, felt keenly this gap between his inner vision and the realities of daily life.

In 1940, he was nominated for the Nobel Prize. Of sixty-five total recommendations submitted to the selection committee, three named Berger. Future Nobel laureate Ulf von Euler, a renowned expert in neurotransmitters and physiology, supported Berger's nomination, noting the widespread international acknowledgement of his EEG. That same year the awards were suspended as war raged across Europe and Asia. Berger had no idea that his name was being considered.

The following spring, Berger was misdiagnosed with an incurable heart condition. It was all too much. His country was at war; his lifelong career seemed ruined by political intrigue; and now he faced slow physical degeneration and death. He ended his life by hanging on June 1, 1941.

Twenty-first-century readers may condemn Berger's final act or dismiss him as mentally unstable. Before rushing to judgment, we might pause to consider that his compulsions, expectations, limits, and desperations were his own. And yet from a life of heartbreak was born the hope of millions.

My father suffered from heart disease. Thanks to an invention created one hundred years ago, Dad enjoyed decades of health that he might not have had otherwise. When my father-in-law lingered on the brink of death, his life quite literally depended on accurate measurements of the electrical impulses of his heart by an electrocardiogram (ECG or EKG)—a direct descendant of the EEG. We're not alone. Across the world, modern hospitals use technology based on Hans Berger's genius to save lives every day.

COMPASSION SAVES A NATION

"The blow overwhelmed me."

> *The king was shaken. He went up to the room over the gateway and wept. As he went, he said: "O my son Absalom! My son, my son Absalom! If only I had died instead of you—O Absalom, my son, my son!"*
>
> 2 SAMUEL 18:33

Abraham Lincoln burst into the office of his secretary, John Nicolay. "My boy is gone," he sobbed. "He is actually gone." The president turned and left the room. His eleven-year-old son Willie had just died. It was 5 p.m. on Thursday, February 20, 1862.

Willie had developed symptoms after a vigorous pony ride in a "chilly rain" two weeks earlier. The horse was a gift from his father. He rode it every day, whatever the weather. By February 5, the boy was sick with fever.

Lincoln was hosting a long-planned dinner the night Willie fell ill. Five hundred invited guests arrived to commemorate the First Lady's refurbishing of the White House. The evening was a success for their callers, who stayed until 3:00 a.m., but the Lincolns were distracted and frequently absent. Lincoln and his wife Mary slipped away from the festivities in shifts so one of them could always be at Willie's bedside.

Within hours, Willie's eight-year-old brother Tad started showing similar symptoms. The younger boy ultimately recovered, but Willie, after enduring painful cramps and diarrhea, fell into a coma on February 18. He died two days later.

Weather did not cause Willie's death. The brothers fell ill with "bilious fever," now believed to be typhoid fever. This life-threatening infection came from their drinking water. The White House, like the rest of Washington, drew from the Potomac. The city's population had grown from 60,000 to 200,000 that winter. Army camp latrines and ruptured sewage pipes soon contaminated the river.

"It is hard, hard to have him die," Lincoln said in a choked whisper the first time he saw his son's body. "I know that he is much better off in heaven, but then we loved him so." Elizabeth Keckly, Mary's dressmaker, was tending to the remains when the president walked in. She watched him lift the cover and gaze into Willie's face. "I never saw a man so bowed down with grief," Keckly recalled. "He buried his head in his hands, and his tall frame was convulsed with emotion. . . . His grief unnerved him."

The sight of Willie's washed and dressed body in the Green Room stayed with Lincoln for years. The next Thursday, and many Thursdays after, the president sought seclusion in the room where his son had lain. He also spent a good deal of time in the stables with Willie's horse. "The blow overwhelmed me," he told a visitor. "It showed me my weakness as I had never felt it before."

Lincoln was no stranger to death. A thoughtful review of the president's many sorrows, informed by modern research, indicates that his grief was healthy, normal, and precisely what is expected after such an overwhelming loss. Years before Willie's death, in the fall of 1844, Lincoln wrote a lament after visiting the graves of his mother and sister in southern Indiana. He sent the piece to Andrew Johnston, who published it in the May 5, 1847, issue of *Quincy Whig* under the title "The Return." Lincoln requested that the poem be published anonymously.

> Oh! memory—thou mid-way world
> 'Twixt earth and Paradise,
> Where things decayed, and loved ones lost,
> In dreamy shadows rise.

In September of 1848, Lincoln took Mary and their two young sons, five-year-old Robert and two-year-old Eddie, to Niagara Falls. The grandeur of nature stunned Lincoln into a rare moment of rhapsody, calling the sight a "world's wonder," and adding, "Its power to excite reflection, and emotion, is its great charm. . . . It calls up the indefinite past."

Two years later, on February 1, 1850, three-and-a-half-year-old Eddie died. "He was sick fifty two days & died the morning of the first day of this month," Lincoln wrote his stepbrother John Johnston. "We miss him very much."

The Reverend James Smith of Springfield's First Presbyterian Church in Illinois conducted the funeral service. Soon Mary rented a pew and the couple began regular attendance. Lincoln rarely spoke of his son's passing, but the loss changed him. "From the time of the death of our little Edward," Mary wrote in 1870, "I believe my husband's heart was directed towards religion." Others too noticed the difference in Lincoln.

He was no longer "open souled," according to his lifetime friend Joseph Gillespie. "If he had griefs he never spoke of them in general conversation. . . . He was tenderhearted without much shew of sensibility." Mary understood this about her husband, commenting on the depth and breadth of his feelings. "[H]e was *not* a demonstrative man," she said, "when he felt most deeply, he expressed, the least."

In today's therapy-conditioned society, we may mistake private, introspective mourning as unhealthy. Failure to *talk out* grief is seen as detachment, denial, or repression. This common misconception is out of touch with the last three decades of grief research and therapy. Experts have long acknowledged the complex nature of mourning. Physical, emotional, cognitive, behavioral, and spiritual expressions are unique to each individual. Some people share their sorrow; others demonstrate their emotions in thought or action. These are not the signs of unresolved mourning that popular entertainment depicts. Many bereaved parents find solace in private, silent expressions of sorrow.

Lincoln's reticence and contemplative reaction to grief could at times be vocal; at others it was demonstrated in changed behaviors. Ever after, according to his friend and bodyguard Ward Lamon, "He was a plain, homely, sad, weary-looking man, to whom one's heart warmed involuntarily, because he seemed at once miserable and kind."

On February 11, 1861, Abraham Lincoln and his sons Robert, Willie, and Tad labeled their trunks: A. LINCOLN, THE WHITE HOUSE, WASHINGTON, D.C., and headed to the Springfield, Illinois, Great Western railroad depot. Well-wishers had gathered to see them off. "Here I have lived a quarter of a century, and have passed from a young to an old man," he told the crowd. Even on this momentous day, Eddie was on his mind. "Here my children have been born, and one is buried. I now leave, not knowing when, or whether, ever I may return."

Mary joined them later. When the family was together in Washington, Lincoln and his wife settled on worshipping at New York Avenue Presbyterian Church. They first attended services on March 10 and were regular congregants throughout Lincoln's presidency.

Robert was seventeen and soon left for Harvard. Tad and Willie were at home in the White House, where they hitched their pair of goats to chairs and carts to drive them through the halls, Tad crying, "Get out of the way there!" to visitors and staff. They adored their father's dog, Jip, who often sat on the president's lap at lunch. Lincoln's secretary John Hay described Tad as a "tricky little sprite . . . bubbling over with health and high spirits." This displayed itself in endearing ways. The boys discovered a collection of calling cards in the White House attic. They immediately put on a minstrel show, using the historic artifacts to create a "snowstorm."

Lincoln was indulgent with the youngsters. One visitor was shocked that while he spoke with the president, his "two little boys, his sons, clambered over those legs, patted his cheeks, pulled his nose, and poked their fingers in his eyes, without causing reprimand or even notice." This tolerant attitude might have been in reaction to Lincoln's strained relationship with his own father, as well as the loss of Eddie over a decade before. One psychiatric study of thirty-seven bereaved mothers found that the participants thought "indulging in the little things" was fruitful and meaningful with their surviving children. Lincoln may have agreed. "It is my pleasure that my children are free—happy, and unrestrained by parental tyranny," he said. "Love is the chain whereby to lock a child to its parent."

Willie was the most like his father, "a peculiarly religious child," his mother wrote, "with great amiability & cheerfulness of character." The blue-eyed, good-natured boy enjoyed interacting with visiting royalty, playing with other children, or simply reading with his father. He was thoughtful, too, and savvy. When Tad busted a large mirror with a new ball, Willie promptly observed that there was more at stake than their father's vanity. "It's not Pa's looking glass," he told his brother. "It belonged to the United States government."

Willie's observant nature displayed itself in other endearing ways. "This town is a very beautiful place," he wrote of the hotel when he and Lincoln went to Chicago. "Me and father have a nice little room to ourselves." He was also fascinated with railroad timetables and delighted in conducting an imaginary trip, with all the stops, from Chicago to New York.

"The most lovable boy I ever knew," wrote sixteen-year-old Julia Taft when she met Willie, "bright, sensible, sweet-tempered and gentle-mannered." Taft's two younger brothers, fourteen-year-old Bud and twelve-year-old Holly, were inseparable from the Lincoln boys. When Willie slipped into a coma, Bud refused to leave his side. "If I go he will call for me," he told the President.

Willie died less than a year after the Lincolns arrived in Washington. Tad and his mother were inconsolable for the first month after the loss. Lincoln spent time each Thursday in the room where Willie had lain, then paced in his private quarters, asking again and again why his son had to die.

Mary also wrestled with this question. "There are hours of each day," she wrote, "that my mind, cannot be brought to realize, that *He*, who is considered, so great and good, a God, has *thus* seen fit to afflict us!"

These reactions are quite common with sudden, unexpected loss. *Why did our loved one have to die?* we may ask. *Where was God when we needed him? Where is the justice? The grace? The mercy?* Rabbi Earl Grollman said that such doubts are a healthy part of faith. Asking *why*, he wrote, is a howl of anguish and a natural reaction to pain: "The statement: 'Dear God, why me? Why us?' may be not only a question but your own normal cry of distress, a plea for help."

Lincoln asked their minister, the Reverend Phineas Gurley, to conduct the funeral in the White House East Room. Before the service, Lincoln, Mary, and their son Robert asked to be left alone with Willie for a half hour.

Gurley's eulogy was calm and compassionate. "We may be sure, — therefore, bereaved parents, and all the children of sorrow may be sure," he said, "while they mourn He is saying to them, as the Lord Jesus once said to his Disciples when they were perplexed by his conduct, 'What I do ye know not now, but ye shall know hereafter.'" The president asked for a copy of the sermon.

"I will try to go to God with my sorrows," Lincoln said as the procession accompanied Willie's body up the rise to Oak Hill Cemetery in Georgetown. His son was placed in a small chapel for a concluding prayer service and later moved to the Carroll family vault at the northwest end of the cemetery. Lincoln once confided to journalist Noah Brooks, "I have been driven many times upon my knees by the overwhelming conviction that I had nowhere else to go."

The heartbroken father frequently visited his son's tomb and twice had the crypt opened so he could see Willie again. This may strike modern readers as disturbing or morbid, but it was in fact an act of grieving love, according to John Updike, who added, "Our ancestors looked gravely and steadily upon things that we cannot."

In Lincoln's day, bodies were not hastily removed by discreet morticians. Open coffins were the norm, usually resting at home until the burial service. Pictures of corpses, dressed in their finest clothes, were commonplace and "make up the largest group of nineteenth-century American genre photographs," observes Stanley Burns, professor of Medical Humanities at New York University. In our time, these mourning rituals might seem unhealthy, but it may be that we have lost something valuable. "The piety of the previous century," Updike concludes, "clung to the Christian tenet, unemphasized in today's churches, that the body is the person, with a holy value even when animation ceases."

Lincoln took to re-reading Gurley's eulogy in his darkest moments of grief. "There was something touching in his childlike and simple reliance on Divine aid," Brooks wrote of this period, "especially when in such extremities as he sometimes fell into." Tad was also prone to extremes after his older brother passed. He was both "a prematurely serious and studious child," Hay wrote, and something of a tyrant in the White House. Mary, who was bedridden for three weeks after the death, dressed in mourning for a year. She noticed her husband's views on an afterlife began to change.

Mary invited Francis Vinton of Trinity Church in New York to the White House. The President welcomed his visit. "Your son is *alive*, in Paradise," Vinton assured the couple. "Alive!" Lincoln moaned. "*Alive!* Surely you mock me." Yet the rector's thoughts on Luke 20:38 ("For he is not a God of the dead, but of the living: for all live unto him") resonated with grieving father. He asked for a collection of Vinton's sermons.

Mary felt this was an important turning point in Lincoln's spiritual life. "When too—the overwhelming sorrow came upon us," she wrote, "Willie was called away from us, to his Heavenly Home, . . . he [Lincoln] turned his heart to Christ." Most biographers agree, chief among them Ida Tarbell, that Lincoln became a believer after Willie's death. Tarbell suggests that this experience caused the President "to look outside of his own mind and heart for help to endure a personal grief." Perhaps, in a way.

Mourners often give priority to finding meaning in their lives. Researchers and therapists note that parental bereavement frequently opens paths to transformation and growth that include a surprising list of coping methods: new appreciation of life; recognition of life's transience and frailty; closer relationships; valuing others; personal strength; humility; a feeling of being fully present; and a marked spirituality. "I had a good Christian mother," Lincoln told Rebecca Pomeroy, an army nurse dispatched by Dorothea Dix to take care of Mary, "and her prayers have followed me thus far through life."

One day Lincoln asked Gurley to join him an hour before breakfast at the White House. "We have talked about the soul after death," the pastor told a friend that same day. "That is a subject of which Mr. Lincoln never tires." The President began attending weekly prayer meetings at the New York Avenue Presbyterian Church. He preferred to sit in the pastor's study with the door ajar. This practice, he told Gurley, provided spiritual solace shorn of ostentation or unwanted attention.

Such private mourning can be surprisingly helpful. Mental health counselor and poet Miriam Greenspan insists that our dark feelings hold within them kernels of emotional well-being. "We need to honor three basic emotions that are an inevitable part of every life: grief, fear, and despair," she writes. Such feelings are not negative in themselves, but we may deal with them in negative ways. In his rare moments alone, Lincoln faced the reality of his loss and the spiritual pain of grief. "Ever after there was a new quality in his demeanor," observed artist Alban Jasper Conant, who painted Lincoln's first portrait, "something approaching awe."

Lincoln lavished attention on Tad and was careful of Robert's safety. This irritated the young man, who insisted that he should enlist and do his part in the war. Lincoln finally relented and secured a nominal rank and position on General Ulysses S. Grant's staff.

The President gave few signs of sorrow during the daily duties of his office, Hay noticed, but all the while "was profoundly moved by this death." In the spring of 1862, English journalist Edward Dicey also observed: "You cannot look upon his worn, bilious, anxious countenance and believe it to be that of a happy man."

In May, 1862, Lincoln visited Fort Monroe in Virginia. He asked General John Wool if he might borrow a copy of Shakespeare's works. After reading for a few hours, Lincoln asked Colonel Le Grand Cannon if he might share a few selections with him. The President recited from *Macbeth* and *King Lear*. Then he read a passage from *King John*, written shortly after the playwright's son, Hamnet, had died. Lincoln's voice began to shake.

> Grief fills the room up of my absent child,
> Lies in his bed, walks up and down with me,
> Puts on his pretty looks, repeats his words,
> Remembers me of all his gracious parts,
> Stuffs out his vacant garments with his form.

When Lincoln finished the verse, he set his book aside. "Did you ever dream of some lost friend, and feel that you were having a sweet communion with him, and yet have a consciousness that it was not a reality?" he asked. "That is the way I dream of my lost boy Willie." The president then broke down into convulsive weeping, as did Colonel Cannon.

Lincoln had what is known as a *lucid dream*, during which we are aware that we're dreaming. This is not unexpected. In fact, it can be quite healthy. These dreams are not easily dismissed as hallucinations nor are they readily accepted as spiritual visitations. In either case, it is clear that they provide insight into the emotional impact of death and the mystical union it inspires.

The President had a lifelong interest in dreams and their possible meaning in the waking world. "Think you better put 'Tad's' pistol away," he once wrote to Mary in June, 1863. "I had an ugly dream about him." Mary also had recurring dreams of their son. "Such a dream as I had of my idolized Willie, last night," Mary wrote in 1869. "Some day I will tell you *all*."

In July of 1862, Mary took a short trip to New York and Boston. The joy she felt in the sights naturally brought Willie to mind: "Yet, in this sweet spot, that his bright nature, would have so well loved, *he is not with us*, and the anguish of the thought, oftentimes, for days overcomes me."

In the first extremity of loss, during the period counselors call acute grief, Mary felt she experienced Willie—and occasionally Eddie—standing at the foot of her bed. The boys seemed happy and loving. This led her to mediums. In an effort to be supportive, Lincoln accompanied Mary to two séances: one in Georgetown, the other in the White House.

A disheartening number of biographers have subjected Mary's obvious emotional distress to ridicule, inserting snide comments, or presenting her in an unfavorable light. I might have done the same before my daughter died. But grief research paints a different picture.

Bereaved adults show increased corticosteroid activity during the first few years after a death. In some cases, this can result in psychiatric difficulties, which in turn can lead to exhaustion, stress, and diminished immunocompetence. It occurs to me that before we judge Mary's reactions, we might consider that few of us know how *we* might respond to losing two children. Sorrow is unique for each mourner. Mary dealt with loss in her own way, as did her husband. "Be aware of the general picture of grief," psychiatrist M. Katherine Shear advised caregivers, "but try not to have preconceived expectations about the specific constellation of symptoms or their time course."

Time is important in understanding Mary's grief. "It is impossible, for *time*, to alleviate, the anguish, of *such irreparable losses*—" Mary wrote in 1865 after Lincoln's assassination, "only the grace of God, can calm our grief & still the tempest." Four years later, in 1869, she admitted to a friend, "Time brings to me, no healing on its wing."

It is easy to dismiss such thoughts as the complicated grief of a widow and bereaved mother who refuses to "move on." Nothing is further from the truth, according to sociologist and death studies pioneer Geoffrey Gorer. Parental bereavement, Gorer observes, is "the most distressing and long-lasting of all griefs," adding that "it seems to be literally true, and not a figure of speech, that the parents never get over it."

On February 20, 1863—one year after Willie's death—Mary Jane Welles sat with the First Lady on what she knew was a difficult day. Wells and her husband,

Gideon, the Secretary of the Navy, had lost six children, including young Hubert, who had died in November, 1862. Mary thanked her visitor, adding, "Only those, who have passed through such bereavements, can *realize*, how the heart bleeds at the return, of these anniversaries." Mary's use of the word *realize* deserves attention.

During and after the American Civil War, thousands of people wrote they could not quite *realize* the deaths of their loved ones. The term meant, in essence, that they could not "make it real" in their minds. "When I can bring myself to realize that he has indeed passed," Mary wrote of Willie on May 29, 1862, "my question to myself is, 'can life be endured?'" Seven months later, on December 16, she wrote that her grief was not lessened, but the finality of her loss was brought home to her: "My precious little Willie is as much mourned over & far more missed (now that we realize he has gone)."

Lincoln too used this familiar expression. "You can not now realize that you will ever feel better," he wrote to twenty-two-year-old Mary Frances "Fanny" McCullough when she lost her father in December of 1862. For Fanny to experience life's joys on some distant day, Lincoln wrote, she must also *realize*, or make real, her current sorrow. Then, Lincoln assured her, "The memory of your dear Father, instead of an agony, will yet be a sad sweet feeling in your heart, of a purer, and holier sort than you have known before. . . . I have had experience enough to know what I say."

The Lincolns' attention to kindness in the wake of their son's death is another common characteristic of those who grieve. Studies show there is a sense of transcendence or transfiguration in the hearts of many bereaved parents: In their search for meaning they turn outward, commiserating with the suffering of others. "Grief itself is a bridge that reminds us of our shared human capacity for love and comfort," observed respected grief experts Robert Neimeyer, Darcy Harris, and Gordon Thornton. This isn't always easy.

Mary admitted that she shied away from missives that recalled the pain of losing her son. But when Hannah Shearer's eldest son, Edward, died in November of 1864, Mary was prompt to take up her pen. "Now, in this, the hour of *your* deep grief, with all my *own wounds* bleeding afresh," she wrote her friend, "I find myself, writing to you, to express, my deepest sympathy, *well knowing* how unavailing, *words*, are, when we are broken hearted."

Lincoln also found himself reaching out to others. In 1864, he invited sixteen-year-old sculptress Vinnie Ream to the White House for a five-month series of sittings. Willie would have been thirteen at the time, and the President seemed to enjoy the artist's company. "I made him think of Willie," Ream recalled. "He often said so and as often wept." The time was not wasted. Ream's sculpture of Lincoln was to be hailed as "one of the best literal representations" of the President.

The next year, on April 10, 1865, fire broke out in the White House stables. Lincoln rushed to the burning barn, calling for help. Security guards physically pulled him away from the conflagration. One of the guards, Robert McBride, came upon Lincoln weeping in the East room as he watched the fire. Tad then explained that the stable housed Willie's horse. "The thought of his dead child had come to his mind," McBride wrote, "and he had rushed out to try to save the pony from the flames."

"I am satisfied that when the Almighty wants me to do or not to do a particular thing," Lincoln once said, "he finds a way of letting me know it." By July of 1862, five months after Willie died, the President was speaking of emancipation.

This was not unexpected. Lincoln's views on slavery were well known. But the suddenness of his announcement, after the Confederate retreat at Antietam, shocked his cabinet. "He had made a vow, a covenant," wrote Secretary of the Navy Gideon Welles on September 22, 1862, "that if God gave us the victory in the approaching battle, he would consider it an indication of Divine Will, and that it was his duty to move forward in the cause of emancipation."

The President candidly shared his reasoning with others. "When Lee came over the river," Lincoln wrote Massachusetts congressman George Boutwell, "I made a resolve that when McClellan drove him back . . . I would send the Proclamation after him." Later, he explained to Secretary of the Treasury Salmon Chase the seriousness of his decision: "I made a solemn vow before God that if General Lee was driven back . . . I would crown the result by the declaration of freedom to the slaves."

The Emancipation Proclamation was issued less than a year after Willie's death: January 1, 1863. That same day the White House held its first public reception since the boy's passing.

Eleven months later, on November 19, 1863, Lincoln delivered his famous address at Gettysburg. He nearly didn't go. Two days earlier Tad had again fallen seriously ill. Lincoln and Mary were distraught, reminded of Willie's death, but the President felt strongly that he must make the trip. A methodical man, Lincoln wrote a draft of his speech at the White House with his usual thorough edits. He made the six-hour journey to Gettysburg on November 18 and stayed at the home of David Wills.

Lincoln rose early the next morning. He was slotted to deliver brief dedicatory remarks for the Soldiers' National Cemetery, following the afternoon's main oration by Edward Everett. The president spoke no more than three minutes, his high Kentucky tenor easily carrying to the closest of the twenty thousand spectators. As with his views on emancipation, the President's thoughts on American national purpose had for years been leading up to this point. Still, even today we are stunned by his compassion and resolve. Lincoln's search for meaning had raised him to new heights of eloquence.

Good Friday, April 14, 1865, seemed full of hope. Lincoln woke, read a few pages of the Bible, as was his habit, and breakfasted with Robert, now a captain in the Army. He later related to his cabinet a recurring dream that he'd had the night before. He felt he was floating on a phantom ship across a vast expanse to an uncharted shore. This dream, Lincoln said, was invariably followed by some important change or disaster. Nicolay and Hay described the President as "singularly happy."

Around 5:00 p.m., Lincoln and Mary took a carriage ride. Two days earlier, on April 12, General Robert E. Lee had completed the infantry surrender ceremony that formally ended hostilities. "Mary, I consider *this day*, the war, has come to a close," Lincoln said. They were in good spirits and yet, as with many bereaved parents, their dead son was not far from their minds.

"We must *both*, be more cheerful in the future—" Lincoln said. "Between the war & the loss of our darling Willie—we have both, been very miserable." They rode together in comfortable silence, then he added, "I have never felt so happy

George Peter Alexander Healy,
Abraham Lincoln, 1869,
The White House Historical Association (White House Collection)

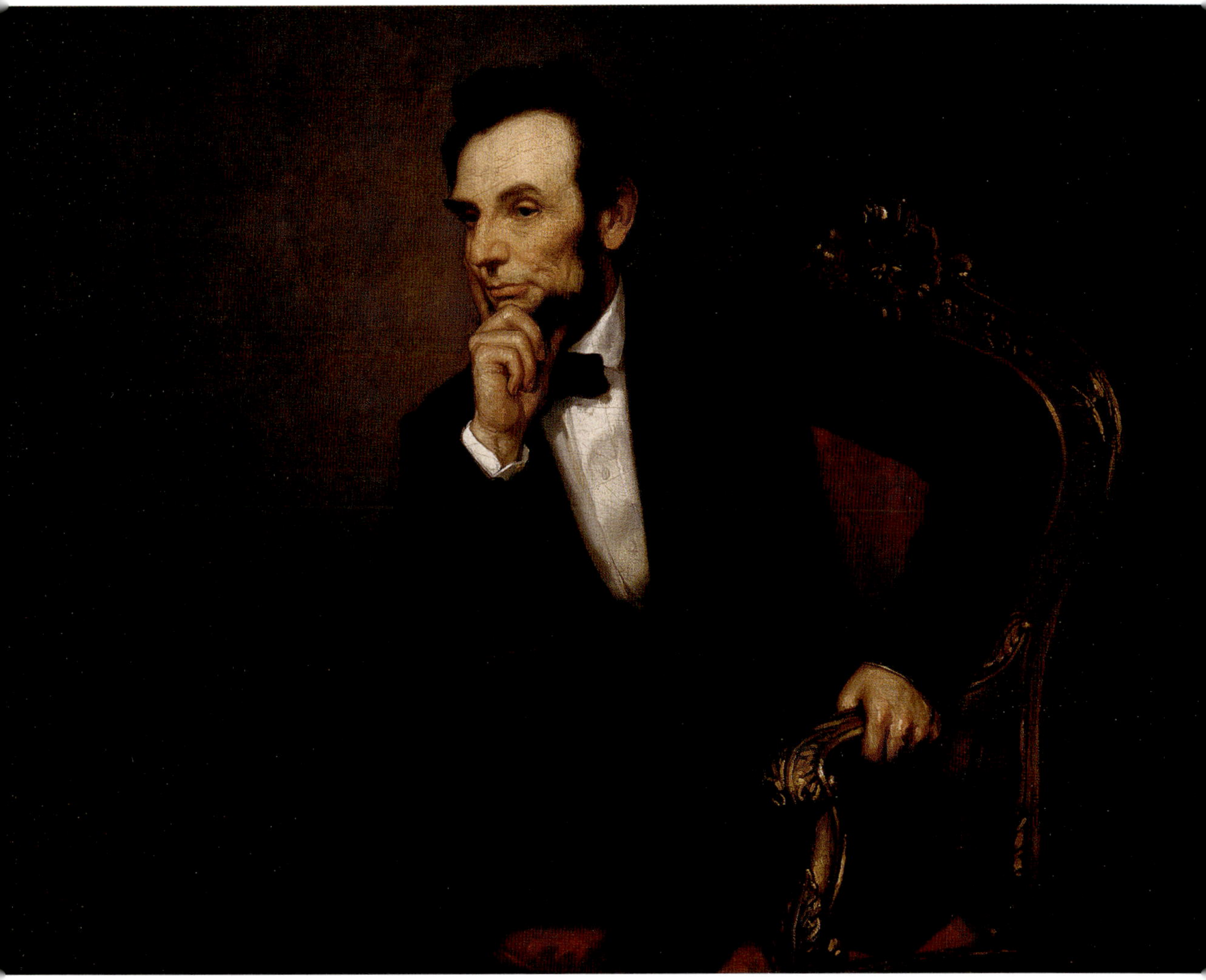

I PRAY THAT OUR HEAVENLY FATHER MAY ASSUAGE THE ANGUISH OF YOUR BEREAVEMENT, AND LEAVE YOU ONLY THE CHERISHED MEMORY OF THE LOVED AND LOST, AND THE SOLEMN PRIDE THAT MUST BE YOURS TO HAVE LAID SO COSTLY A SACRIFICE UPON THE ALTAR OF FREEDOM.

—ABRAHAM LINCOLN, NOVEMBER 21, 1864

in my life." Mary was shocked. "Don't you remember feeling just so," she said, "before our little boy died?"

That night Lincoln was struck by an assassin's bullet. He died on April 15, 1865. Tad, barely twelve years old, wept openly when he saw his father's body two days later. "I can hardly believe that I shall never see him again," he told his nurse. "Well, I will try and be a good boy, and will hope to go someday to Pa and brother Willie, in heaven." Tad died of tuberculosis on July 15, 1871, at the age of eighteen.

Mary wore black for the rest of her life. "When I reflect, as I am always doing," she wrote in November of 1865, "upon the overwhelming loss, of that, *most* idolized boy, and the crushing blow, that deprived me, of my *all in all* in this life, I wonder that I retain my reason & live." Later Mary turned away from the desperate measures of spiritualism, instead thinking of her dead son as "my Angel boy, in Heaven," and waiting, she wrote, "to be rejoined to my dearly loved ones, who have 'gone before.' . . . to be forever reunited to my idolized husband & my darling Willie."

On April 21, 1865, Willie's casket was disinterred to accompany his father's coffin on Lincoln's funeral train to Springfield, Illinois. They rode together on the sixteen-wheel coach that had been built to transport the Commander-in-Chief to battlefields during the war. Six other cars carried mourners, with one more reserved for a military honor guard.

Today Willie rests with Eddie, Tad, and his parents in the Lincoln Tomb at Oak Ridge Cemetery.

TWENTY YEARS WITH PHILIP

"Letters are the most precious, most immediate breath of life."

> *The Son of Man came eating and drinking, and they say, "Here is a glutton and a drunkard, a friend of tax collectors and sinners." But wisdom is proved right by her deeds.*
>
> MATTHEW 11:19

Pen pals seem to be a thing of the nineteenth century, or the early twentieth, unsuited to our modern age of email and text. This strikes me as sad. Perhaps we've lost something without noticing it. We may have let the comforting words of distant companions slip away.

"During the early months of the COVID-19 pandemic," writes Chelsea Butkowski of American University, "people in the US reported sending more personal mail to stay in touch with friends and family." At the time, Instagram posts sprang up supporting popular letter-writing campaigns like Letters Against Isolation, The Big Send, and Penpalooza. Dr. Butkowski suggests that this rebirth of letter writing can help build an intermingling of online and offline relationships across the world.

A pen pal is not limited to handwritten letters. In fact, one of my most valued friends writes to me nearly every week via email. Over two decades we have shared much laughter and much sorrow. His compassion and advice have helped shape my life. His name is Philip.

I wrote my first letter to him in 2004. "Can God forgive me?" I asked. I had read two of his books on the subject and truly wanted to know the answer to this haunting question about God's capacity for forgiveness—for things I presented myself as having done (but did not), and deeper, in my secret heart, things I had done but dared not admit. I don't recall the contents of Philip's reply, but we've been pen pals ever since.

Having a pen pal is a curious experience. As with any relationship, we start slow, perhaps waiting for the proverbial shoe to drop. Well, he seems nice enough, we may muse, but what's he after? I was solidly involved in a life of grifts at the time. To my astonishment, I discovered that I really wanted to be a friend to my new correspondent.

Our first foray focused on Wendell Berry's *The Gift of Gravity*. I sent it to Philip and, with his usual penchant for precise language, he pronounced it "most apt" in relation to one of his popular books. So began twenty years of swapping letters, poetry, prose, art, and music.

With a few breaks.

We had been writing semi-regularly when, in January, 2006, I was filming a documentary near Philip's home in Colorado. I asked my pen pal and his wife to join me at Boulder's famed teahouse. He was in the middle of writing his latest volume and declined the invitation. He didn't miss much. I was arrested for criminal impersonation that same week.

Later, at my hearing, the court officer asked if I knew anyone locally. "Oh, sure," I said. "But they wouldn't touch me with a ten-foot pole now." She tilted her head and spun a sheet of paper round for me to read. "Don't be so sure," she said. Her notes had a column entitled ATTEMPTED CONTACT and under it, one name: *Philip*.

The court system dominated my life for a while. I lost touch with my pen pal for eight years. Then something strange happened.

My mother died in 2013. The following spring I spent a few weeks with my dad in Washington state. My connecting flight on the return trip was a fifty-seater from Arizona to South Carolina. Wiggling along the crowded aisle, I looked down and there he sat, my old friend, all crazy hair and crooked smiles.

When we disembarked, I reintroduced myself and our acquaintance began anew. But our letters changed. Philip's new notes held an undertone of genuine concern for my well-being. The fact that I was no longer on the grift—and full of odorous cattle manure—may have had something to do with it.

Less than a year later, on January 16, 2015, my daughter died of a fentanyl-laced heroin overdose. She was twenty-six. "Jess is dead," I wrote to Philip. "Please pray for us." He replied almost immediately: "No one knows your pain."

My pen pal hasn't left me alone since. His personal, weekly letters have become an important part of my life. They also contribute to my efforts in service of fellow sufferers.

In those first few months after Jess died, Philip shared his thoughts on the nineteenth-century German poet Friedrich Rückert, who wrote some five hundred laments in the wake of losing his two youngest children. Three years earlier, Philip told me, he had been asked to speak in Newtown, Connecticut, after the Sandy Hook Elementary School shooting. His remarks included a reading of Rückert's "In this weather." Now we talked over the poem via email, as was our habit, but this time with far deeper resonance.

I downloaded a copy of Rückert's 1872 German-language book, *Songs on the Death of Children* [Kindertotenlieder]. In it I discovered a communion of grief that I dared not imagine might exist. I translated one of his best, "Over all Graves," and sent it to Philip on a whim.

> "Over all graves grass must grow,"
> "time heals all wounds," such is the solace,
> the worst thing to say, as consolations go;
> poor heart, not that, not a healed wound.
> It is something, at least, this pain;
> we amputate the numb and the dead.

Philip was on a flight to Georgia when he replied that the piece is "very fine." He encouraged me to render into English more songs from this classic. Soon we were sharing Rückert's poems in our letters. At times Philip could be snarky, insisting a piece made no sense; or stunned that a moving verse had never before been translated. We weighed each according to its merits, back and forth, the good and the bad. Three years later, ten of the laments seemed ideal for inclusion in my first book on grief, *Wounded in Spirit.*

We can thank my pen pal for that, too.

In December, 2017, I thought to send artistic masterpieces via email to Philip as a sort of digital Advent devotional. I chose painters who had also known loss, as we both had, and wrote letters describing their journeys of grief. A few weeks into the month, Philip began urging me to turn these missives into a book.

A pen pal can offer insight that we might miss on our own. It never occurred to me that there was a book in our letters. Philip was right. A publisher picked up the manuscript a month later. By the next Christmas, it was in the hands of other mourners.

My second book on grief is an English translation of Rückert's *Songs on the Death of Children*, the same German book that my pen pal had introduced to me shortly after Jess's death. As it happened, Philip and I were sharing a long lunch with our wives the day before this new volume arrived from the publisher.

Our pen pal connection has extended in unexpected ways. A few years ago, Philip introduced me to Tim, a writer and former rector of a cathedral located a few blocks from where my daughter lived before her death. I have also become friends with Rudolf in Germany, thanks to a shared love of Rückert's verse. It is a rare week in which I don't hear from these two new pen pals, as well.

It's not all letters and email. Philip's sister-in-law lives near our small town. She is the guiding force behind grief programs at our local community center. I facilitate support groups there.

Over the years Philip and I have lost beloved family members. We've survived illness and accidents, disappointments and successes, and at times simply needed a safe space to grouse. "Letters are the most precious, most immediate breath of life," observed Goethe. Perhaps so, in a way. We are occasionally shocked when Philip's letter to me, or mine to him, seems to arrive at just the right moment.

My pen pal was recently diagnosed with Parkinson's disease. Our weekly emails have grown shorter. He's as sharp as ever, but at times he seems a tad distracted as he wrestles with this progressive disorder.

Social media focuses on bite-sized nuggets of information. Who needs pen pals and the long letters they inspire? What's in it for us in an age of instant gratification? Not much, I suppose. Other than relationships that matter, that require attention and patience, that mean more than thousands of texts shot off without thought.

Books come and go, as do essays, but no effort is too great for a friendship that lasts over the years, through our happiest and most grief-stricken moments. For this lesson, and many others, thank you, my pen pal, Philip.

Gabriel Metsu,
Man Writing a Letter, 1665,
National Gallery of Ireland

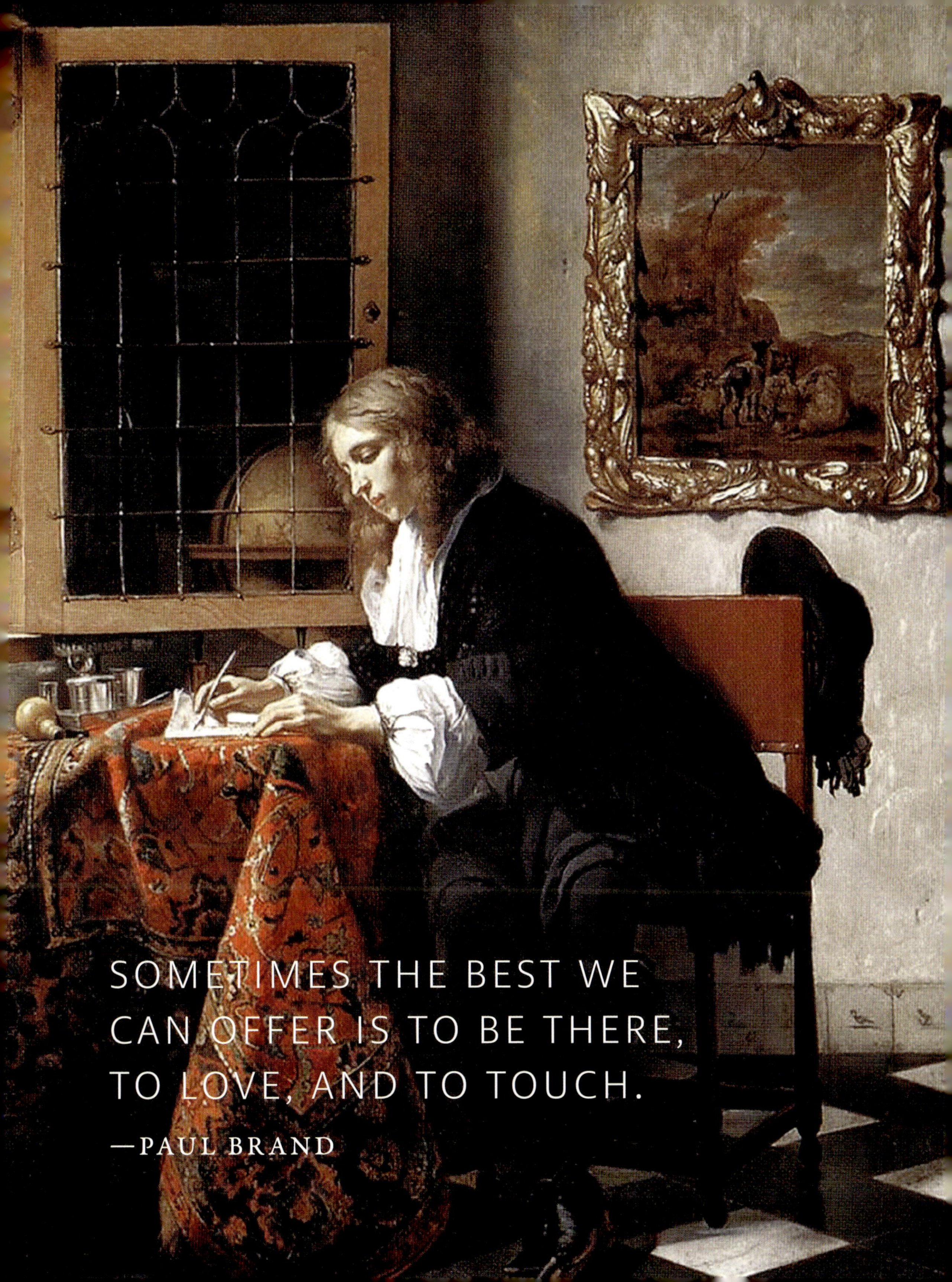

SOMETIMES THE BEST WE CAN OFFER IS TO BE THERE, TO LOVE, AND TO TOUCH.

—PAUL BRAND

SAFE AT LAST

"'Come!' will be heard when I enter the presence of the righteous."

So teach us to count our days, so that we will become wise.

PSALM 90:12 (CJB)

I sit with my daughter, Jess, as the sun rises. In the predawn calm beside her grave, I watch spiders spin glorious webs between nearby trees. Various insects investigate my presence. Most quickly turn away at a whiff of my repellent, but not the beetles. If I am still, I spot them feeding. One or two may crawl onto my boots. They usually disappear by mid-morning, but with the sun's rising, they are tranquil companions.

In ancient Egypt, scarabs were thought to be the harbingers of universal harmony. They emerge at dawn and fly to heaven in the same way that our souls leave our bodies at death. They return each day, as the sun appears and reappears, as the souls of our loved ones live on through eternity.

Beetles were named *kheper*, meaning to become, to be, to exist. Khepera, the scarab deity, was revealed through the ascending sun, a symbol of regeneration and rejuvenation. This is why heart scarabs of gold and precious stone were interred with the deceased, placed on the breast as amulets of power beyond all others.

Jess knew where she wanted to be buried. In the fall of 2014, she and her mother visited the Ramsey Creek nature preserve in South Carolina. Spotting the graves there, she said that this is where she hoped to rest. A few months later my daughter was dead from an overdose. She was twenty-six.

"I'll die young, Dad," Jess often informed me in matter-of-fact tones. From an early age, she knew her life would be short. Sometimes I didn't reply; at others, I insisted this was not the case. What stunned me then, as it does now, was her pragmatic assurance.

Jess's prescient words register in my mind and deeper, in my secret heart, but before her death their reality seemed distant and confusing. Now I face them each day. Questions of eternity are no longer ethereal or esoteric. They matter.

When I came across this poem inscribed in the Theban tomb of Neferhotep, I was shocked by a sense of recognition, heartbreak, and hope:

> I've heard songs from tombs of our ancestors
> "celebrating life" and ignoring our afterlife.
> Why do we treat eternity so? Our loved ones
> have been there since the beginning
> and will remain, for all must go:
> our time on earth is a dream. Yet when
> we reach that distant land, we are greeted
> with the words, "Welcome, safe at last!"

The ancient Egyptians would have understood Jess's practical approach. They saw death as a perfectly normal manifestation of life and prepared for their ends accordingly, albeit in extravagant ways. Modern readers might dismiss such preoccupations, but it occurs to me that our views may be equally skewed in the opposite direction.

To the ancients, death was our common heritage, an integral part of life. Pretending it did not exist was naive. "The day of our death is unknown to us," wrote Egyptian scribe Ani some 3,500 years ago. "Death comes, to steal the child from a mother's arms, just as it comes for the elderly." They believed that death was a transition from the joys and admitted miseries of this life to a new existence of peace and fulfillment.

A much later poet, King David, expressed a similar view when he asked God to "teach us to count our days, so that we will become wise." Counting our days is not an act of despair nor is it an act of resignation. David was echoing the ancients when he urged us to experience joy fully in this life, as we will enjoy it far more in the next.

"The Egyptian way of death is comprehensible on the basis of a few simple assumptions," suggests Egyptologist Barbara Mertz, perhaps best known as the author of the Amelia Peabody series under her pseudonym Elizabeth Peters. The first assumption is that an aspect of our essence survives physical death; the second, that how we treat the body of the deceased matters. "But we also find a unifying theme," Mertz observes. "The desire for survival in some, perhaps any, form."

Egyptians had as many euphemisms for death as modern Americans. "He has joined his father the sun," for example, or "she mingles now with the gods," and in a land dependent on the Nile, the poignant expression, "the final mooring." Perhaps the most common Egyptian expression equals our own culture's emphasis on eternal peace: "final rest from life."

The ancient Egyptian view of the soul was as simple—and as complex—as our own. When a body is created at birth, a person's *ka* is also created: invisible, spiritual, as much life force as individual personality. After death, the *ba*, or essence of the deceased, also comes into existence. The difference is a question of timing: the *ka* accompanies the living, whereas the *ba* only exists after death. During the funerary rituals, the *ka* and *ba* unite into the *akh*, the closest approximation to our concept of an immortal soul. In the *akh*, a new soul is born, combining both the old life (*ka*) and the new (*ba*), to continue on into eternity.

Such terms do not follow a simple mathematical precision, of course. Just as we vaguely refer to such words as spirit, essence, life force, and soul, so too did the ancient Egyptians flail about to express the ineffable. "Beneath their extravagance," Mertz concludes, they displayed "a common human terror and a common hope."

Names for the afterlife were equally plentiful and spoke with promise of a better existence: Peaceful Paths of the West; Field of Fulfillment; Eternal Land. The east, west and underworld (*duat*) were all mentioned as realms of the dead. Paradise was known as the Field of Reeds. The north, lit by circumpolar stars that do not set, was considered remote, ethereal, and endless. Wherever the soul ends up, it was thought, it would spend eternity in a place "beautiful and just, free of trouble," where the dead will be reunited with their families in joy and love.

Death had a name in ancient Egypt: "Come!" In many poems this imperative verb is used as a pronoun, calling our demise simply The Day of Come. A prayer from the reign of Ramesses II exclaims, "'Come!' will be heard when I enter the presence of the righteous."

The tomb of Ramesses's beloved wife, Nefertari, is one of the most impressive edifices of Egypt. But the scale of her grave does not resonate with me. Instead, I pause at her grieving mate's devotion, the care taken with each carving and painting. Nothing was done in haste. A little over 2,100 years ago, another deceased woman spoke to her husband from the grave in this poignant tomb inscription:

> Let me face a north wind on the bank of the Nile;
> there my grief will cool.
> Death—"Come!" is its name—calls whom it will
> and each must answer.

Modern poets echo this wisdom. In his poem "Drum," Langston Hughes suggests death beckons to life: *Come!* Egyptians knew grief: emptiness at the passing of a spouse; rending pain when losing a child. Yet they saw life and death as interwoven and inseparable. This pragmatic view is not as foreign as it may seem. It persists in an old Gregorian chant that is now part of twenty-first-century burial services: "In the midst of life we are in death; to whom may we turn but you, Lord?"

The ancients believed that death permeates our lives. "The tomb served life, not death," observes Egyptologist Jan Assmann. This was a source of surprising hope. Egyptian verse is rich with admonitions to enjoy our loved ones while time remains in anticipation of a greater day of reunion in death. "Listen, death matters little," wrote Hordjedef, the son of Pharaoh Khufu, nearly 5,000 years ago. "Listen, life matters a great deal to us; the house of death counts as life."

Ancient mourners believed that their loved ones needed a heart at the time of judgment. Corpses lack this vital organ, so a scarab amulet—about three inches in length—was placed on the throat, over the heart, or within the chest of the dead. Some pieces were crafted with astonishing beauty.

We have similar traditions today.

I worked at a funeral home for years. The bereaved frequently asked that we place a cross around the neck of their loved one. Rosaries, Bibles and precious mementos were also included in the coffins. Grandparents were often buried with photos of their grandchildren; the very young, with beloved toys. Usually the dead were dressed in carefully selected clothes: Sunday best or favored outfits—including cowboy boots or flannel shirts. After the funeral, cemetery visitors continued to leave precious keepsakes along with flowers. Seeing such gentle gestures, the words of Washington Irving are brought home in a way I had not understood before: "The love which survives the tomb is one of the noblest attributes of the soul."

I have my own custom in the nature preserve where Jess rests. I scour the gullies and the creek bed for a rock. I have no idea which stone will suit me that day. In

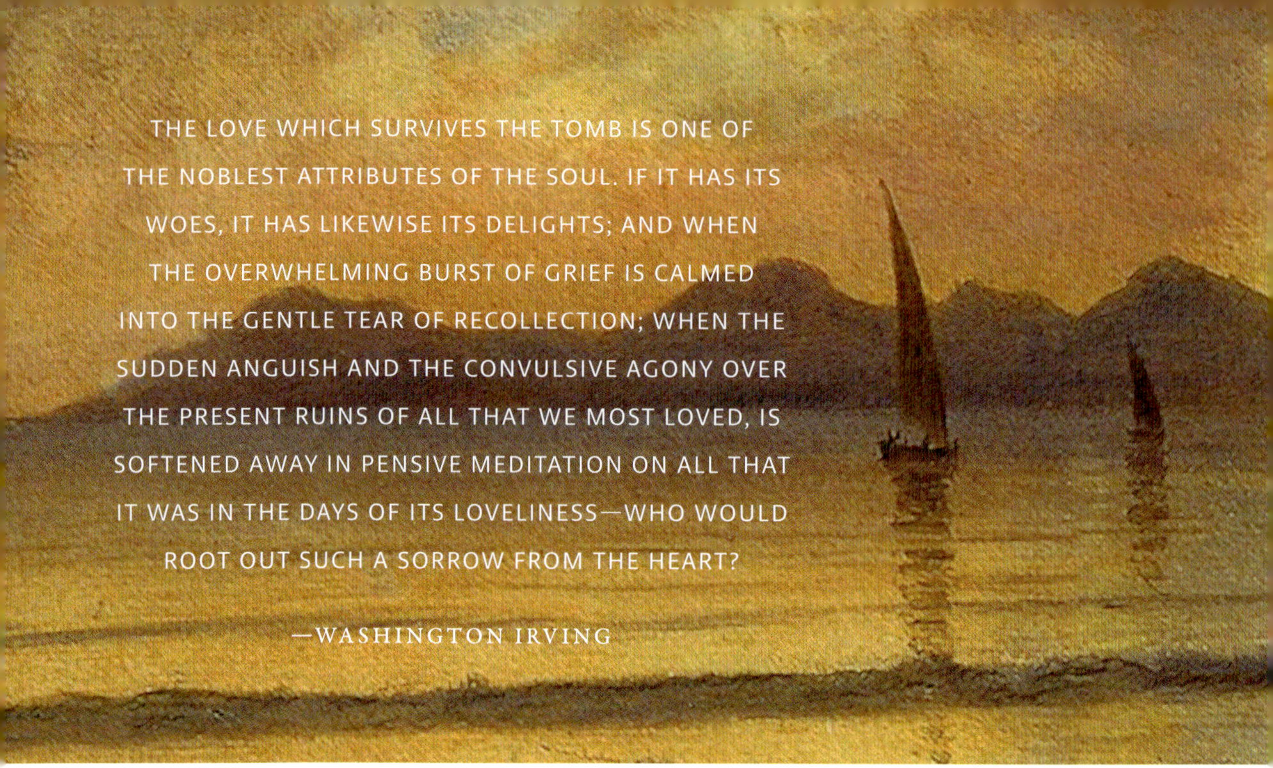

THE LOVE WHICH SURVIVES THE TOMB IS ONE OF THE NOBLEST ATTRIBUTES OF THE SOUL. IF IT HAS ITS WOES, IT HAS LIKEWISE ITS DELIGHTS; AND WHEN THE OVERWHELMING BURST OF GRIEF IS CALMED INTO THE GENTLE TEAR OF RECOLLECTION; WHEN THE SUDDEN ANGUISH AND THE CONVULSIVE AGONY OVER THE PRESENT RUINS OF ALL THAT WE MOST LOVED, IS SOFTENED AWAY IN PENSIVE MEDITATION ON ALL THAT IT WAS IN THE DAYS OF ITS LOVELINESS—WHO WOULD ROOT OUT SUCH A SORROW FROM THE HEART?

—WASHINGTON IRVING

this quiet search, my aloneness invites openness to the world around me. Once I find a stone that seems just right, I place it alongside Jess's grave. Its contours may lack the elegance of a heart scarab, but for me its natural beauty lies in this ritual that I share with my daughter. She has quite a collection at this point.

As the sun rises over the Nile or my daughter's grave, it occurs to me that the ancient Egyptians may have been onto something. Jess lives on; her soul soars to heaven, yet she returns each day, as close as a whispered web or a patient beetle on my boots.

Since Jess passed, my awareness of death is the opposite of morbid. I find solace in the knowledge that physical dissolution is not the end, that our loved ones are mindful of us and looking out for us. "And all along the valley, by rock and cave and tree," writes Tennyson, "The voice of the dead was a living voice to me."

When I visit Jess's grave in the Ramsey Creek nature preserve, I do not enter a place of death. The earth there is precious to me, as tombs have been sacred to mourners for millennia. When I run my fingers over her gravestone or place my hands on the rich soil, I am reminded of her life on this earth and her continued life in eternity. "Come!" I hear her call. "Welcome, safe at last."

Albert Bierstadt,
Sunset Over A Mountain Lake, c1882,
Location unknown

Love

O death, where is thy sting? O grave, where is thy victory?

1 CORINTHIANS 15:55 (KJV)

Jesus replied, "You do not realize now what I am doing, but later you will understand."

JOHN 13:7

HELD FAST IN GOD'S CLOAK

"My love for you is the one image of God permitted us."

> *Hear my cry, O God; listen to my prayer. From the ends of the earth I call to you, I call as my heart grows faint.*
>
> PSALM 61:1–2A

She was once a darling of Berlin's literati, recipient of the prestigious 1932 Kleist Prize for Literature. Now, less than a year later, she is threatened, beaten, and forced out of the city. Her only son is dead, and she is running for her life. Brilliant poet and playwright Else Lasker-Schüler is a Jew in Nazi Germany.

She emigrates to Zurich, then Palestine, "my Hebrew country," as she calls it. Lasker-Schüler ultimately settles in Jerusalem in 1937. There she forms a literary salon at the French Cultural Center, an artistic gathering called *Kraal* (Dutch for corral), that opens with Martin Buber on January 10, 1942. Such luminaries as Austrian author Karl Kraus consider her "the greatest poet of modern Germany." Five-time Nobel Prize in Literature nominee Gottfried Benn goes a step further, pronouncing Lasker-Schüler "the finest lyric poet of the century." But these distinctions are only part of her life.

Biographers often consign Lasker-Schüler to a single type, suggests Nina Berman with Arizona State University: "Either artist, woman, German, or Jew." They frequently ignore or explain away complex aspects of grief and spirituality that inform her life. This seems unjust. She was more than a few lines of verse, a gender, a national or ethnic identity.

Born in 1869, Lasker-Schüler was deemed a prodigy by the age of four. Such labels are especially hard on children, who feel constrained to measure up to improbable expectations. She was the youngest of six children. All too soon, grief replaced art as the dominant factor in her life.

Her brother Paul died when she was thirteen. A few months after Lasker-Schüler's twenty-first birthday, her mother, Jeanette, passed in 1890, followed by her father, Aaron, seven years later. Jeanette was to figure prominently in her daughter's poetry, often addressed directly as "dear Mother."

On August 24, 1899, Lasker-Schüler gives birth to a son. She names him Paul after her brother. The boy is a child of many gifts. His mother sees in him hope for all that has been blurred and withered in herself, she writes. His playfulness, talent, and candor are to her "a blossom, a breath from God." Her son's promise is never fulfilled. Paul dies from tuberculosis at the age of twenty-eight on December 14, 1927. Later, Lasker-Schüler writes this poem of faith and loss:

> *To My Child*
>
> You die over and over as
> the year passes, my child,
>
> when leaves flow down
> and branches grow narrow.
>
> Your taste of death was
> bitter: as with red roses,
>
> you were spared no
> withering blow.
>
> And so, endless, I weep . . .
> in the night of my heart.
>
> Still I sigh the lullabies that
> sobbed you into death's sleep,
>
> and my eyes no longer turn
> to the world; the green
>
> of leaves hurts them so.
> —yet Eternity dwells in me.

My love for you is the one
image of God permitted us.

Angels wept with me, I saw
them in the wind, in the sleet.

They floated . . .
on the air of heaven.

A moon in bloom is like
your life, my child.

And I dislike the light of carefree
butterflies as they pass.

I did not foresee death
—hunting you, my child—

And I love these walls in the room
I am painting with your boyish face.

These stars, this very month,
fall radiant in life to drop
heavy on my heart.

Lasker-Schüler's lament is steeped in desperation, longing, and sorrow. She hints at Paul's continuing influence in her life. Psychiatrist Karl Goodkin with the University of Miami's School of Medicine describes these normal aspects of grief as "searching for the deceased, the sense of the deceased being present, and the sense of being in ongoing communication with that person." Lasker-Schüler infuses her brief lines with undertones of inevitability, resignation, regret, and self-recrimination. Then she surprises us with a source of unexpected hope: *Angels wept with me, I saw them in the wind, in the sleet.* But such hope does not come easily.

Respected grief experts Robert Neimeyer and David Kessler write in separate books that *meaning-making* is of paramount importance to parents. It is perhaps their sole means of survival.

Most bereaved parents count their child's death as the single defining moment in their lives. They relate that their personal calendars were reset that day. This has been true for me since my daughter, Jess, died on January 16, 2015. Yet my love for her endures; so, too, does my sorrow, an expression of that love. As with Lasker-Schüler, grief and love now inhabit my life, my decisions, my perspectives, and each word I write.

Lasker-Schüler's lament for Paul does not speak of healing or recovery; it merely proffers occasional glimpses of relief. This is quite common. For those so inclined, creative arts allow us to express complex images and impressions of mourning. Poetic responses, rather than analyses of feelings, allow sorrow to be shared in fresh and unanticipated ways, according to Barbara Thompson of Russell Sage College and Dr. Joy Berger, a hospice educator. For Lasker-Schüler, poetry offers simple but powerful solace while simultaneously providing a productive outlet for grief. In verse she finds brief liberation from despair. And something more.

Lasker-Schüler took religion seriously, but saw her relationship with God as both beautiful and vexing. This led to a certain amount of whimsy. "Once the stars read the Bible among themselves," she quips. "And God spun the moon on his finger." In the same poem, "Oh God," she places lines of deep yearning among her flights of fancy: "Could I but once feel God's hand in mine. Oh God, oh God, how far I am from you!" And in another piece, "Oh God, hold me fast in your cloak."

She frequently spoke and wrote of angelic visitations. These interactions with the invisible world, she said, were no different than the tangible existence we experience each day. In this she was not far from her friend the philosopher Martin Buber, who observes that God may be wholly other, wholly mysterious, but he is also wholly present, "nearer to me than my *I*." Lasker-Schüler's admirers praised her as a mystic; others derided her as mentally unstable. Both may have been right.

She refused remuneration as a medium or psychic, flatly stating that her ability was as much curse as blessing. She expressed frustration at the heavy emotional, mental, and physical toll exacted by her connection with the incorporeal. Her antipathy reminds me of French Catholic mystic Thérèse of Lisieux, who was plagued by headaches, convulsions, shivering, and chronic pain. "I would say and do things that I wasn't thinking," Thérèse writes, as translated by Robert Edmonson. "I almost always seemed to be delirious, saying words that had no meaning, and nevertheless I'm *sure* that I wasn't *deprived for a single instant of the use of my reason.*"

Lasker-Schüler's friends noticed that her behavior could seem as unsettling as her visions. A leading figure in the Expressionist movement, which values emotional experience over physical reality, she occasionally spoke in tongues or wrote of communicating with the dead. She also created an alter-ego, dubbed "Prince Jussuf," and dressed exotically as part of her decidedly bohemian lifestyle. All of this made her a little hard to take. Her confidant, poet and artist Hans Cohn, joked that she had "a gift for making friends and also for antagonizing them."

Before we scoff, however, we might recall that Lasker-Schüler's views and behavior were part and parcel of a hardscrabble life. And she was in good company. After all, Isaiah stripped and strolled around in the buff. Jeremiah hid his undergarments and stumbled for months with a cattle yoke on his shoulders. Theologian Abraham Heschel, another refugee from Hitler's Europe, suggests that a lifetime of interaction with the divine nearly drove Jeremiah mad.

This may be one reason that some mystics seem simultaneously inspired and disturbed. Samuel Kottek with Hebrew University's Hadassah Medical School agrees. Even in the time of Jesus, he says, "The frontiers between insanity and prophecy could at times be blurred and difficult to define." First-century rabbi Yohanan ben Zakkai cites Psalm 116, *the Lord watches over the simple*, to demonstrate that innocents are open-minded and unconscious of societal constraints. "Since the Temple was destroyed," he writes, "prophecy was taken from the prophets, and given to the simple and the very young."

Our image of a mad German poet wandering Jerusalem in the garb of Prince Jussuf seems an easy target for mockery. But the more I read Lasker-Schüler's poetry and the letters of those who dearly loved her, the less I am inclined to dismiss those eccentricities that her friends adored. They described her alternately as archangel, bird of paradise, herbalist, genius, or fortune-teller. "I'm not a human being," she said in reply. "I am weather."

Whatever Lasker-Schüler's mental state, it is clear that she knew the emotional and mental anguish of grief. "All at once my sorely orphaned heart hurts," she muses. "I have taken much harm in this life. I walk the earth timidly, on tiptoe." Her companions insisted that this gave her unique spiritual insight. Perhaps. Her work is certainly redolent of sorrow and, as she describes it, the eternity that dwells within her. But her words also carry hope and surprising faith that she will see her son again. "I love these walls in the room I am painting with your boyish face," she writes. "My love for you is the one image of God permitted us."

"To My Child" was published in her last volume of verse, *My Blue Piano* (1943). The once-famous poet printed only 330 copies of what is often considered her finest work. Else Lasker-Schüler died of a heart attack on January 22, 1944. She was seventy-five, penniless, and alone. She rests on the Mount of Olives in Jerusalem.

"I wander!" Lasker-Schüler confesses on the last page of *My Blue Piano*. "My mind flits about like a bird, dear Mother. Yet no one will rob me of my freedom. If I die on the side of a road, dear Mother, lift me up to the blue of Heaven. I know you are touched by my lonely wavering, and the playful tick-tock of our hearts—mine and my precious son's."

PRAYER, TOO, IS FREQUENTLY AN INNER *vision*, AN INTENSE DREAMING FOR GOD—THE REFLECTION OF THE DIVINE INTENTIONS IN THE SOUL OF MAN. . . . TO PRAY IS TO *dream* IN LEAGUE WITH GOD, TO ENVISION HIS HOLY VISIONS.

—ABRAHAM HESCHEL

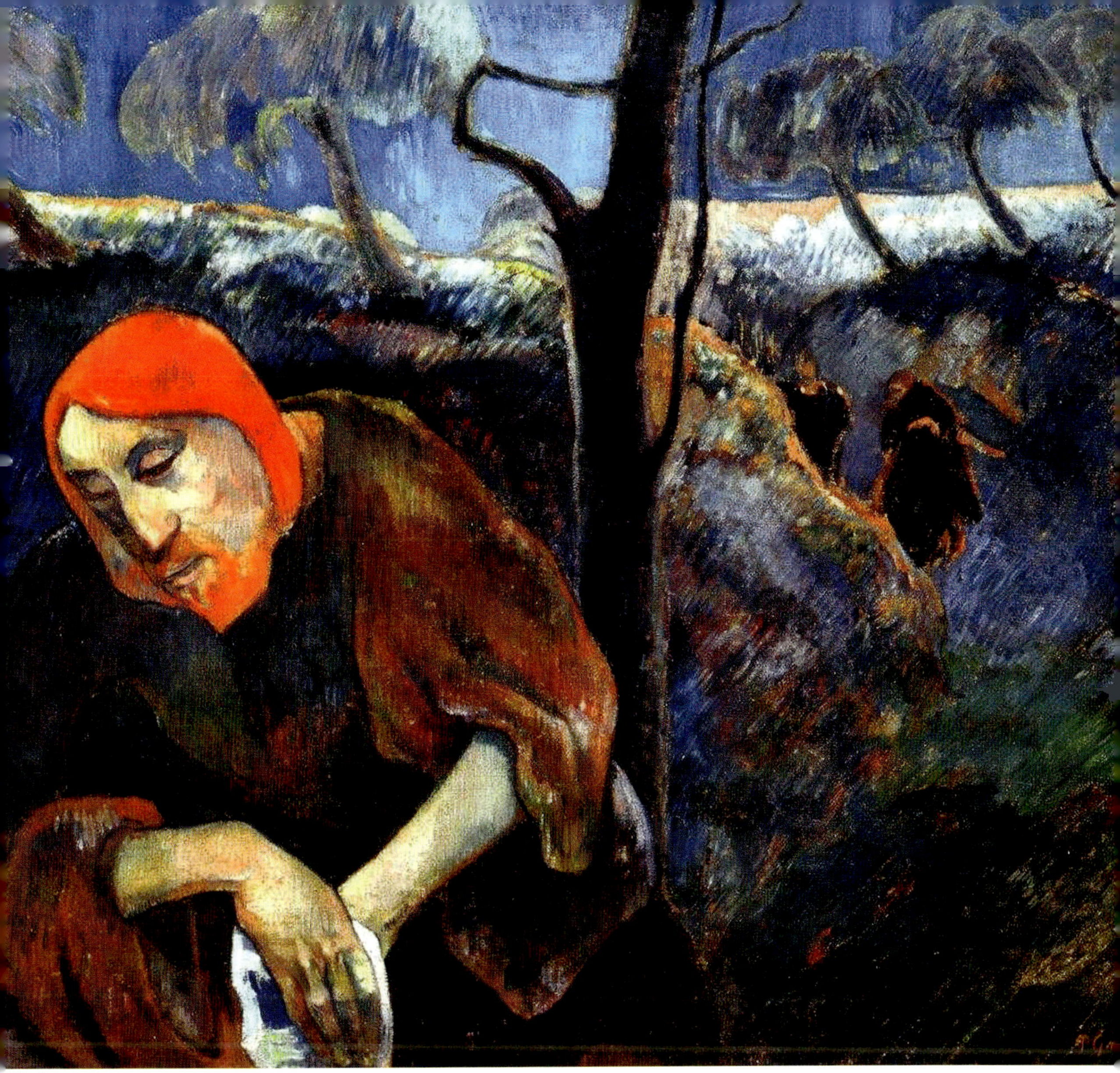

Paul Gauguin,
Christ on the Mount of Olives, 1889,
Gift of Elizabeth C. Norton, Norton Museum of Art

AS GRIEF METAPHORS GO, GODZILLA IS BETTER THAN MOST

"Sometimes the only way to heal our wounds is to make peace with the demons who created them."

> *Is it nothing to you, all you who pass by? Look around and see. Is any suffering like my suffering?*
>
> LAMENTATIONS 1:12A

My daughter, Jess, loved King Kong. We watched the films, swapped trading cards, posters, magazines, even the novel by Edgar Wallace. Godzilla was different. She never understood why her stepmother and I enjoy the movies. "Sure, Godzilla's really big," she laughed. "But so what?"

Jess had a point. Godzilla is not horrifying or even slightly creepy. The film's warning about unchecked nuclear testing still rings true, but as with all myth, modern or ancient, we sense there is something else going on. When this allegorical behemoth lumbers through our lives, we can do little more than deal with the damage. We are helpless in the wake of its devastation.

My daughter died in 2015. She was twenty-six. The loss is so primal that I can think of no metaphor more apt. Godzilla has arrived.

"This is a bad movie," Roger Ebert writes of the original *Godzilla* (1954). "But it has earned its place in history." The treatment by novelist Shigeru Kayama was a basic giant monster story. Writer Takeo Murata and director Ishirō Honda then reworked his outline into their morality tale of a leviathan born of nuclear weapons testing. Later, writing a young adult novelization of the film, Kayama saw wisdom in their changes. "Atomic and hydrogen bombs," he observes, "have taken on the form of Godzilla in this story."

Godzilla was released two years after American occupational forces left the Japanese islands. Prior to that, creative artists labored under strict governmental controls on how they discussed nuclear weapons. The film broke a powerful cultural taboo about atomic testing. But it did more.

Godzilla was a metaphor for the monster in the room—Japan's national grief over war, loss, and the devastation of atomic bombs. Audiences left theaters in tears. "Godzilla is equipment for living through trauma," writes rhetorician Shannon Stevens with the University of Nevada. "A film that explores trauma metaphorically allows viewers to revisit their past trauma simultaneously with the characters on the screen . . . but in a guided and safe way."

Over the decades, Godzilla has taken many forms: some thoughtful; others silly. Yet each incarnation adds a new interpretation to this creature that seems at once mythological and modern. Why does such a callous force of nature speak to us? Perhaps because, like death and grief, Godzilla is unstoppable.

Bereavement is permanent. There is no solution, no good news, no consolation that will return our dead to us right now. Yet we will always love them and will forever feel their absence in our lives. Grief is a natural and healthy expression of that love. It can also seem *monstrous*.

This paradox may be difficult for others to understand. And so we turn to metaphors.

Grief comes in *waves*, we say: slow, relentless, consuming, receding. This is accurate enough, but to avoid swells we need simply leave the seashore. A *storm* is another popular comparison. Again, with inclement weather, we might choose to evacuate or at least head indoors. Alas, there is no running or hiding from grief.

Perhaps death is analogous to *losing a limb*, we suggest. It will never grow back, never "heal," per se. We must adjust and adapt to its lack. C. S. Lewis said this about the loss of his wife, adding that he would always be aware of the stump. Later he changed his mind. "I was deceived," he writes, "because it has so many ways to hurt me that I discover them only one by one."

Psychologist and bereaved parent Catherine Sanders also sees grief as an amputation. "It is like having a part of ourselves sliced away," she writes. "The pain is unbearable. Even when scar tissue has formed, the agony of living without that part of ourselves leaves us feeling isolated and different, awkward and unsure. There is no prosthesis."

One staple of early Lutheran funeral poetry described parental bereavement as a *gaping wound* that requires timely treatment or it will fester. In 1690, Margarethe Susanna von Kuntsch's nine-year-old daughter died, the eleventh child she had lost. She wrote that the new death was a wound that reopened her ten others, specifically comparing it to Jeremiah's cry of Israel in Lamentations: "Is it nothing to you, all you who pass by? Look around and see. Is any suffering like my suffering?"

I facilitate bereavement support groups. We do a good bit of sharing, but ultimately words fail us. Our grief is beyond metaphors of the physical. I frequently suggest that the pain of loss may be described in literal, rather than figurative, terms: *Our souls have taken harm*. This is certainly true for me. True healing will be mine the moment I hold Jess in my arms again. Until then, I love her in absence. But I never feel completely alone.

Some time ago I was working under our truck, replacing a starter, when I chanced to look aside. The sunset was breathtaking, a moment like so many I have shared with Jess. It seemed that if I turned my head, I might see her beside me banging away at an errant rusted part. Suddenly, grimy and lying on my back beneath a half-repaired engine, I was weeping. These moments still sneak up on me. They force me to pause and take time to mourn. Sorrow cannot be denied, pushed to the side, ignored, or "worked through." It is the price we pay for love.

Grief arrives unbidden, stays as long as it will, lumbers through uncaring, leaves on a whim. It offers no pact or truce. But even in the face of such devastation, I am not helpless. I choose grief because I choose love. In mourning my daughter, I am loving her. "Sometimes the only way to heal our wounds is to make peace with the demons who created them," one character tells a bereaved father in *Godzilla: King of the Monsters* (2019). "There are some things beyond our understanding. We must accept them and learn from them. Because these moments of crisis are also potential moments of faith."

As grief metaphors go, Godzilla is better than most.

Gustave Doré,
The Destruction of Leviathan, 1866,
Doré's English Bible

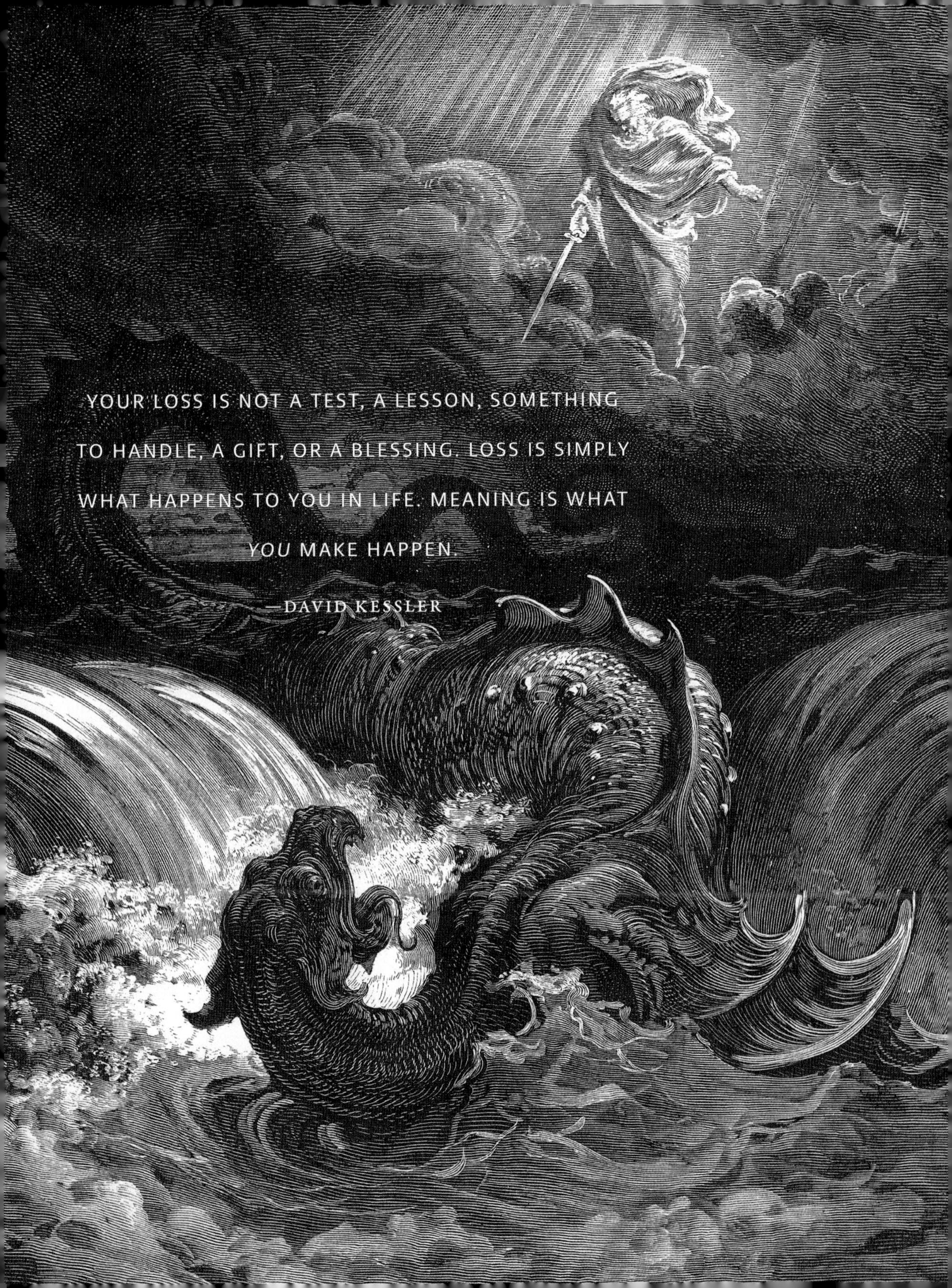

YOUR LOSS IS NOT A TEST, A LESSON, SOMETHING TO HANDLE, A GIFT, OR A BLESSING. LOSS IS SIMPLY WHAT HAPPENS TO YOU IN LIFE. MEANING IS WHAT *YOU* MAKE HAPPEN.

—DAVID KESSLER

LOVE REDEEMS US

"I shall see my boy again"

Humans look at the outward appearance, but Adonai looks at the heart.

1 SAMUEL 16:7B (CJB)

William Shakespeare thought his family was safe from the plague. His eldest, Susanna, and the twins, Judith and Hamnet, were with their mother in Stratford-upon-Avon in Warwickshire.

Stratford was a prosperous market town some eighty miles from London, a journey of two or three days on horseback along the convoluted byways of Elizabethan England, including a stop for the night in Oxford. Stratford's central location between Wales, London, and the north made it a crossroads for commerce and culture. It also had something the capital did not: an abundance of trees, lush foliage, and a peaceful rural setting.

Shakespeare's children seldom if ever visited London. Their education didn't suffer—schooling was free and widespread for the middling ranks of society in Stratford. In 1594 Shakespeare had co-founded a successful acting company, the Lord Chamberlain's Men. His family was planning to purchase a large house and was eagerly anticipating the College of Heralds award of arms in autumn of 1596. It seemed that their future was assured.

But disease plays no favorites.

When Shakespeare was an infant, a pandemic ravaged the capital in 1563. The following year it killed 200 of Stratford's 1,800 inhabitants, including four children of the miller Roger Green's family, who lived a few doors down from the Shakespeares. The epidemic passed only to return in 1592–93. It claimed nearly 11,000 lives of the 125,000 London inhabitants, closing theaters in London and stubbornly lingering outside the capital.

In 1596 the provinces suffered their greatest mortality, among them Shakespeare's eleven-year-old son, Hamnet. The younger twin had always been prone to sickness. He fell ill in early August 1596 and died within days. Shakespeare would never be the same.

Loss must inevitably find expression, all the more for creative artists. Shakespeare was no different. His future plays were steeped in grief. "Give sorrow words," he wrote in *Macbeth* ten years after his son's death. "The grief that does not speak whispers the o'erfraught heart and bids it break."

Shakespeare never shied away from tough questions, nor did he offer easy answers. He spoke to the worst and best of life, exploring themes of spirituality and meaning, loss and resurrection, twin figures, paternal guilt, father-daughter relations, family strife and reunion. With prescient insight, Shakespeare threw light on many aspects of grief.

Kenneth Heaton, Reader in Medicine at the University of Bristol for three decades, examined Shakespeare's work for evidence of physical manifestations of grief. Heaton looked at 39 plays and 3 long narrative poems, finding 140 instances of 31 different grief-associated symptoms. "Shakespeare's empathy with grieving humanity was unrivalled," Heaton concludes.

Shakespeare was no stranger to sorrow. His parents lost two children before he was born. Shakespeare's younger sister, Anne, died at the age of seven in 1579. He was to see his parents and four younger siblings pass: At the time of the playwright's death in 1616, only his sister Joan survived.

Then as now, the death of a younger sibling receives scant social acknowledgement despite having marked similarities to losing a child. It casts a long shadow, as in *Richard II*, which uses the word *grief* more than any of his other works. Shakespeare wrote *Richard II* in 1595, two years after the epidemic had cost the lives of many Londoners and remained an active fear in the provinces.

The play is set in the fourteenth century. The Black Death has weakened the foundations of the Plantagenet monarchy. Richard inherited a throne surrounded by death. His consolers offer the usual glib solutions to mourning: time, logic, resolve, distraction. But none satisfies. The play suggests that sorrow does not end: It must be endured, faced, and accepted. Grief is a teacher and a constant companion. "The shadow of your sorrow," observes Bolingbroke, "hath destroyed the shadow of your face." To this Richard replies:

Say that again:
'The shadow of my sorrow'—ha, let's see.
'Tis very true: my grief lies all within,
And these external manners of laments
Are merely shadows to the unseen grief
That swells with silence in the tortured soul.

Modern experts have identified the pattern Shakespeare described. "Shadow grief," as they call it, is not overt, nor is it debilitating. The bereaved continue in a more or less normal life. But their sorrow is never completely resolved, nor can it be. It will always be part of their new existence, an "unseen grief that swells with silence."

By the sixteenth century societal constraints regarding what to do and say when faced with death had become particularly vexing. The bereaved were offered traditional platitudes: It is God's will, he is at peace, and so on. These well-meant expressions of sympathy do little to ease the devastation of losing a child, as Shakespeare was aware. "Everyone can master a grief but he that has it," he wrote in *Much Ado About Nothing*, two years after Hamnet's death.

Others expected Shakespeare to refrain from overt expressions of sorrow, or at least to mourn in quiet and within a suitable time frame. But Shakespeare's grief found its way into his plays for the rest of his career.

When Hamnet died, Shakespeare had been working on *King John*. What started as a desultory historical epic, filled with the same jingoism as *Richard II*, was after Hamnet's death transformed by some of the poet's most poignant verse. John's role is small, nearly unimportant. Political conflicts between good and evil are replaced with introspection. "I'll go with thee," declared a character who echoed Shakespeare's grief, "and find th'inheritance of this poor child, his little kingdom of a forcèd grave."

King John is a human play. In it, Cardinal Pandolf reprimands Constance for her displays of mourning: "You hold too heinous a respect of grief." Constance lashes out at his pious judgment: "He talks to me that never had a son." King Philip chimes in on the same note, "You are as fond of grief, as of your child." Constance replies:

Then have I reason to be fond of grief. . . .
O Lord, my boy, my Arthur, my fair son,
My life, my joy, my food, my all the world,
My widow-comfort, and my sorrows' cure!

This scene eloquently details acute grief—the overwhelming burden of sorrow that is often accompanied by a sense that the lost loved one is present. Shakespeare may well have felt the same. "I have heard you say that we shall see and know our friends in heaven," Constance tells Cardinal Pandolf. "If that be true, I shall see my boy again."

Shakespeare gave himself time to grieve his son, whether by choice or necessity. He completed the wildly successful *The First Part of Henry the Fourth* shortly after Hamnet's passing. Then his output was considerably diminished. He wrote only three plays between 1596 and 1598.

The Merry Wives of Windsor, begun within a few months after Hamnet's death in early 1597, is a comedy that has little to recommend it. Many of the elements for engrossing theater are there, but they do not combine well: The result is dull and lifeless. However, Giuseppe Verdi spotted hidden gems in the play. Himself a bereaved parent, Verdi often took inspiration from Shakespeare's work. His operatic version of *The Merry Wives of Windsor* shears away Shakespeare's uncharacteristic dross to deliver the masterpiece *Falstaff*.

Shakespeare also wrote the second part of *Henry the Fourth* in 1597 and followed it the next year with the brilliant comedy *Much Ado About Nothing*. This timeline is not surprising. It usually takes three to five years to put a death in perspective, often longer for bereaved parents. The first two years can be excruciating; it is remarkable that Shakespeare wrote anything at all.

The death of an only child (or a sole heir, as with Hamnet) carries a dual loss: Whatever future the parent envisioned with grandchildren and the family name is now gone forever. This reaction was part of Shakespeare's mourning. Hamnet would have inherited the large house and estate, the family coat of arms, and the Shakespeare sword. The playwright's work from this period is preoccupied with father–son relationships: the flawed older man's frustrated attempts to communicate what he has learned about life, the future, and the inevitability of time.

The sonnets also reveal a number of allusions to Hamnet. This is not surprising: Shakespeare started work on them in 1593 when London theaters closed in the face of epidemic. He finally finished the sonnets in 1600, four years after his child's death, but did not publish them until 1609, preferring instead to share them with friends.

The sonnets speak of the cruel destructions of time and how the youth addressed in the poems is immortalized in verse. In this light, discussions in the early sonnets of marriage and the possibility of future generations are especially poignant. Sonnets 55, 60, 65, and 68 were probably influenced by Hamnet's death. Of them all, however, 33 is most clearly a lament. As one scholar observed, the metaphor of "sun" for "son" identifies the addressee as Hamnet:

> . . . my sun one early morn did shine,
> With all triumphant splendour on my brow;
> But out, alack, he was but one hour mine;
> The region cloud hath masked him from me now.
> Yet him for this, my love no whit disdaineth:
> Suns of the world may stain, when heaven's sun staineth.

Shakespeare experienced a spiritual crisis after the death of Hamnet. This revealed itself in many aspects of Shakespeare's work, most tellingly in *Hamlet*, which he wrote in 1600. Both *Richard II* and *Hamlet* deal with self-absorbed men. The characters are melancholic and grieving, but where Richard revels in wit, Hamlet is faced with a believably real quandary: "To be or not to be" is more than an exercise in clever linguistics.

Hamlet also offers profound insight into the complex nature of masculine mourning. The obvious similarity of the names Hamlet and Hamnet aside, the play itself is preoccupied with twinning: The act of sublimation, doubling themes, the use of two points to describe a single complex meaning, a play within a play—all are delivered in a masterpiece of lyricism. The title character displays much of the terrifying anxiety and exhausting nature of grief while examining internal struggles that lead ultimately to transformation.

Hamlet's first soliloquy reveals his growing despair over the death of his father and his mother's remarriage. He has not yet heard the Ghost's story. It is the first hint that he is considering ending his life:

> O God, God,
> How weary, stale, flat, and unprofitable
> Seem to me all the uses of this world!

Near the end of the play, Hamlet has learned to live with his heartbreak. He throws himself into dangerous situations, but not in self-punishment. Rather, Hamlet is unconcerned. Shakespeare had a similar experience.

Friends of bereaved parents often despair that the grieving appear to have given up, when actually the opposite is true. Many parents say they have come to appreciate life in ways they did not before, now cherishing its preciousness and transience. Shakespeare expressed this awareness in the 1599 play *As You Like It*, when the just and carefree character Duke Senior "finds tongues in trees, books in the running brooks, sermons in stones, and good in every thing." Time spent in nature can indeed offer profound solace to the grieving, but Shakespeare did not ignore the daily realities of living with loss.

Through Hamlet the playwright acknowledged the terrible vulnerability of our existence. Having faced the worst that life can offer, he had lost his fear of the future and of death:

> There's a divinity that shapes our ends, rough hew them how we will. . . . There is special providence in the fall of a sparrow. If it be, 'tis not to come. If it be not to come, it will be now. If it be not now, yet it will come. The readiness is all. Since no man of aught he leaves knows, what is't to leave betimes? Let be.

Shortly after *Hamlet* was finished, in 1601, Shakespeare's father died. Shakespeare began work on *All's Well That Ends Well*, finishing sometime between 1603 and 1605. This is one of the poet's notorious "problem plays": an experiment in genre that blends dark themes and anguish with comic elements and unsettling endings.

The story surprises us with its compassionate view of a somewhat unsavory Bertram. It is also the only play in which Shakespeare opens with a speech by an ordinary woman: a mother and a widow. The opening scene sets the tone of loss that will be an undercurrent throughout the play. Bertram is taking his leave:

COUNTESS
In delivering my son from me, I bury a second husband.

BERTRAM
And I in going, madam, weep o'er my father's death anew.

As always with Shakespeare's comedies, the plot is too convoluted to adequately describe here (or anywhere, for that matter). Suffice it to say that amid the laughs there is an underlying theme that binds together grief and loss. The play is a creative meditation on death and renewal.

Grief often leads to a quest for meaning and new discoveries of what that entails. Crystal Park, a respected clinician whose research focuses primarily on bereavement and spirituality, has found that the bereaved must inevitably give some significance to the belief that their loved ones go on. Shakespeare was no exception. He was to return again and again to themes of belief, suffering, and reunion.

Shakespeare's career kept him away from his family, that much is certain, but that does not signify a lack of affection for his son. Love is not measured by time spent with a child, nor is grief measured by time spent without a child. Modern research has confirmed that parental bonds are usually immediate, persistent, and absolute.

Fifteen years after Hamnet's death, Shakespeare described in *The Winter's Tale* how the mere mention of a name still had the power to wound:

Prithee no more, cease. Thou know'st
He dies to me again when talked of.

One of Shakespeare's last plays, *King Lear*, is also his most grim. Written in 1605, nine years after Hamnet died, it is different from anything that came before.

Where Richard is plagued by shadow grief, Lear's mourning is described in violent terms: Tears break forth from him perforce, staining his cheeks, robbing his masculinity. This was a new side of sorrow. *Hamlet* is Shakespeare's great work on fathers and sons. *King Lear*, on the other hand, deals with the complicated relationships between fathers and daughters.

Shakespeare's eldest, Susanna, had married reasonably well. The youngest, Hamnet, was the favored twin while alive and now, in death, was treasured in memory. Shakespeare's love for his lost son was tempered by guilt over the time he had missed while Hamnet was alive; now the years had slipped away with his surviving children as well.

Susanna, two years older than her sister, was Shakespeare's favorite, but the fictional struggle between Lear and his youngest daughter, Cordelia, is closer to the acrimony Shakespeare felt with Judith. Both characters can communicate clearly but are incapable of deciphering their own intentions and needs, leading to the father's rebuke: "Nothing can come of nothing."

King Lear is a testament to a perennially late father's attempt to pour his love into his daughters. The play is steeped in regret. Today Lear's three daughters have become stereotypes: the assertive eldest, the gregarious rebel in the middle, and the much-loved youngest.

Early performances usually used the same actor for Cordelia and the mad king's companion, the Fool. This casting added a particular pathos to Lear's lament over his daughter, "And my poor fool is hanged," reminding the audience that Lear was cruelly and finally alone:

> She's gone for ever. . . . No, no life.
> Why should a dog, a horse, a rat have life,
> And thou no breath at all? O, thou wilt come no more,
> Never, never, never, never, never!

Shakespeare was fascinated with relationships between the bereaved and the deceased. Ten years after Hamnet's death and five years after the death of his father, Shakespeare wrote two plays that deal powerfully with what links us to our dead.

Macbeth, finished in 1606, includes heartbreaking passages of paternal loss: The characters are tied to their dead in grief and regret. "I must also feel it as a man," MacDuff laments after the murder of his family. "I cannot but remember such things were that were most precious to me." Memory and self-recrimination are universal aspects of bereavement. Such guilt could lead to madness and despair, as in *King Lear*, if not for MacDuff's hope of reunion:

> Sinful MacDuff,
> They were all struck for thee. Naught that I am,
> Not for their own demerits, but for mine,
> Fell slaughter on their souls. Heaven rest them now.

After completing *Macbeth* Shakespeare wrote another play on loss and guilt. *Timon of Athens* suggests that though we are bound to our dead, it is precisely in these ties that we may blot out the wrongs of the past. These continuing bonds provide a hope for presence and reunion.

Shakespeare would soon have need of solace. His brother Edmund, sixteen years his junior, had followed him to London to be an actor. Shakespeare was pleased. He had always taken a paternal interest in Edmund. Then in 1607, while the playwright was working on *Timon of Athens*, Edmund died. He was twenty-seven. That same year Shakespeare launched himself into a new genre: the romance.

Shakespeare's romances were a dramatic shift for the playwright. Situations that in earlier plays would have led to tragedy are now met with unexpected healing. His first three romances deal with reunion and the joy felt by those who realize that a loved one they thought was dead is actually alive. Shakespeare had touched upon this theme in 1598, two years after his son's death, in *Much Ado About Nothing*. Now he was to explore it fully.

The playwright started work on *Pericles* in late 1607. This was followed by *Cymbeline* in 1608–09 and *The Winter's Tale* in 1609–10. All three plays focus on similar themes of separation and reconciliation, death and rebirth.

In *Pericles*, the revival of Thaisa in her coffin has undertones of the miraculous. By the end of the play, Pericles, who believed his wife and daughter were dead, is reunited with both. *Cymbeline* tells of a jealous husband who orders his wife's

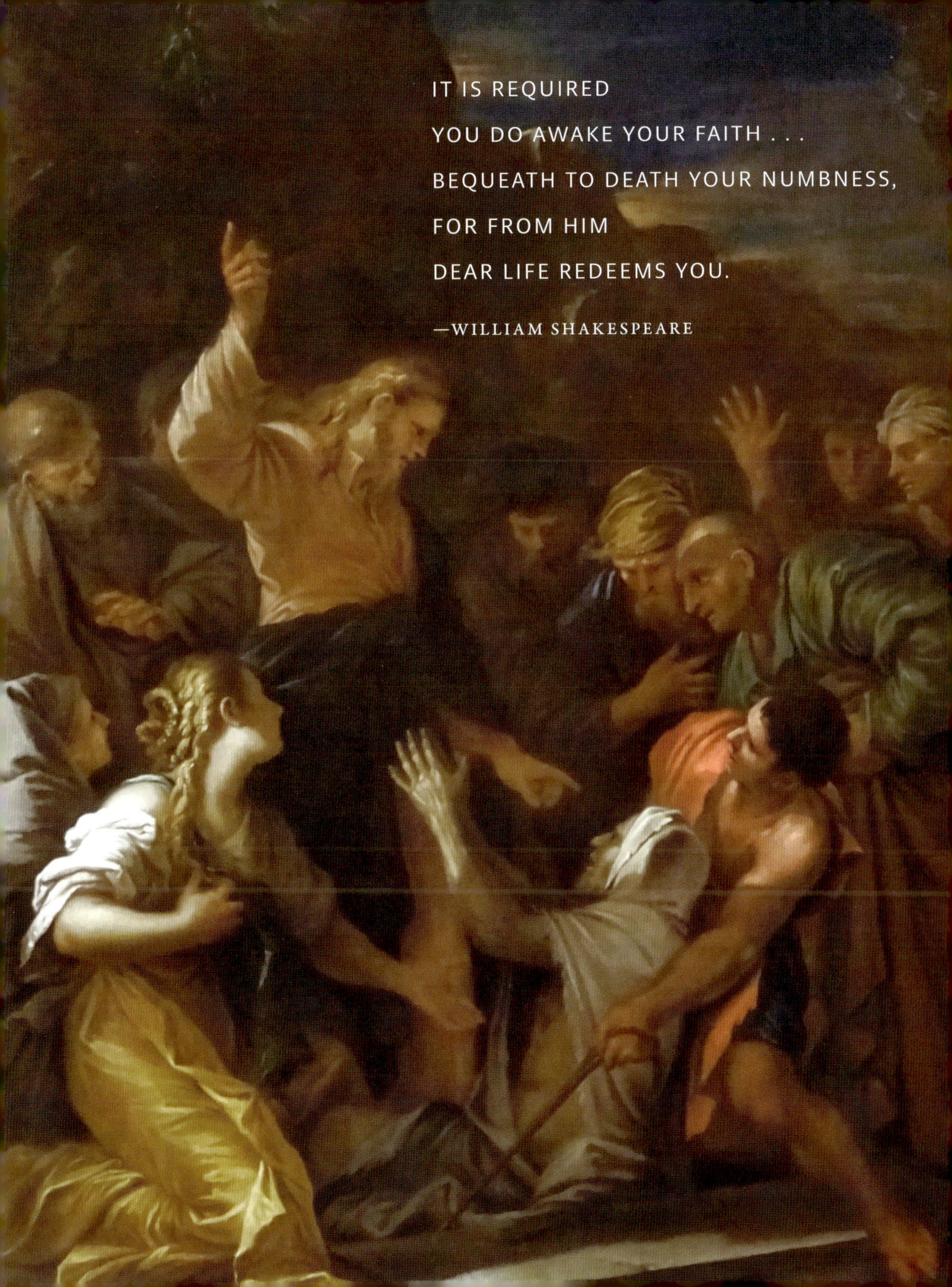

IT IS REQUIRED
YOU DO AWAKE YOUR FAITH . . .
BEQUEATH TO DEATH YOUR NUMBNESS,
FOR FROM HIM
DEAR LIFE REDEEMS YOU.

—WILLIAM SHAKESPEARE

death only to have her restored to him years later, vindicated and in good health. "Be cheerful, wipe thine eyes;" one character declares. "Some falls are means the happier to arise." In both plays, the audience knew the wives were alive.

This was not so in Shakespeare's next work. His mother died in 1608. After a brief hiatus, Shakespeare began writing a powerful study of human frailty, guilt, and forgiveness: *The Winter's Tale*.

Early in the play a doomed Mamillius, a surrogate for Hamnet, warns that "a sad tale's best for winter." Much of the performance takes place in suffering and bitter cold. After Mamillius's death, his mother, Hermione, dies from grief. Her husband, Leontes, had wronged her, believing her unfaithful. When the death of their son brings him to his senses, it is too late. For sixteen years he is wracked with guilt and regret, saying many a prayer over their graves.

Then in the coming of a new spring, Leontes is presented with a memorial statue of Hermione. He reaches to touch it—"O, she's warm!" he exclaims—and suddenly the cold stone has the heat of flesh and blood. It is not a statue but Hermione, who had been alive and in hiding all along. They embrace in silence. The moment has the force of a resurrection.

We are struck by the power of Hermione's forgiveness: Years have passed; her son is dead; she is reunited with the husband she still loves; the daughter that she thought was dead is returned. Rather than waste another moment in recrimination, Hermione instead offers only acceptance. W. H. Auden, lecturing on the romances in 1947, concluded that "like a fairy-tale story, this is the world as you want it to be, and nothing makes one more inclined to cry."

Shakespeare's loss had no such happy ending. Two more younger brothers died in 1612 and 1613. His daughters, his wife, and his sole remaining sibling might bring joy but never forgetfulness. They too mourned their loved ones. It comes as no surprise that Shakespeare kept writing about sorrow and the bonds of love beyond death. Through art he found a way to make peace with himself and his grief. Four hundred years later he is helping us to do the same.

(PAGE 185) Salvator Rosa,
The Raising of Lazarus, c1662-1673,
Condé Museum

WANDERING IN SOLITUDE

"These are the music and pictures of the most ancient religion."

> *For ever since the world was created, people have seen the earth and sky. Through everything God made, they can clearly see his invisible qualities—his eternal power and divine nature.*
>
> ROMANS 1:20A (NLT)

Since my daughter died, I often hike for hours and miles each day. I find solace in these jaunts through the Carolina woodlands. Does it help? Yes. And no. Many mourners relate that in nature they feel their dead loved ones near, joining them as surely as fish or birds or chattering squirrels. "Most wanderers have lost something," observes David Brown Morris, Emeritus Professor at the University of Virginia. "Solitude comes to embrace emotional experiences ranging from social isolation to cosmic interconnection." This has certainly been true for me.

Nature may not be safe, but it is *communal.* I usually walk along the creek, resting for up to an hour at a time on large rocks in the stream. Birds stop by, and deer, often in small herds. Now and then an otter passes, sometimes quite close, unaware of my presence or uninterested. Beavers, though nocturnal, rear their heads to see what I'm up to.

There's an occasional black bear, terrifying but relatively congenial, as long as we both understand which of us runs the wood. (It isn't me.) Our local bobcat is intriguingly bold. I've spotted him around dawn. He approaches the water, pauses, looks my way, then drinks, stealing glances. Bobcats rarely stalk large mammals. This one seems to have little interest in me other than as a potential threat.

The deep wood is a dangerous place. I make plenty of noise before sitting down on whichever rock I find that day, splashing through the creek, coughing, or daring a Pavarotti impersonation. This chases away the snakes and small critters. Even lumbering skunks and porcupines saunter off if I alert them to my presence in advance.

More than once, alone in the wood, I've whispered lines from Wendell Berry's poem "The Peace of Wild Things." He observes that nature's inhabitants do not burden themselves with anticipation of grief. The poet refers to *inner* quiet in his verse, but at times I chuckle at the complete lack of *outer* peace on my walks. Once the birds and frogs have grown accustomed to me, there's no shutting them up. Sudden silences alert me to keep an eye out for predators.

Hawks float overhead, circling, sometimes hunting, but often as not seeming to catch the wind out of pure joy. One memorable week, a male broad-wing joined me for breakfast each morning. It was early spring. I walked to the creek, about a mile into the wood, and settled onto a large boulder beside the stream. There I ate fruit and nuts. Within minutes, a young hawk gracefully settled on a branch no more than ten feet overhead. He often stayed there as long as I did.

Samuel Taylor Coleridge and William Wordsworth, working together on *Lyrical Ballads*, suggest that when wandering alone "accidents of light and shade" may transform the known and familiar into places of unforeseen discovery. Wordsworth reportedly walked some 175,000 miles in his lifetime. He spoke of "the bliss of solitude" that combines specific locations with reality and memory.

Coleridge and Wordsworth helped to launch the Romantic Age in English literature. They saw reconciliation between self, nature, and the invisible world as possible and desirable. There was no Romantic School, per se, merely brilliant, like-minded and highly creative individuals who indelibly influenced nineteenth-century culture.

They were a cantankerous lot. Most did not consider themselves part of the fraternity and sought distance from such epithets. In Germany, for example, to be called a *Romantiker*, or romantic writer, was an insult, not a compliment. The word *Romantische* was usually spoken with a sneer by those we now describe as, well, Romantics.

One early Romantic tradition held that a person could transform his perception of the world by looking *inward* while reaching *outward*. In this regard, Romantics acknowledged a profound debt to nature, without which there could be no artistic creation at all. "—these are the music and pictures of the most ancient religion," Ralph Waldo Emerson observed.

Nature's benefits for the bereaved have been acknowledged for centuries. Francis Bacon prescribed "contemplations of nature" for sadness. This led English poet Joseph Addison to observe that panoramas of nature "are able to disperse grief and melancholy." One modern researcher, based in Montana, concluded that experiences of weeping and other deep emotions in response to nature provide transformation and unity of mind and body.

Put another way, in nature our grief is not *easier* but may at times be *eased.* Wandering grounds us in ways we may miss otherwise, providing unhurried accidents of clarity that assure us we are not alone.

Another inveterate walker, Friedrich Rückert, was a post-Romantic poet whose work is at once hopeful *and* pessimistic about life's transience. In a deliciously wry and popular poem, Rückert writes in the voice of al-Khidr, the eternally youthful wanderer of Islamic tradition first alluded to in the Qur'an.

Khidr visits the same location every five hundred years. At first it is a city. *How long has this been here?* Khidr asks. "It's always been this way," a man tells him, "as it will forever and a day." Five centuries later, Khidr finds a vast grassy knoll in the same spot. A shepherd is tending his flock as he plays a fife. *How long has the city been gone?* Khidr asks. "Things come and go their way," the shepherd replies. "This has been my pasture forever and a day."

Another five hundred years, and on the same road is a sea. A fisherman gives Khidr an identical answer, as does a woodsman—yet another five centuries later—who insists that his ancestors had always lived in the forest that now thrives there. In the final stanza of Rückert's poem, the wandering Khidr returns:

> 500 years went by and then
> I passed that way again.
> I came upon a city: the hue, the cry,
> the bustle of people rushing by.
> I asked, *How long has this city been here?*
> *Where is the wood, the sea, the fife?*
> They yelled back at me in their strife:
> "It's always been this way,
> as it will forever and a day."
> I'll wait 500 years and then
> I will pass this way again.

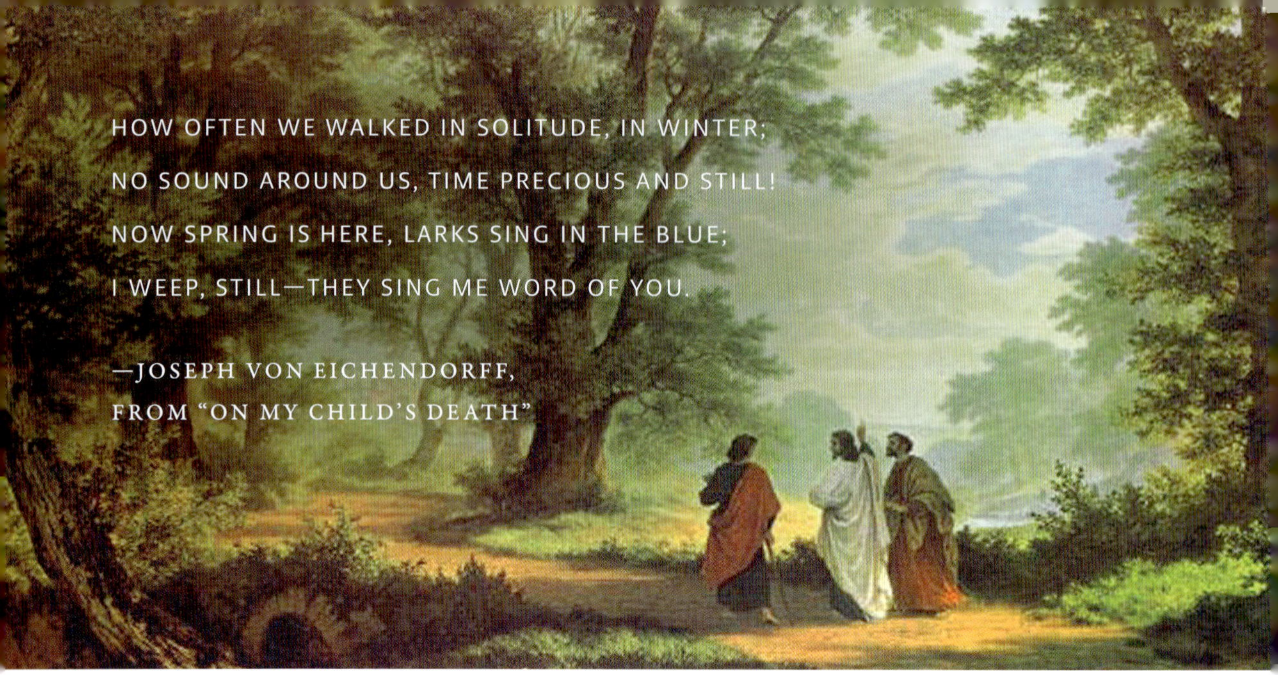

Time brings slowness to grief. Respected expert Dennis Klass notes in his book *The Spiritual Lives of Bereaved Parents* that all mourners must adjust psychologically and socially to loss, whether we would or not. But there is something more going on. We also face a new "transcendent reality," as Klass puts it, in which we see the spiritual world with new eyes. This may include changed views of the sacred, nature, and time itself.

For example, in our new calendar of grief, many of us seem to measure days and years differently. Three months after our loved one dies, we may feel as though only a day has passed. After a year, it seems no more than a week; five years, and the pain is as fresh as last month. Time seems to shrink. Conversely, it also seems endless. Our new perception gives weight and meaning to the briefest moments, as though we might slip sideways and disappear.

Grief often has an aspect of delayed, continuous shock. Because of this, walking in nature holds great risks. We are not as alert as we should be. We may miss the dangers around us. But nature also offers unexpected rewards. "Everybody needs beauty as well as bread," observed John Muir, "places to play in and pray in, where nature may heal and give strength to body and soul alike." In the deep wood, surrounded by so much life, I feel my daughter near and the concern of an attentive God. I may wander in solitude, but I am not alone.

Robert Zünd,
Gang nach Emmaus (Road to Emmaus), 1877,
St. Gallen Museum of Art

OUR LOVE GOES ON

"It seemed she was a messenger of God."

> *Dear friends, let us love one another, for love comes from God. Everyone who loves has been born of God and knows God.*
>
> 1 JOHN 4:7

I dream of my daughter nearly four months to the day after her death. I run to Jess, hold her tight, kiss her. "You don't have to hug me every time you see me, Dad," she says, something she often muttered as an adult. "Yes, I do," I reply, as always.

Clarity is a weak word for such a dream, if indeed dream it is. It has the kind of hyperreality that is described by many mourners: far more "real" than any other dreams. My day-to-day existence is a poor copy.

A vision? Perhaps. Experiences like these are almost commonplace for the bereaved. They relate being surprised at the *reality* of them. In fact, more mourners have had such waking or sleeping visions than have not. In a tangible way, our bond engenders this continuing connection.

Dreams of our dead reflect a deep need for spiritual union after a loss. They facilitate adjustment to the death by helping us process trauma and understand the many complex emotions of mourning. These *grief dreams*, as researchers call them, are linked to our spiritual awareness of self in relation to others. They often awaken a growing sense of compassion while serving as a coping mechanism.

"Each time I dream about her (and I dream only of her)," Roland Barthes wrote of his late mother, "it is in order to see her, believe her to be alive, but other, separate." Her death led the notorious atheist Barthes to rethink what a life of faith might mean, making a distinction between what he saw as the ills of organized religion and his mother's unwavering religious devotion.

Shortly after my dream of Jess, I came across this song by Friedrich Rückert, written in July, 1834, after the deaths of his two youngest children. It speaks to me today as if the poet had written it that first summer of my sorrow:

> I often looked up in the
> night to view the Evenstar,
> and always, it seemed, she
> was a messenger of God.
> But I never saw her shine
> in quite the way she does
> now falling full upon
> these distant graves.
> As if she grasps the
> essence of things;
> as befits a herald of peace
> she speaks: "Look up
> from the grave and learn.
> Your dead shine like
> the star above you;
> you flow on and they rest,
> as you will rest, in God."

Rückert is using a common occurrence—seeing a star—to address a paradox that disturbs many believers: *Our loved ones are with God, yet it seems that they are also here with us.* The poet often speaks of feeling his dead children near, yet he knows they rest in God while his life flows on.

His Evenstar in this poem refers to the planet Venus or its eastern Semitic counterpart, Ishtar. Writing of the star of love, or the evening star, was a common trope in nineteenth-century poetry. Readers usually spotted the reference and expected mooning verse or mourning lament.

Here the grieving father surprises us. He sees the star as a messenger from God, and with good reason. Venus is just as often called the Morning Star, another appellation of Jesus. The poet's astronomical allusion underscores his suggestion that our physical and invisible worlds interact. We might agree with him.

But something isn't right.

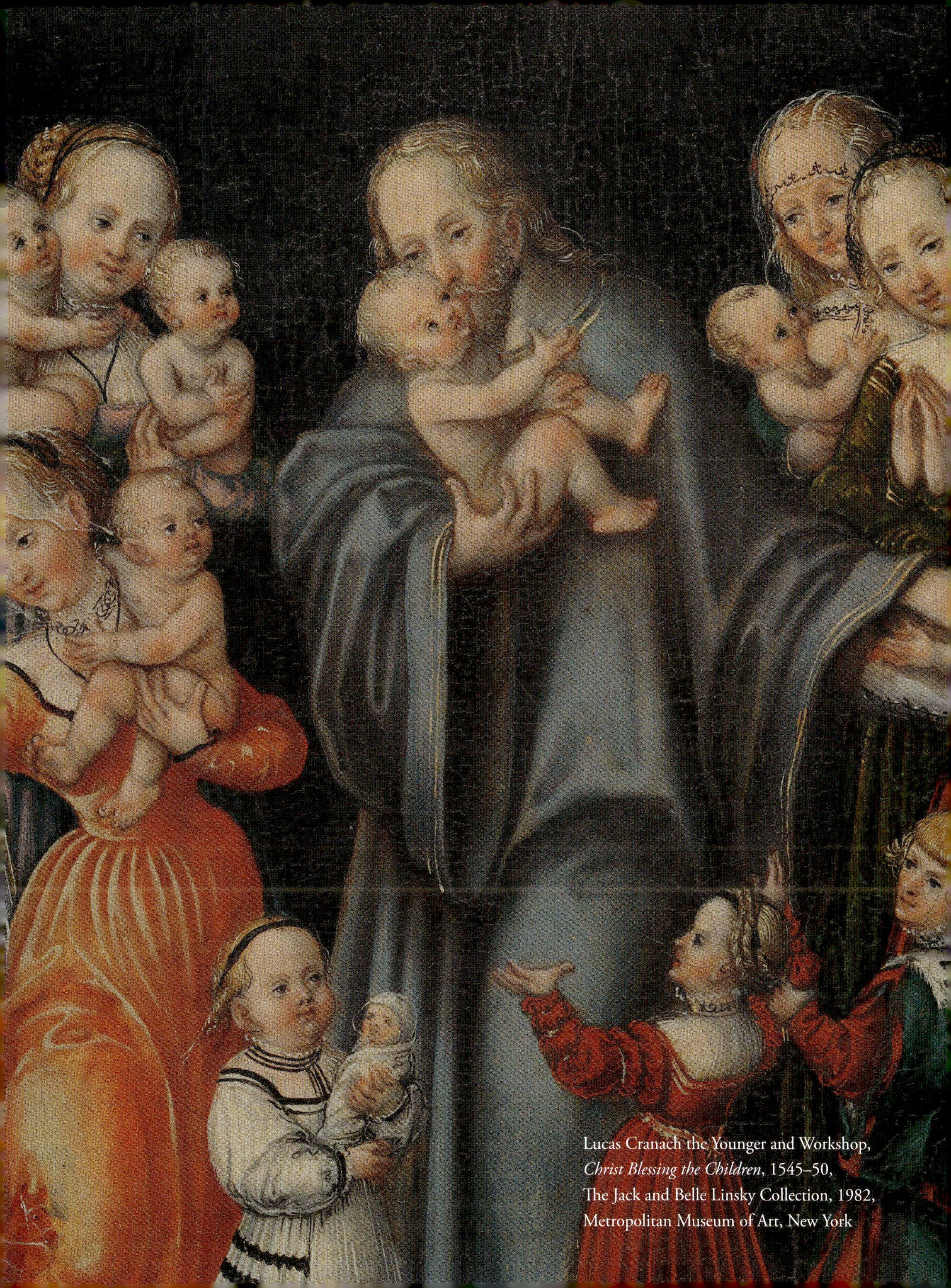

Lucas Cranach the Younger and Workshop,
Christ Blessing the Children, 1545–50,
The Jack and Belle Linsky Collection, 1982,
Metropolitan Museum of Art, New York

Our dead are still dead. We are alone with a love that seems to have no place to go. Death did not sever the bonds we feel with those we have lost. Today is another day without them.

Today we may pause over memories of what *was*. These can be a great comfort. We may also wonder what our loved ones *might say* if they were here. *Would he be proud of how I'm handling my sorrow? Would she cry with me, knowing how much I miss her? What gentle words might they say to me now?*

Today these quiet suppositions are a source of strength in their absence. They are a healthy way to continue a connection that will remain with us all of our days. This is a good thing. After all, relationships evolve in life. It is only natural that they take on new shape in separation.

Today, this very day, we know our love does not end. Our bonds continue; our dreams will one day be reality. We never have to lose them again.

THE TRUTH IS THAT WE ARE BELOVED, EVEN IN OUR CURRENT CONDITION, BY SOMEONE; *we have loved and been loved. We have also known the abyss of love lost to death or rejection, and that it somehow leads to new life. We have been redeemed and saved by love, even as a few times we have been nearly destroyed.*

—ANNE LAMOTT

NOTHING, ABSOLUTELY NOTHING, CAN BE DONE WITH THE THOUSAND MISERIES OF LIFE, *our fate of sin and death; all existence is too small to fill this gaping hole. Accept it: Everything fails, there's no way out! Save for a miracle; no, not* a *miracle,* the *miracle, the miracle of God, God's incomprehensible, saving intervention and compassion, his all-encompassing renewal from death to life, God's creative call, God's word of life:* Resurrection!

—KARL BARTH

WHY *A HOPE OBSERVED*?

Love and hope are part of grief—for me, the part that matters most. Grief is love. Love is an act of hope. Hope can be an aspect of grief. These emotions seem inseparable. And maybe they are.

As respected bereavement expert Colin Murray Parkes famously observes: "The pain of grief is just as much a part of life as the joy of love; it is, perhaps, the price we pay for love." We will never stop loving those we have lost, never stop hoping for reunion the other side of death. Grief is closely tied to our love, our hope, and the meaning we find in life.

This is why psychologists Mai-Britt Guldin (Aarhus University) and Carla Leget (University of Humanistic Studies in Utrecht) note that grief cannot be removed, treated, or cured. Suggestions to the contrary are often viewed by mourners as disrespectful and intrusive. "Expressing and honoring our grief can be seen as an expression of the very essence of our being," they write. "Grief is as much a fundamental part of being human and developing as a human being as love is. There is no end to grief because there is no end to love."

For example, when philosopher Nicholas Wolterstorff loses his son Eric to a climbing accident in Austria on June 11, 1983, he says that he knows only that he loves his child. His book, *Lament for a Son*, is an expression of that love. Twenty-eight years later, in 2011, he tells an audience at the Mayo Clinic's The Veritas Forum that when he wrote his lament he knew nothing of grief, nor did he have the energy to understand it. "The book is not about grief; it's a cry of grief." In 2024, he adds that his lament is not a *generic* cry of grief, but rather, "*My* cry of grief."

German poet Friedrich Rückert loses his two youngest children to scarlet fever. He too gives voice to love through some five hundred poems of lament, written in the first six months after their passing, known today as *Songs on the Death of Children* (Kindertotenlieder). Like Wolterstorff and Rückert, C. S. Lewis also leaves a poignant record of his heartbreak at the loss of his wife in *A Grief Observed.*

I treasure these books. Each has pride of place on my shelf. I too know the pain of unanswered keening, the desperation of a love that seems to have no place to go. I observe and honor their grief.

And something more.

In the ten years since my daughter died, I've devoured books, papers, poetry, and laments from across the globe on many aspects of loss. I'm often struck by the hope so many mourners feel. Even those who do not believe in an afterlife; those who have no place for God in their worldview: They too write of hope that their loved ones continue on, that reunion is possible. Despite all reason, in the face of our daily reality of loss, hope persists. This is their gift to us, a view not detached but visceral, vital, as much a part of our lives as it is theirs—*a hope observed.*

Acknowledgements

Many thanks to Jeff Bilbro; Bob Edmonson; Lorraine Hedtke; Ann Johnson; Tim Jones; Rudolph Kreutner; Lillian Miao; Alisa Ruddell; Libby Sweatt-Lambert, her staff, and participants in the bereavement support groups at the Fort Lawn Community Center (South Carolina); the staff of the Chester County Library (South Carolina); Johannes Wilkes; Philip and Janet Yancey; and my true love, my wife: Thank you all.

About the Author

David Bannon is the author of two previous books on grief: *Wounded in Spirit: Advent Art and Meditations* (Paraclete Press, 2018) and *Songs on the Death of Children: Selected Poems from* Kindertotenlieder (Toplight/McFarland, 2022). He taught college for many years and has appeared on The Discovery Channel, A&E, The History Channel, NPR, Fox News, and in *The Wall Street Journal.* David and his wife currently live in South Carolina.

Permissions and Credits

The following essays first appeared in *Front Porch Republic* (frontporchrepublic.com): William James's Grief (December 17, 2024); Mary Shelley's Grief (December 5, 2024); Joan of Arc's Grief (November 15, 2024); Else Lasker-Schüler's Grief (November 6, 2024); Falling is Not Failure, and Getting up is Not the Point (October 22, 2024); Sigmund Freud's Grief (August 26, 2024); Safe at Last (August 6, 2024); The Heartbreak behind the EEG (July 30, 2024); The Consolation of Silence (July 18, 2024); Grief in Eternity (July 10, 2024); Emerson's Grief (June 24, 2024); Lincoln's Grief (June 13, 2024); 98.6 Percent of Us Sense our Dead (June 3, 2024); Wandering in Solitude (May 20, 2024); Shakespeare's Grief (April 23, 2024); Facing Loss with Job and *Faust* (April 8, 2024); A *Really Real* God (March 29, 2024); Eisenhower's Grief (March 21, 2024); Twenty Years with Philip (March 6, 2024); Roosevelt's Grief (February 22, 2024); Confession (January 26, 2024).

The following essays first appeared in *Christ and Pop Culture* (ChristAndPopCulture.com): The Grace of Phantom Pain (October 7, 2024); Let's Talk About Abbott and Costello Movies (and a Communion of Grief) (August 30, 2024); As Grief Metaphors Go, Godzilla Is Better than Most (July 8, 2024); A Separate Bargain: How Grief Is an Act of Love (July 1, 2024); Love and Loss with Metalcore (June 10, 2024).

"Over all graves grass must grow" is from *Wounded in Spirit: Advent Art and Meditations* by David Bannon. Copyright © 2018 by David Bannon. Reprinted by permission of Paraclete Press. All rights reserved.

"The maid brings news of their"; "Nightwatch"; "Once I held the reality of you"; "You are a shadow in the day"; "We each face an image"; "500 years went by and then"; "In loss it is difficult to begin"; "O Christmas tree"; an earlier version of "From the silver bloom of morning," published here as "From a silver bloom of dawn emerges"; "*Christmas*—fresh and healthy"; adapted material in "A Separate Bargain"; "Love and Loss with Metalcore," "The Heartbreak behind the EEG," "The Promise of Easter"; and other brief excerpts are from *Songs on the Death of Children: Selected Poems from* Kindertotenlieder by Friedrich Rückert, translated and annotated by David Bannon, © 2023 David Bannon, by permission of McFarland & Company, Inc., Box 611, Jefferson NC 28640. www.mcfarlandbooks.com.

Linda Pastan's "The Five Stages of Grief" first appeared in *Chicago Review 28*(4) (Spring, 1977): 128-9. © 1977 Linda Pastan. Reprinted by permission of W. W. Norton & Company, Inc.

All references to "In Memory of Sigmund Freud" are to *W. H. Auden: Collected Poems*, ed. Edward Mendelson (Vintage, 1991): 273-276.

"Phantomschmerz" is © Sony/atv Music Publishing (Germany) Gmbh, Emma's Park Music. Songwriters: Madeline Juno and Oliver Samuel Epsom.

"I'd Rather Go Blind" is © BMG Platinum Songs o/b/o Arc Music Corp. Songwriters: Ellington Jordan and Billy Foster with Etta James.

The images in this book are exact, faithful photographic reproductions of two-dimensional, public domain works of art taken from Wikimedia Commons (additionally page 19: Photograph by GoldenArtists, CC BY-SA 4 / page 185: Photograph by Pierre Poschadel, CC BY-SA 4.0 / page 193: CC0). The works of art themselves are in the public domain. Every attempt has been made "to reproduce the underlying works with absolute fidelity" in accordance with the United States District Court for the Southern District of New York ruling that "exact photographic copies of public domain works of art would not be copyrightable under United States law because they are not original." The images in this book are "'slavish copies' of public domain works of art" as defined by the court's ruling; as such, "Copyright is not available in these circumstances." [Bridgeman Art Library, Ltd., Plaintiff v. Corel Corporation, 36 F. Supp. 2d 191 (S.D.N.Y. 1999); see also Bridgeman Art Library v. Corel Corp., 25 F.Supp.2d 421 (S.D.N.Y. 1998)].

Selected Bibliography

Our Permissions and Credits section lists the Friedrich Rückert poems that appear in this book and where to find them. Academic papers are indicated by author in the readings and may easily be located on the Internet. This bibliography focuses on some of the books I cited or referenced, noting those I recommend, and that are considered important in their fields.

A good biography or memoir is always a pleasure. I enjoyed Anne Mellor's *Mary Shelley: Her Life, Her Fiction, Her Monsters* (Routledge, 2012). Likewise, Edmund Morris's Pulitzer- and National Book Award-winning trilogy (*The Rise of Theodore Roosevelt, Theodore Rex,* and *Colonel Roosevelt*). I also recommend *The Lion's Pride: Theodore Roosevelt and His Family in Peace and War* (Oxford University Press, 1999). Jean Edward Smith wrote one of the best single-volume biographies of his subject, *Eisenhower in War and Peace* (Random House, 2013). Abraham Lincoln's grief is detailed with compassion and precision in Jon Meacham's *And There Was Light: Abraham Lincoln and the American Struggle* (Random House, 2022) and Joshua Wolf Shenk's *Lincoln's Melancholy: How Depression Challenged a President and Fueled His Greatness* (Mariner Books, 2006). Two other rich sources: *The Collected Works of Abraham Lincoln*, v1, ed. Roy Basler (Rutgers University Press, 1953) and *Abraham Lincoln's Speeches and Letters: 1832-1865*, rev. ed., ed. Paul Angle (Dutton & Col, 1957). *Psychoanalysis and Faith: The Letters of Sigmund Freud and Oskar Pfister* (Porirua, 2025), eds. Heinrich Meng and Ernst Freud, trans. Eric Mosbacher, offers insight into the subjects' complex relationship, as does *Sigmund Freud and Oskar Pfister on Religion: The Beginning of an Endless Dialogue* (Routledge, 2023) by Carlos Domínguez-Morano, trans. Francisco Javier Montero. Volume three of Ernest Jones's multivolume *The Life and Work of Sigmund Freud* (Basic Books, 1957) addresses the loss of Freud's daughter and grandson. I often revisit Donald Spoto's *Joan: The Mysterious Life of the Heretic Who Became a Saint* (HarperOne, 2009) as a rational introduction by a respected biographer and theologian. Régine Pernoud's *Joan of Arc: By Herself and Her Witnesses* (Scarborough House, 1990) is a groundbreaking work that is worth a read, as is Helen Castor's delightfully chatty *Joan of Arc: A History* (Harper, 2015). And speaking of chatty, Barbara Eden's *Jeannie Out of the Bottle* (Crown Archetype/Random House, 2011) has a moving chapter on her son. Chris Costello also offers insights in a biography of her father, *Lou's On First* (St. Martin's Press, 1981). I recommend Isabel Allende's *Paula* (HarperVia, 1994), trans. Margaret Sayers Peden, for her remarkable sense of family and place in loss; and Celia Correas Zapata's *Isabel Allende: Life and Spirits*, trans. Margaret Sayers Peden (Arte Público Press, 2002). While C. S. Lewis's *A Grief Observed* (HarperOne, 1961, 1996) is justifiably famous, please don't overlook *The Collected Letters of C.S. Lewis, vIII: Narnia, Cambridge, and Joy 1950-1963*, ed. Walter Hooper (HarperCollins, 2007). This also goes for Nicholas Wolterstorff's *Lament for a Son* (Eerdmans, 1987). His later thoughts on loss are equally important, especially in *Grief: Is There More Than Moving On?* (VeriTalks) (The Veritas Forum, 2013) and *Living with Grief* (Cascade Books, 2024). Another bereaved father, Lewis Smedes, writes on the death of his infant child in *My God and I: A Spiritual Memoir* (Eerdmans, 2013). To learn about William James, Ellen Kappy Suckiel offers a rigorous overview in *Heaven's Champion: William James's Philosophy of Religion* (University of Notre Dame Press, 1998). Otherwise, I suggest going straight to James's books: *Human Immortality: Two Supposed Objections to the Doctrine*, third ed. (Archibald Constable & Co., 1899), *The Varieties of Religious Experience: A Study in Human Nature* (Longmans, Green & Co, 1902), and *The Principles of Psychology*, v2 (MacMillan & Co., 1922). This is also true with William Shakespeare, who needs no introduction, though I'm particularly fond of *The Oxford Shakespeare: The Complete Works*, second ed. (Oxford University Press, 2005). Ralph Waldo Emerson is also enriching when we read his own words: *Essays: The First and Second Series* (Houghton Mifflin, 1883) and *The Selected Letters of Ralph Waldo Emerson* (Columbia University Press, 1997). There isn't a lot on Hans Berger in English, but if science biographies are of interest, Cornelius Borck gives Berger a fair hearing in *Brainwaves: A Cultural History of Electroencephalography* (Routledge, 2018), trans. Ann Hentschel. Robert Newton writes a solid introduction and translates some evocative verse in his collection *Your Diamond Dreams Cut Open My Arteries: Poems by Else Lasker-Schüler* (University of North Carolina Press, 1982). For a pleasant trip to Egypt, try Bob Brier's *Egyptomania: Our Three Thousand Year Obsession with the Land of the Pharaohs* (St. Martin's Press, 2013), Toby Wilkinson's *The Nile: A Journey Downriver Through Egypt's Past and Present* (Penguin, 2014), and Barbara Mertz's *Red Land, Black Land: Daily Life in Ancient Egypt* (HarperCollins, 2009).

Turning to books on the Holy Bible, Frederick Buechner speaks candidly about his loss in *Telling the Truth* (Harper & Row, 1977) and *Secrets in the Dark: A Life in Sermons* (HarperSanFrancisco, 2006). John Donne also has his say in the eminently readable *A Companion in Crisis: A Modern Paraphrase of John Donne's Devotions*, ed. and paraphrased by Philip Yancey (Illumify, 2021). Yancey tackles the challenges of suffering with *The Question that Never Goes Away* (Zondervan, 2013) and his memoir, *Where the Light Fell: A Memoir* (Convergent, 2021). Holocaust survivors also face this difficult subject, notably in Ekkehard Schuster and Reinhold Boschert-Kimmig's *Hope against Hope: Johann Baptist Metz and Elie Wiesel Speak Out on the Holocaust* (Paulist Press, 1999) and Viktor Frankl's *The Unheard Cry for Meaning: Psychotherapy and Humanism* (Simon & Schuster, 1978). I find these volumes on Job helpful: Ann Astell, *Job, Boethius, and Epic Truth* (Cornell University Press, 1994); Stephen Vicchio, *The Book of Job: A History of Interpretation and a Commentary* (Wipf & Stock, 2020); Harold Kushner, *The Book of Job: When Bad Things Happened to a Good Person* (Penguin Random House, 2012); and Stephen Mitchell's informative notes and remarkable translation of *The Book of Job* (Harper Perennial, 1994). Kushner also talks about death and sorrow in *The Lord Is My Shepherd: Healing Wisdom of the Twenty-third Psalm* (Knopf, 2003). Other books that cover the psalms of lament: Claude Goldsmid Montefiore, *The Book of Psalms* (MacMillan and Co., 1901); Kristin Swenson, *Living Through Pain: Psalms and the Search for Wholeness* (Baylor University Press, 2005); and a collection of insightful readings, *Lament in Jewish Thought: Philosophical, Theological, and Literary Perspectives*, eds. Ilit Ferber and Paula Schwebel (de Gruyter, 2014). Étienne Gilson suggests that thinking on these questions is worthwhile in *God and Philosophy*, second ed. (Yale University Press, 1941, 2002). Two more authors have been close companions in my grief: Abraham Heschel, *Man Is Not Alone: A Philosophy of Religion* (Farrar, Straus and Giroux, 1951), *The Insecurity of Freedom: Essays on Human Existence* (Farrar, Straus and Giroux, 1966), and *The Prophets: Two Volumes in One* (Prince Press, 2000); and James Kugel, *The God of Old: Inside the Lost World of the Bible* (Free Press, 2003), *The Great Poems of the Bible: A Reader's Companion with New Translations* (Free Press, 2012), and *The Great Shift: Encountering God in Biblical Times* (Houghton Mifflin Harcourt, 2017).

If theodicy asks why we suffer, we may also wonder how much we dare believe. A few books that have meaning to me and are referenced in this volume: Marcus Borg and John Dominic Crossan, *The First Christmas: What the Gospels Really Teach About Jesus's Birth* (HarperOne, 2007); Christopher Cook's surprisingly helpful *Hearing Voices, Demonic and Divine: Scientific and Theological Perspectives* (Routledge, 2019); John Dominic Crossan, *The Essential Jesus: What Jesus Really Taught* (HarperSanFrancisco, 1994) and *The Birth of Christianity: Discovering What Happened in the Years Immediately After the Execution of Jesus* (HarperCollins e-books, 1998); Benedict Groeschel, *Behold, He Comes: Meditations on the Incarnation* (St. Anthony Messenger Press, 2001); David Hay, *Religious Experience Today: Studying the Facts* (Mowbray, 1990); Søren Kierkegaard, *Purity of Heart Is to Will One Thing*, trans. Douglas Steere (Harper Torchbooks, 1956); Thomas Merton's *The Seven Storey Mountain* (Harcourt Brace, 1948) and *Love and Living*, eds. Naomi Burton Stone and Patrick Hart (Harvest/HBJ, 1979); John Milton's *Paradise Lost Books IX and X*, ed. R. E. C. Houghton (Oxford University Press, 1969); Henri Nouwen, *Bread for the Journey: A Daybook of Wisdom and Faith* (HarperOne, 1997) and *Love, Henri: Letters on the Spiritual Life* (Convergent, 2016); John O'Donohue, *Anam Cara* (HarperCollins, 1997) and *Eternal Echoes* (HarperCollins, 1999); and Franz Rosenzweig, *The Star of Redemption*, trans. Barbara Ellen Galli (University of Wisconsin Press, 2005).

I mention poets and musicians. Here are a few of the sources: All references to "In Memory of Sigmund Freud" are to *W. H. Auden: Collected Poems*, ed. Edward Mendelson (Vintage, 1991); Emily Dickinson, *The Complete Poems of Emily Dickinson*, ed. Thomas Johnson (Little, Brown & Co., 1890, 1960) and *The Poems of Emily Dickinson*, v2, ed. Ralph W. Franklin (The Belknap Press of Harvard University Press, 1998); Etta James, Ellington

Jordan and Billy Foster's "I'd Rather Go Blind" is © BMG Platinum Songs o/b/o Arc Music Corp; Frederic Lawrence Knowles, *On Life's Stairway* (L. C. Page & Co., 1901); Henry Wadsworth Longfellow, *Poems of Henry Wadsworth Longfellow* (Crowell, 1901) and *The Sonnets of Henry Wadsworth Longfellow*, ed. Ferris Greenslet (Houghton, Mifflin & Co., 1907); John Muir, *My First Summer in the Sierra* (Houghton Mifflin, 1911) and *The Yosemite* (The Century Company, 1912); Linda Pastan's "The Five Stages of Grief" first appeared in *Chicago Review 28*(4) (Spring, 1977): 128-9, © 1977 Linda Pastan, reprinted by permission of W. W. Norton & Company, Inc.; Alfred Tennyson, *In Memoriam*, ed. William Rolfe (Houghton Mifflin, 1895); Mark Twain, *Autobiography of Mark Twain*, v1 (University of California Press, 2010); Marie Josephine Bennett and David Gracon, eds., *Music and Death: Interdisciplinary Readings and Perspectives* (Emerald Publishing, 2020) includes an introspective paper on metal and grief by the artist Nachthexe (Jasmine Hazel Shadrack); Robert Walser discusses metal masses for the greater glory of God in *Running with the Devil: Power, Gender, and Madness in Heavy Metal Music* (Wesleyan University Press, 1993); Peter Hühn, *Facing Loss and Death: Narrative and Eventfulness in Lyric Poetry* (De Gruyter, 2016); William Wordsworth and Samuel Taylor Coleridge, *Lyrical Ballads* (J. and A. Arch, 1798) and Wordsworth's *Poems in Two Volumes* (Longman, Hurst, Rees and Orme, 1807).

Some of the German works referenced in this book: *Dietrich Bonhoeffer Werke, Widerstandund Ergebung: Briefe und Aufzeichnungenaus der Haft*, v8, eds. Christian Gremmels, et al. (Gütersloher Verlagshaus, 1998, 2011); Martin Buber, *Ich und Du* (Shocken Verlag, 1923); Meister Eckhart (Eckhart von Hochheim), *Reden der Unterweisung* (Insel-Verlag, 1963): Sigmund Freud, *Briefe 1873-1939* (S. Fischer, 1960); Johann Wolfgang von Goethe, *Goethes Werke: Vollständige Ausgabe letzter Hand*, v1 (J. G. Cotta'sche Buchhandlung, 1827), *Goethes Briefe an die Gräfin Auguste zu Stolberg, Verwitwete Gräfin Von Bernstorff* (Brockhaus, 1881), *Goethes Briefe*, v4, 01 Januar 1779 - 07 November 1780 (Hermann Böhlau, 1889), *Goethes Werke in zwei Bänden*, ed. Gerhard Stenzel (Bergland-Buch, 1891), *Goethes Sämtliche Werke*, v5, ed. Franz Schultz (Theodor Knaur Nachf, c.1920), *Gedenkausgabe der Werke, Briefe und Gespräche*, ed. Ernst Beutler (Artemis. 1948-54); Madeline Juno and Oliver Samuel Epsom's "Phantomschmerz" is © Sony/atv Music Publishing (Germany) Gmbh, Emma's Park Music; Martin Luther, *D. Martin Luthers Werke, Kritische Gesamtausgabe*, v23 (Hermann Böhlaus Nachfolger, 1901); Rainer Maria Rilke, *Das Stunden-Buch* (Insel-Verlag, 1905), *Erste Gedichte* (Insel-Verlag, 1913), *Duineser Elegien* (Insel-Verlag, 1923), *Briefe*, 2 vols. (Insel, 1950); Rüdiger Safranski, *Goethe: Kunstwerk des Lebens: Biographie* (Carl Hanser, 2013); *Narrative Bewältigung von Trauma und Verlust*, ed. Carl Scheidt, et al. (Schattauer, 2015); Friedrich Schlegel, *Sämmtliche Werke*, v7 (J. Mayer, 1822) and *Friedrich Schlegel, 1794-1802: Seine Prosaischen Jugendschriften*, v2, ed. J. Minor (Carl Konegen, 1882).

Finally, grief. Here is a selected list of the books I cited in *A Hope Observed*, or referenced in preparing relevant material. I find them helpful and hope that one or two speaks to you.

Aberbach, David. *Surviving Trauma: Loss, Literature and Psychoanalysis*. Yale University Press, 1989.

Al-Chokhachy, Elissa. *Our Children Live On: Miraculous Moments for the Bereaved*. Llewellyn, 2012.

Attig, Thomas. *The Heart of Grief: Death and the Search for Lasting Love*. Oxford University Press, 2000.

Attig, Thomas. *How We Grieve: Relearning the World*. Oxford University Press, 1996.

Avery, Gilian and Kimberley Reynolds, eds. *Representations of Childhood Death*. Palgrave Macmillan UK, 1999.

Bernstein, Judith. *When the Bough Breaks: Forever After the Death of a Son or Daughter*. Andrews and McMeel, 1997.

Blum-Hyclak, Kimberlyn. *In the Garden of Life and Death: A Mother and Daughter Walk*. Main Street Rag, 2014.

Boddice, Rob. *The History of Emotions*. Manchester University Press, 2018.

Bowlby, John. *Attachment and Loss: Vol. 1, Attachment*. Basic Books, 1969.

Bowlby, John. *Attachment and Loss: Vol. 2, Separation: Anxiety and Anger*. Basic Books, 1973.

Bowlby, John. *Attachment and Loss: Vol. 3, Loss: Sadness and Depression*. Basic Books, 1980.

Bowlby, John. *A Secure Base: Parent-Child Attachment and Healthy Human Development*. Basic Books, 1988.

Buckle, Jennifer and Stephen Fleming. *Parenting After the Death of a Child: A Practitioner's Guide*. Routledge, 2010.

Buckley, Kelly. *Gratitude in Grief*. AuthorHouse, 2010.

Calhoun, Lawrence and Richard Tedeschi, eds. *Handbook of Posttraumatic Growth: Research and Practice*. Psychology Press/Taylor & Francis, 2006.

Calhoun, Lawrence and Richard Tedeschi, eds. *Posttraumatic Growth in Clinical Practice*. Routledge, 2013.

Cholbi, Michael and Travis Timmerman, eds. *Exploring the Philosophy of Death and Dying: Classical and Contemporary Perspectives*. Routledge, 2021.

Cholbi, Michael and Travis Timmerman, eds. *Grief: A Philosophical Guide*. Princeton University Press, 2022.

Cleiren, Marc. *Adaptation After Bereavement: A Comparative Study of the Aftermath of Death from Suicide, Traffic Accident, and Illness for Next of Kin*. Leiden University Press, 1991.

Davies, Douglas. *Death, Ritual and Belief: The Rhetoric of Funerary Rites*, third edition. Bloomsbury Academic, 2017.

Davies, Douglas and Alastair Shaw. *Reusing Old Graves: A Report on Popular British Attitudes*. Shaw & Sons, 1995.

Davis Bush, Ashley (published under Ashley Davis Prend). *Transcending Loss: Understanding the Lifelong Impact of Grief and How to Make it Meaningful*. Berkley, 1997.

Dickinson, George, Michael Leming, and Alan Mermann. *Dying, Death, and Bereavement 98/99* fourth edition. McGraw-Hill, 1998.

Doka, Kenneth, ed. *Disenfranchised Grief: Recognizing Hidden Sorrow*. Lexington, 1989.

Doka, Kenneth, ed. *Living with Grief: After Sudden Loss*. Taylor & Francis/Hospice Foundation of America, 1996.

Doka, Kenneth, and Joyce Davidson, eds. *Living with Grief at Work, at School, at Worship*. Taylor & Francis/Hospice Foundation of America, 1999.

Doka, Kenneth, ed. *Living with Grief: Children, Adolescents, and Loss*. Routledge, 2000.

Doka, Kenneth, ed., *Living with Grief: Loss in Later Life*. Hospice Foundation of America, 2002.

Doka, Kenneth. *Disenfranchised Grief: New Directions, Challenges, and Strategies for Practice*. Research Press, 2002.

Doka, Kenneth and Marcia Lattanzi-Light, eds. *Living with Grief: Coping with Public Tragedy*. Routledge/Hospice, 2003.

Doka, Kenneth, ed. *Living with Grief: Before and After the Death*. Hospice Foundation of America, 2007.

Doka, Kenneth and Amy Tucci, eds. *Living with Grief: Children and Adolescents*. Hospice Foundation of America, 2008.

Doka, Kenneth and Terry Martin. *Grieving Beyond Gender: Understanding the Ways Men and Women Mourn*, revised edition. Routledge ebook, 2010.

Doka, Kenneth. *Grief Is a Journey: Finding Your Path through Loss*. Atria, 2016.

Drautzburg, Anita and Jackson Oldfield. *Making Sense of Suffering: A Collective Attempt*. Brill, 2019.

Dyregrov, Kari and Atle Dyregrov. *Effective Grief and Bereavement Support: The Role of Family, Friends, Colleagues, Schools and Support Professionals*. Kingsley, 2008: 45-8.

Edelstein, Linda. *Maternal Bereavement: Coping with the Unexpected Death of a Child*. Praeger, 1984.

Fagan, Andrew, ed. *Making Sense of Dying and Death*. Rodopi, 2004.

Finkbeiner, Ann. *After the Death of a Child: Living with Loss through the Years*. Johns Hopkins University Press, 1996.

Fitzgerald, Helen. *The Mourning Handbook*. Simon and Schuster, 1994.

Gorer, Geoffrey. *Death, Grief, and Mourning*. Doubleday, 1965.

Goss, Robert and Dennis Klass. *Dead but Not Lost: Grief Narratives in Religious Traditions*. AltaMira/Rowman & Littlefield, 2005.

Greenspan, Miriam. *Healing through the Dark Emotions: The Wisdom of Grief, Fear and Despair*. Shambhala, 2003.

Grollman, Earl, ed. *Concerning Death: a Practical Guide for the Living*. Beacon, 1975.

Grollman, Earl. *Living When a Loved One Has Died*. Beacon Press, 1977.

Guldin, Mai-Britt and Carlo Leget. *Loss, Grief and Existential Awareness: An Integrative Approach*. Routledge, 2025.

Haig, Robin. *The Anatomy of Grief: Biopsychosocial and Therapeutic Perspectives*. Charles C. Thomas, 1990.

Haugk, Kenneth. *Experiencing Grief: Journeying through Grief—Book Two*. Stephen Ministries, 2004.

Hedtke, Lorraine and John Winslade. *Remembering Lives: Conversations with the Dying and the Bereaved*. Routledge, 2004.

Hedtke, Lorraine. *Bereavement Support Groups*. Taos Institute, 2012.

Hedtke, Lorraine and John Winslade. *The Crafting of Grief: Constructing Aesthetic Responses to Loss*. Routledge, 2017.

Hendin, David. *Death as a Fact of Life*. W. W. Norton & Co., 1973.

Howarth, Glennys and Peter Jupp. *Contemporary Issues in the Sociology of Death, Dying and Disposal*. Palgrave Macmillan, 1996.

Jackson, Edgar. *The Christian Funeral: Its Meaning, Its Purpose, and Its Modern Practice*. Channel Press, 1966.

Jedan, Christoph, Avril Maddrell, and Eric Venbrux, eds. *Consolationscapes in the Face of Loss: Grief and Consolation in Space and Time*. Routledge, 2018.

Kessler, David. *Finding Meaning: The Sixth Stage of Grief*. Scribner, 2019.

Klass, Dennis. *Parental Grief: Solace and Resolution*. Springer, 1988.

Klass, Dennis, Phyllis Silverman, Steven Nickman, eds. *Continuing Bonds: New Understandings of Grief*. Taylor & Francis, 1996.

Klass, Dennis and Edith Steffen, eds. *Continuing Bonds in Bereavement: New Directions for Research and Practice*. Routledge ebook, 2017.

Knapp, Ronald and Larry Peppers. *Motherhood & Mourning: Perinatal Death*. Praeger, 1980.

Knapp, Ronald and Larry Peppers. *Beyond Endurance: When a Child Dies*. Schocken Books, 1986.

Kroen, William. *Helping Children Cope with the Loss of a Loved One: A Guide for Grownups*. Free Spirit, 1996.

Kübler-Ross, Elisabeth and David Kessler. *Life Lessons*. Scribner, 2000.

Leick, Nini and Marianne Davidsen-Nielsen. *Healing Pain: Attachment, Loss, and Grief Therapy*, trans. David Stoner. Routledge, 1991.

Leming, Michael and George Dickinson. *Understanding Dying, Death, and Bereavement*, Fourth Edition. Holt, Rinehart & Winston, 1998.

Levine, Stephen and Ondrea Levine. *Who Dies? An Investigation of Conscious Living and Conscious Dying*. Penguin, 1989.

Linton, Anna. *Poetry and Parental Bereavement in Early Modern Lutheran Germany*. Oxford University Press, 2008.

McCoyd, Judith and Carolyn Ambler Walter. *Grief and Loss Across the Lifespan: A Biopsychosocial Perspective*, second edition. Springer, 2016.

Malchiodi, Cathy. *The Art Therapy Sourcebook*, second edition. McGraw-Hill, 2006.

Malchiodi, Cathy and David Crenshaw, eds. *Creative Arts and Play Therapy for Attachment Problems*. Guilford Press, 2014.

Mills, Liston, ed. *Perspectives on Death*. Abdingdon Press, 1969.

Morgan, John, ed. *Ethical Issues in the Care of the Dying and Bereaved Aged*. Routledge, 1996.

Neimeyer, Robert, Darcy Harris, Howard Winokuer, and Gordon Thornton, eds. *Grief and Bereavement in Contemporary Society: Bridging Research and Practice*. Routledge, 2011.

Neimeyer, Robert. *Lessons of Loss: A Guide to Coping*. Center for the Study of Loss and Transition, 2006.

Neimeyer, Robert, ed. *Meaning Reconstruction & the Experience of Loss*. American Psychological Association, 2001.

Neimeyer, Robert, ed. *Techniques of Grief Therapy: Assessment and Intervention*. Routledge, 2015.

Neimeyer, Robert, ed. *New Techniques of Grief Therapy: Bereavement and Beyond*. Routledge, 2021.

Neimeyer, Robert. *Living Beyond Loss: Questions and Answers about Grief and Bereavement*. Routledge, 2025.

Neuhaus, Richard John, ed. *The Eternal Pity: Reflections on Dying*. University of Notre Dame Press, 2000.

O'Connor, Mary-Frances. *The Grieving Brain: The Surprising Science of How We Learn from Love and Loss*. (HarperOne, 2023).

O'Connor, Mary-Frances. *The Grieving Body: How the Stress of Loss Can be an Opportunity for Healing*. HarperOne, 2025.

Parkes, Colin Murray and Holly Prigerson. *Bereavement: Studies of Grief in Adult Life*, fourth edition. Routledge, 2009.

Parkes, Colin Murray, Joan Stevenson-Hinde, and Peter Marris, eds. *Attachment across the Life Cycle*. Routledge, 1991.

Peale, Norman Vincent. *The Healing of Sorrow*. Inspiration Book Service/Doubleday, 1966.

Rando, Therese, ed. *Parental Loss of a Child*. Research Press, 1986.

Raphael, Beverly. *The Anatomy of Bereavement*. Aaronson, 1983, 1994.

Redfern, Suzanne and Susan Gilbert. *The Grieving Garden: Living with the Death of a Child*. Hampton Roads, 2008.

Reif, Stefan, Andreas Lehnardt, and Avriel Bar-Levav, eds. *Death in Jewish Life: Burial and Mourning Customs among Jews of Europe and Nearby Communities*. de Gruyter, 2014.

Rosof, Barbara. *The Worst Loss: How Families Heal from the Death of a Child*. Henry Holt, 1994.

Rynearson, Edward, ed. *Violent Death: Resilience and Intervention Beyond the Crisis*. Routledge, 2006.

Samuel, Julia. *Grief Works: Stories of Life, Death, and Surviving*. Simon & Schuster, 2018.

Sanders, Catherine. *Surviving Grief ... and Learning to Live Again*. John Wiley & Sons, 1992.

Sandy, Mark. *Romanticism, Memory and Mourning*. Routledge, 2014.

Schiff, Harriet Sarnoff. *The Bereaved Parent*. Penguin, 1977.

Seigal, Catherine. *Bereaved Parents and their Continuing Bonds: Love after Death*. Kingsley, 2017.

Solomon, Sheldon, Jeff Greenberg, and Tom Pyszczynski. *The Worm at the Core: On the Role of Death in Life*. Penguin, 2015.

Spargo, R. Clifton. *The Ethics of Mourning: Grief and Responsibility in Elegiac Literature*. Johns Hopkins University Press, 2004.

Stephenson, John. *Death, Grief, and Mourning: Individual and Social Realities*. Free Press, 1985.

Stroebe, Margaret, Wolfgang Stroebe, Robert Hansson, and Henk Schut, eds. *Handbook of Bereavement Research: Consequences, Coping, and Care*. American Psychological Association, 2001.

Stroebe, Margaret, Robert Hansson, Henk Schut, Wolfgang Stroebe, eds. *Handbook of Bereavement Research and Practice: Advances in Theory and Intervention*. American Psychological Association Press, 2008.

Tarlow, Sarah, ed. *The Archaeology of Death in Post-medieval Europe*. de Gruyter, 2015.

Tedeschi, Richard and Lawrence Calhoun. *Helping Bereaved Parents: A Clinician's Guide*. Routledge, 2003.

Thompson, Barbara and Robert Neimeyer, eds. *Grief and the Expressive Arts: Practices for Creating Meaning*. Routledge, 2014.

Valentine, Christine. *Bereavement Narratives: Continuing bonds in the Twenty-first Century*. Routledge, 2008.

Williamson, John and Edwin Shneidman, eds. *Death: Current Perspectives*. Mayfield, 1995.

Worden, J. William. *Children and Grief: When a Parent Dies*. Guilford, 2001.

Worden, J. William. *Grief Counseling & Grief Therapy: A Handbook for Mental Health Practitioners*, second edition. Springer, 1991.

ABOUT PARACLETE PRESS

Paraclete Press is the publishing arm of the Cape Cod Benedictine community, the Community of Jesus. Presenting a full expression of Christian belief and practice, we reflect the ecumenical charism of the Community and its dedication to sacred music, the fine arts, and the written word.

YOU MAY ALSO ENJOY:

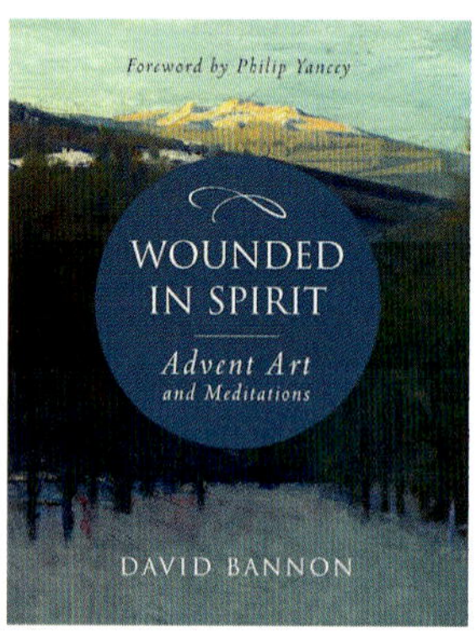

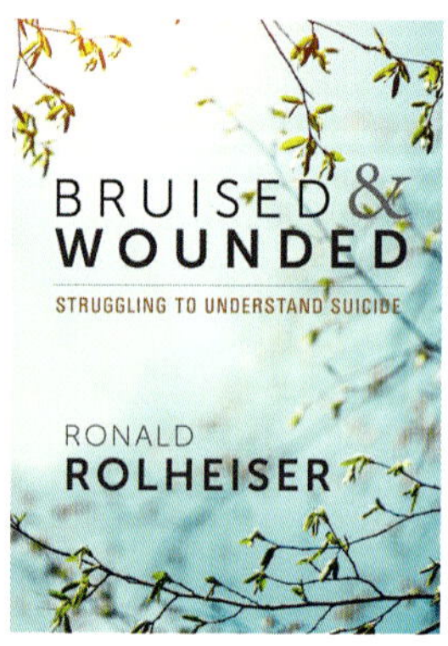